Genre Relations

Equinox Textbooks and Surveys in Linguistics
Series Editor: Robin Fawcett, Cardiff University

Also in this series:

Language in Psychiatry by Jonathan Fine
Multimodal Transcription and Text Analysis by Anthony Baldry and Paul J. Thibault
Intonation in the Grammar of English by M. A. K. Halliday and William S. Greaves

Forthcoming titles in the series:

Text Linguistics: the how and why of meaning by Jonathan Webster
The Rhetoric of Research: a guide to writing scientific literature by Beverly Lewin

Genre Relations
Mapping culture

J. R. Martin and David Rose

LONDON   OAKVILLE

Published by

Equinox Publishing Ltd

UK: Unit 6, The Village, 101 Amies St, London, SW11 2JW
USA: DBBC, 28 Main Street, Oakville, CT 06779

www.equinoxpub.com

Genre Relations by J. R. Martin and David Rose
First published 2008
Reprinted 2009

British Library Cataloguing-in-Publication Data
A catalogue record for this book is available from the British Library.

ISBN-13 (Hardback)   9781845530471
ISBN-13 (Paperback) 9781845530488

Library of Congress Cataloging-in-Publication Data
Martin, J. R.
  Genre relations : mapping culture / J.R. Martin and David Rose.
     p. cm. -- (Equinox textbooks and surveys in linguistics)
  Includes bibliographical references and index.
  ISBN 1-84553-047-0 (hb) -- ISBN 1-84553-048-9 (pb)
  1. Discourse analysis. 2. Literary form. 3. Literacy programs. 4. Language and culture. 5. Linguistic analysis (Linguistics) I. Rose, David, 1955- II. Title. III. Series.
  P302.M3728 2005
  401'.41--dc22
                        2005006062

Typeset by Catchline, Milton Keynes (www.catchline.com)
Printed and bound in Great Britain and USA

Contents

Acknowledgements

Frank Brennan and University of Queensland Press for permission to reproduce an extract from *Tampering with Asylum: a universal humanitarian problem* (Brennan 2003).

Mona Green, P. Lofts and Scholastic for permission to reproduce an extract from *The Echidna and the Shade Tree* (Green and Lofts 1984).

HK Magazine for Mourning.

D. Horton and Aboriginal Studies Press for the Australian Institute of Aboriginal and Torres Strait Islander Studies for permission to reproduce a photograph from *The Encyclopaedia of Aboriginal Australia: Aboriginal and Torres Strait Islander history, society and culture* (Horton 1994).

Doris Pilkington and University of Queensland Press for permission to reproduce an extract from *Follow the Rabbit-Proof Fence* (Pilkington 1996).

Lyn Scott and Sally Robinson for permission to reproduce illustrations and text from *Australian journey: environments and communities* (Scott & Robinson 1993).

NSW AMES for permission to transcribe Lavina Gray's autobiography (Wanyarri 1997).

Elaine Russell, cover illustration.

For Joan

Preface

For this book we have tried to write an accessible introduction to the genre theory underpinning the literacy programmes of what has come to be referred to as the 'Sydney School'. Jim began working with Joan Rothery and Fran Christie on this initiative in 1979, to address the literacy needs of primary school students. David was first drawn to the project in 1989, by the literacy needs of the Indigenous communities he worked for. Pedagogy and curriculum have always been important aspects of this action research, but we won't deal directly with questions of practice here. Rather our focus is on the way we have theorised genre as part of a functional model of language and attendant modalities of communication. Our aim is that this description will continue to inform the pedagogic work, as well broader research in language and culture.

The first phase of this research (1980–1987), the 'Writing Project', involved a study of student writing in Sydney schools. Jim worked closely with Joan Rothery and with Suzanne Eggins, Radan Martinec and Peter Wignell analysing text types across the curriculum in primary school, with a focus on geography and history in secondary school. This phase of schools based work was considerably enhanced by studies of various community genres undertaken by post-graduate students in the Linguistics Department at the University of Sydney, including work by Eija Ventola on service encounters, Guenter Plum on narrative and Suzanne Eggins on casual conversation. It was during this period that Fran Christie developed her interest applying genre theory to classroom discourse, leading to her ongoing focus on what she calls curriculum genres.

From 1986 the Disadvantaged Schools Program in Sydney played a critical role in the development of this work, beginning with the primary school focused 'Language and Social Power Project' (1986–1990) and continuing with the secondary school and workplace focused 'Write it Right Project' (1990–1995). Jim acted as chief academic adviser and David coordinated work on the discourse of science based industry. Mary Macken-Horarik worked closely with Joan Rothery on both of these projects, the second of which involved important contributions from Caroline Coffin, Sally Humphrey, Maree Stenglin and Robert Veel (school genres), from Susan Feez, Rick Iedema and Peter White (workplace genres) and from David

McInnes who worked with both the school and workplace teams. Inspired by our work on science discourse, Len Unsworth undertook his detailed study of scientific explanations, which he later extended to his work on multimodal discourse.

We were fortunate throughout this work to be able to draw on relevant thinking about genre in the Sydney metropolitan region by Ruqaiya Hasan (on narrative, appointment making and service encounters) and by Gunther Kress, who worked with Jim as part of LERN (Literacy and Education Research Network) in its early years. In addition we benefited from having our work taken up in the context of EAP by the Learning Centre at the University of Sydney (under the direction of Carolyn Webb and later Janet Jones) and for ESL by Sue Hood and Helen Joyce at AMES (Adult Migrant English Service). While a major focus of the theory has been on writing in English, it has increasingly been applied to mapping genres across other cultures, such as David's work on the language and culture of Australia's Western Desert.

None of this would have been thinkable of course without the informing systemic functional linguistic theory and guiding hand of Michael Halliday, whose thinking about language underpinned the research, who organised the 'Working Conference on Language in Education' in 1979 where Jim first met Joan Rothery, and who established the undergraduate Linguistics and MA/MEd Applied Linguistics programs at the University of Sydney. It was in these programs that so many of the colleagues noted above became interested in genre, and where Joan Rothery and Guenter Plum first came up with the idea of distinguishing register from genre circa 1980–1981.

In Halliday's linguistics, theory emerges out of a dialectic with practice, and we want to especially thank here all of the students and teachers and language consultants who have tried out our ideas and challenged us to improve them over the years. Our thanks as well to the many colleagues who have taken an interest in this work, in functional linguistics and beyond – at meetings and on the web (and a special thanks to Sue Hood for her help with editing the page proofs for this edition). Like all knowledge, genre theory is a continuing project, and has been an excellent excuse for keeping in touch. Ever more so, we hope, as a result of this particular packaging up of what we've seen so far.

Joan Rothery's name has come up at several points in this discussion, and we would like to acknowledge her contribution as the principal co-architect of the theory we present here by dedicating this book to her – a small tribute to one of the world's most inspiring educational linguists.

1 Getting going with genre

1.1 Back to school

Walk into a primary school in Australia in 1980 and here's the kind of writing you would likely find:[1]

> **[1:1]**
>
> On Sunday the 9th of November Jesse my friend and me Conal, went to the park called Jonson park me and Jesse played on the playaquitmint and it was very fun but me and Jesse both like the same peace of equipment I don't know wa…

What can we say about it? As for the text itself, the spelling and punctuation are far from standard; the grammar is quite spoken, unfolding serially from clause to clause; and the writing is unfinished, arresting in the middle of a word beginning 'wa'. Alongside the writing we would very likely find a colourful drawing, of Jesse and Conal playing in the park. The writer could be around 7, 8, 9 or 10 years old, depending on their social background and the school involved. The teacher would be relatively supportive, ready to correct the spelling and punctuation and keen to encourage the young writer to try harder and hand in a complete text next time round.

But what does this text do? As far as meaning goes, the text makes an observation about something that has happened to the writer (going to the park to play); and it makes some comments about how they felt about it (what they liked). Jesse and Conal's teacher would have called it a story, since *story* was the term that primary school teachers used to refer to children's writing in their school. Functional linguists working in the school would have christened it an **observation/comment** text, in order to distinguish it from texts like [1:2] which record a series of events unfolding through time:

[1:2]

Last Sunday me and My family went to the blue Mountains to go and see my dads friends. There were two children as well One of the childrens name was Hamish, Hamish was about 12 years old and his brother was about 19 or 18 years old. So when we arrived we all had lunch and we had chicken, bread, salad and a drink. after we had lunch I went on the tramplen after I went on the tramplen for about half an hour we went to go to a rugby leeg game for about 3 hours and I got an ice-cream and a packet of chips after the rugby leeg game I went on the tramplen agin and I got another ice-cream and after I had finished my ice-cream we went home. I had a great day.

Here the trip to the Blue Mountains north of Sydney is broken down into steps – going to the mountains, having lunch, playing on the trampoline, going to the rugby, playing on the trampoline again and going home; and the steps are explicitly sequenced in time (**when** *we arrived,* **after** *we had lunch,* **after** *I went on the tramplen,* **after** *the rugby leeg game,* **after** *I finished my ice-cream*). The linguists involved called this kind of text a **recount**, and noticed that it became more common as the literacy pedagogy known in Australia as process writing became popular in schools in the early eighties.[2] Process writing experts encouraged teachers to set aside more time for writing on a daily basis, which led to longer texts about children's first-hand experiences. The longer and more unusual the experience, the more kids had to write about:

[1:3]

I woke up and got redy to get on the giant plain. Me my sister my Brother my dad and Sue our house mate all got ready to go so when the taxi came we would be ready so the taxi came at about 9:30 so we got on the taxi and went to the airport and waited for the people to announe when our plain is going to come or if it is here. they finily announced that the plain is here and we got strait on the plain and it left at about 10:00 in the morning it took a day and a harf to get there so when we got off the plain we went on a taxi to Autawa, Autawa is where my grandma and granpa live. On that same day we went to a playce called cascads it was a water park. it was so big there was only about 10 or 11 water slides but they were so fun. My favorite water salide was the gost slide it was pitch black four or five peaple can go at a time because it was lick one of those small pools but it didn't have water in it when you went down you would get a bit scared because you couldn't see everything. There was holes in it shaped lick gost's and there was heps of other rides. We stayed there for about three hours. After three hours we went back to my grandma and grandpas house after one week later we wrang a taxi and asked him to come and tack us t the airport and we got on the plain back home when we got back home we had dinner.

For everyday events kids simply had to go into more and more detail to fill up the time slot set aside for writing and produce the longer texts their teachers desired.

By 1985 there were lots of recounts, although numerically observation/comment texts were still the most common text type. And you couldn't count on children graduating from primary school having written anything other than observation/comments and recounts, although other kinds of text appeared. We found factual texts, written especially by boys:

[1:4] Crocodile

Crocodiles are from the reptile family. Crocodiles are like snakes but with two legs on each side of the crocodiles body.

Crocodiles have four legs and the crocodiles have scales all over its body. Crocodiles have a long gore and they have a long powerful tail so it can nock its enems into the water so it can eat the animal.

Crocodiles live on the ege of a swamp or a river. They make there nests out of mud and leaves.

Crocodiles eat meat lke chikens, cows and catle and other kinds of animals.

Crocdils move by there legs. Crocodiles can walk on legs. Crocodiles have four legs. Crocodiles also have scals all over there body and they have a powerfall tail to swim in the water. Crocdils have eggs they do not have (live) babys.

Crocodiles can carry there egg(s) in there big gore.

Some factual texts, like [1:4] generalised about experience, drawing on research about classes of phenomena; these were called **reports**. Others focused on specific first hand observations, and often expressed the feelings of writers to what they were describing (these were written by both boys and girls):

[1:5] My dog Tammy[3]

My dog Tammy has a lovly reddy brown furr. Here eyes are brown too. Her shape is skinny. She has a fluffy, furry, smooth and shinny texture. She moves by wagging her tail and waving her body. The feelings that I feel of my dog is sweat, loving and cute. My dog is very loved. She smells sweet. My dog is big, tall and very long.

Text of this kind were termed **descriptions**. Beyond this there were occasional 'how to' texts, designated **procedures**:

[1:6] How to brush your teeth

1   Turn the taps on and fill your glass with water.

2   Get your tooth brush.

3   Put tooth paste on your tooth brush

4   put your tooth brush in your mouth and scrub your teeth.

5   When you are finished brushing your teeth rins out your mouth with water.

6...

Sometimes these procedures had been specially adapted to suit the goals of scientific experimentation:

[1:7] The Strongest Parts of a Magnet

Aim:

To find out which part of the magnet is the strongest.

Equipment:

You will need a magnet, pins or some-thing that is mad out of iron.

Steps:

1   Spread your pins out on the table.

2   Put your magnet over your pins.

3   See what happened/s.

4   Repet trying sides with pins.

5   See which side is the strongest by comparing.

Results:

The pins all went to the poles.

Conclusion:

I found out that the poles where the strongest part of the magnet.

Now and again procedures would be complemented by **protocol** – lists of rules which restrict what you can do instead of explaining how to do it:

[1:8] Bus Safety

1   Alwas keep your hands and feet to yourself.

2   Never eat or drink it the bus because you could chock on your food when the bus stops.

3   Don't draw on the bus.

4   Don't litter on the bus because a babby could pick it up and he or she could chock on it.

5   Don't arguw on the bus because it could distrack the bus driver.

And there were some real stories too – or at least attempts at them. In these **narrative** texts there is something that goes wrong, that needs to be set right:

[1:9] The duff children

In the outback in vicktorya in 1918 there was three there names where isack, jane, and frank isack was 4, Jane was 7 and frank was 9. there mother told them to go to some brom bushes so there mother could mack a brom. They left on Friday and when they didn't come back!!!!!!

[A good start, Conal. What next?]

And there were '**just so stories**', that explain how the world came to be the way it is:

[1:10] How the sparow could glide

Once when the white people came to Australia there was a little bird called a sparow. It was a very nice bird but the white people that first came to Australia they thoute that the sparrow as a very annoying bird because it slowly flew around them slowly. One time they got so annoyed that they got a gun out and tride to shote it so he got his gun out and shot his gun but it didn't hit the bird it was write behind the sparow the sparow's aims got so tiyard that he had to stop flapping its wings and it sort of glided just near the ground and he moved and the bullets went away and that is how the sparow's lernt how to glide. And they lived happily ever after.

In general narrative writing reflected the reading and viewing experiences of children, often with girls modelling narrative on what they'd read in books and boys retelling the plot of action drama they had seen on screen.

Other kinds of writing were pretty rare. And teachers not only called everything the kids wrote a story but evaluated everything as if it were a story too. Here's a short **explanation** of the history of the planet written in 1988 by Ben, then 8 years old (Martin 1990):

[1:11] OUR PLANET

Earth's core is as hot as the furthest outer layer of the sun. They are both 6000c°.

Earth started as a ball of fire. Slowly it cooled. But it was still too hot for Life. Slowly water formed and then the first signs of life, microscopic cells. Then came trees. About seven thousand million years later came the first man.

His teacher commented as follows:

[Where is your margin? This is not a story.]

And on his picture of the planet, which accompanied his text, she wrote 'Finish please.' Ben's parents were quite concerned. And as linguists we felt we had some work to do.

One job was to identify and name the kinds of texts we found. We approached this by looking closely at the kinds of meaning involved – using global patterns to distinguish one text type from another and more local patterns to distinguish stages within a text. Recurrent global patterns were recognised as genres, and given names. For example, the distinction we drew between observation/comments and recounts was based on the presence or absence of an unfolding sequence of events; and the distinction between reports and descriptions was based on whether the facts presented were generic or specific.

Recurrent local patterns within genres were recognised as **schematic structures**, and also labelled. For most people the most familiar example of this kind of labelling is the experiment report from school science. Example [1:7] above used the terms Aim, Equipment, Steps, Results and Conclusion for its staging structure. This genre and its staging were normally taught explicitly to students in Australian schools and was thus the sole exception to the prevailing practice in process writing and whole language classrooms of not teaching students genres (or even telling them what to write).

As a working definition we characterised genres as staged, goal oriented social processes. Staged, because it usually takes us more than one step to reach our goals; goal oriented because we feel frustrated if we don't accomplish the final steps (as with the aborted narrative [1:9] above); social because writers shape their texts for readers of particular kinds.

In functional linguistics terms what this means is that genres are defined as a recurrent configuration of meanings and that these recurrent configurations of meaning enact the social practices of a given culture. This means we have to think about more than individual genres; we need to consider how they relate to one another.

Relations among genres implicitly informed the presentation of the examples considered above. To begin, two event and reaction genres were considered and distinguished with respect to the presence of a time line (observation/comment vs recount). Then two factual genres were introduced and opposed in terms of generic or specific reference (report vs description). We then looked at two directive genres, separated according to whether they tell us how to do something or what not to do (procedure vs protocol). Finally we presented two story genres in which complications arose that needed to be set right – one which used drama to entertain, the other which explained (narrative vs just so story).

Overall, we might oppose procedures and protocols to the others, on the grounds that are mainly instructing rather than informing. And within informing genres, we might oppose those organised around sequences of events to those focused on describing things; and those organised around events could be divided into those that present an expectant sequence, and those with complicating actions. An outline of these relationships is presented in Figure 1.1. A network diagram is used here to present genres as a series of choices. The first choice is between genres that instruct or inform, secondly between genres that inform about things or events, and thirdly between event sequences that are expectant or complicating. Each choice is indicated by an arrow leading to further options.

Figure 1.1 gives us an approximate map of the 1980s literacy terrain in Australian primary schools as we presented it above (although it doesn't include Ben's history of the planet, and doesn't show how overwhelmingly common the observation/comment and recount genres were compared with the others). Technically speaking we have a genre system – we have organised what kids wrote into a taxonomy of text types, based on the recurrent configurations of meaning they produced. Network diagrams such as Figure 1.1 are used in SFL to model language as systems of resources

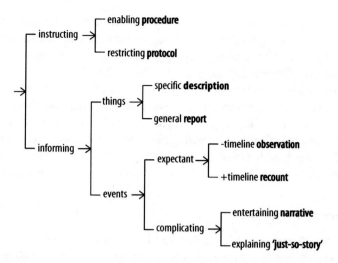

Figure 1.1 Relations among junior primary genres (provisional)

for meaning, that speakers and writers choose from in the process of making meaning. At the level of genre, this system network shows relations among genres that at least some children were able to choose from for their writing tasks.

What kind of literacy world was this? Basically one in which writing was not taught. For models kids had to depend on texts they'd bumped into on their own. These included spoken genres like observation/comment and recount they'd heard in conversation at home, and written genres they might have seen in books or other genres they might have viewed on screen – dependent of course on what they read and viewed (only a few students like Ben drew now and again on factual writing they had encountered in their own research). The school's contribution was pretty much limited to the instructional genres, since writing up science experiments was taught and rules for behaviour were regularly negotiated early in the school year, posted round classrooms and recorded in students' notebooks.

It seemed a bad idea to us to leave all this to chance since by and large students were not being prepared for writing across the curriculum in primary school, nor were they being introduced to the kinds of writing they would have to read and produce in secondary school. And in schools with large populations of non-English speaking children (whether Indigenous or migrant) there was the additional problem that these kids were often the most fluent English speaker in their families and the go-between as far as a range of professional and government services were concerned. The community oriented literacy which could help them out wasn't part of the curriculum either. On top of all this the fact that teachers called every genre a story reflected their own lack of genre consciousness. This impacted heavily on both implicit and explicit evaluation – since everything was treated as good or bad narrative (as was text [1:11] above). Handy if as a student you tweak that this is what teachers have in mind, but debilitating if you can't read between the lines.

It didn't seem like social justice to us and we tried to intervene. This meant identifying and describing the genres we thought every student should learn to write in primary school. And it meant developing pedagogy and curriculum to make sure they learned them (Cope & Kalantzis 1993, Johns 2002). This book is not however about this ongoing intervention in literacy teaching, which over time had considerable influence on Australian primary and secondary schools, adult migrant English teaching and on academic literacy teaching in universities. But this intervention was the context in which Jim and later David began to worry seriously about genres. And it influenced the funding that became available to pursue our research. So we probably have to acknowledge an educational bias in the genre theory we present below.

1.2 Where did we turn?

As systemic functional linguists we had a rich tradition of work on language and social context to draw on, going back through Halliday, Hasan and Gregory to the work of their mentor Firth and his colleagues in Britain. From this tradition two publications were directly related to our concerns – Mitchell 1957 and Hasan 1977. Mitchell was a colleague of Firth's specialising in Arabic; based on his research in the Libyan market place he wrote the classic Firthian study of language in relation to context of situation – focussing on what came to be known as the service encounter genre. Mitchell distinguished market auctions from market stall and shop transactions, and proposed partially overlapping schematic structures for each (the difference between market stall and shop transactions was the optional nature of a Salutation in the former). Mitchell's structures are presented below, using '∧' to mean 'is followed by' (although we must note in passing that Mitchell did recognise the possibility of alternative and overlapping sequencing conditioned by context):

MARKET AUCTION: Auctioneer's Opening ∧ Investigation of Object of Sale ∧ Bidding ∧ Conclusion

MARKET TRANSACTIONS: Salutation ∧ Enquiry as to Object of Sale ∧ Investigation of Object of Sale ∧ Bargaining ∧ Conclusion

In his discussion Mitchell attended closely to the patterns of meaning characterising each genre and elements of schematic structure. Mitchell's article was originally published in the relatively obscure Moroccan journal *Hesperis*, and we were fortunate to have a well-worn photocopy of it; 'The language of buying and selling in Cyrenaica: a situational statement' became more widely available in 1975 when it was republished in a collection of Mitchell's papers, his *Principles of Neo-Firthian Linguistics*.

Hasan was a colleague of Halliday's working at Macquarie University in Sydney and in 1977 she published a paper on text structure which focused on appointment making. Her obligatory stages for this genre were Identification ∧ Application ∧ Offer ∧ Confirmation. For Hasan, these stages, additional optional stages and the linguistic realisation of stages were conditioned by Halliday's three social context variables field, tenor and mode; social context in this sense determined the genre.

Later on Hasan's work on the structure of nursery tales and Australian service encounters also became available to us (Hasan 1984, 1985).[4]

The third major influence on our thinking came from a different tradition, the narrative analysis of the American variation theorist Labov. Labov and Waletzky's 1967 paper on the narratives of personal experience in Labov's corpus also focused on schematic structure, including obligatory and optional staging (parentheses are used to signal optional elements below):

NARRATIVE OF PERSONAL EXPERIENCE: (Abstract) ^ (Orientation) ^ Complication ^ Evaluation ^ Resolution ^ (Coda)

Like Hasan and Mitchell, Labov & Waletzky gave detailed semantic descriptions of each element of structure, relating these as far as possible to linguistic realisations (further elaborated in later work by Labov 1972, 1982, 1984, 1997). This work, alongside Hasan 1984, was a major influence on our analysis of story genres which we present in Chapter 2 below.[5]

To be frank, these three papers were pretty much what we had to go on, although there were obviously lots of concurrent developments going on around the world. We concentrated on making sense of these ideas within the framework of systemic functional linguistics as we understood it at the time. This meant working very hard on the notion of recurrent configurations of meaning, drawing on Halliday's emerging functional grammar of English (Halliday 1994) and Martin's emerging descriptions of discourse semantics (Martin 1992). The most distinctive thing about our approach to genre was probably that it developed within such a rich theoretical framework and drew upon far richer descriptions of meaning-making resources in English than had been available in the past.

1.3 Modelling context

In our emerging interpretation of genre, we were strongly influenced by two developing theories of the social contexts of language, Halliday's model of language as text in context (1978, 1989), and Bernstein's model of the social contexts of language as 'codes' (1971, 1990, 1996). Halliday described social context as 'the total environment in which a text unfolds' (1978:5), building on Firth (1957) and Malinowski for whom 'the meaning of any significant word, sentence or phrase is the effective change brought about by the utterance within the context of the situation to which it is wedded' (1935:213). In an effort to present the discourse of Trobriand Islanders for a European audience, Malinowski interpreted the social contexts of interaction as stratified into two levels – 'context of situation' and 'context of culture', and considered that a text (which he called an 'utterance') could only be understood in relation to both these levels. Conversely we could say that speakers' cultures are manifested in each situation in which they interact, and that each interactional situation is manifested verbally as unfolding text, i.e. as text in context. This stratified theory of text in context is illustrated in SFL as a series of nested circles, as in Figure 1.2.

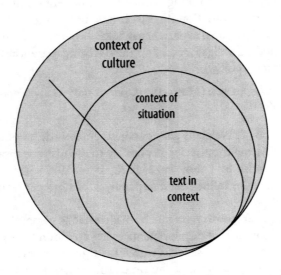

Figure 1.2   A stratal interpretation of the relation of language to social context

The relation between each of these strata of language and social context is modelled in SFL as 'realisation', represented in Figure 1.2 by a line across the strata. We described this concept in Martin & Rose 2003/2007 as follows:

> Realisation is a kind of re-coding – like the mapping of hardware through software to the images and words we see on the screen on our computers. Another way of thinking about this is symbolisation… Symbolising is an important aspect of realisation, since grammar both symbolises and encodes discourse, just as discourse both symbolises and encodes social activity. The concept of realisation embodies the meanings of 'symbolising', 'encoding', 'expressing', 'manifesting' and so on.

The concept of realisation also entails 'metaredundancy' (Lemke 1993) – the notion of patterns at one level 'redounding' with patterns at the next level, and so on. So patterns of social organisation in a culture are realised ('manifested/ symbolised/ encoded/ expressed') as patterns of social interaction in each context of situation, which in turn are realised as patterns of discourse in each text. Furthermore, if each text realises patterns in a social situation, and each situation realises patterns in a culture, then the stratification of context had implications for how we thought of the types of texts we were finding. Should we be modelling the relation between text types and their contexts at the level of situation or of culture? Since each genre can be written and read in a variety of situations, the latter option seems likely. But before we can begin to answer this question, we need to consider Halliday's model of situation in more detail.

1.3.1 Register – variations in situation

Halliday links contexts of situation to three social functions of language – enacting speakers' relationships, construing their experience of social activity, and weaving these enactments and construals together as meaningful discourse. Accordingly contexts of situation vary in these three general dimensions. The dimension concerned with relationships between interactants is known as **tenor**; that concerned with their social activity is known as **field**; and that concerned with the role of language is known as **mode**. Halliday has characterised these three dimensions of a situation as follows:

> **Field** refers to what is happening, to the nature of the social action that is taking place: what it is that the participants are engaged in, in which language figures as some essential component.

> **Tenor** refers to who is taking part, to the nature of the participants, their statuses and roles: what kinds of role relationship obtain, including permanent and temporary relationships of one kind or another, both the types of speech roles they are taking on in the dialogue and the whole cluster of socially significant relationships in which they are involved.

> **Mode** refers to what part language is playing, what it is that the participants are expecting language to do for them in the situation: the symbolic organisation of the text, the status that it has, and its function in the context (Halliday 1985:12).

Taken together the tenor, field and mode of a situation constitute the register of a text. That is, from the perspective of language, we will now refer to the context of situation of a text as its **register**. As register varies, so too do the patterns of meanings we find in a text. Because they vary systematically, we refer to tenor, field and mode as **register variables**.

As language realises its social contexts, so each dimension of a social context is realised by a particular functional dimension of language. Halliday defines these functional dimensions as the 'metafunctions' of language: enacting relationships as the **interpersonal** metafunction, construing experience as the **ideational** metafunction, and organising discourse as the **textual** metafunction. Relations between register variables and language metafunctions are as follows:

	REGISTER	METAFUNCTION	
tenor	'kinds of role relationship'	**interpersonal**	'enacting'
field	'the social action that is taking place'	**ideational**	'construing'
mode	'what part language is playing'	**textual**	'organising'

This set of functional relationships between language and context is illustrated in Figure 1.3, and expanded on as follows.

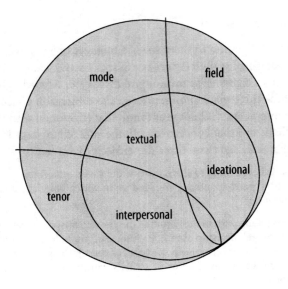

Figure 1.3   Field, tenor and mode in relation to metafunctions

First **tenor**: In a model of this kind, and here we follow Martin 1992 in particular, tenor is concerned with the nature of social relations among interlocutors, with the dimensions of status and solidarity. Status is equal or unequal and if unequal, is concerned with who dominates and who defers (the vertical dimension of tenor). Solidarity is concerned with social distance – close or distant depending on the amount and kinds of contact people have with one another, and with the emotional charge of these relations (the horizontal dimension of tenor). Status and solidarity are complementarities, and both obtain in all of our interactions with one another. The terms status and power are often used interchangeably, but in this discussion we will reserve the term power for more general relationships, beyond specific situations in the wider distribution of resources in a society, discussed below. Examples of varying tenor relations are given in Figure 1.4: close equal relations are characteristic of siblings or close friends, whereas distant equal relations are more likely between acquaintances or co-workers; close contact in unequal relations may be found between a worker and their line-manager, who work together each day, while a distant unequal relationship is more likely between a junior worker and a senior manager, who rarely meet.

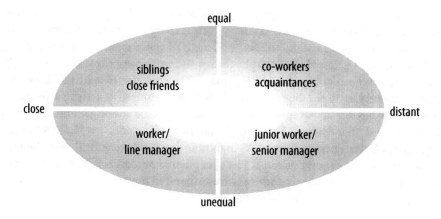

Figure 1.4 Dimensions of variation in tenor

Some important realisation principles for status and solidarity are outlined by Poynton 1985. For status, 'reciprocity' of choice is the critical variable. Thus social subjects of equal status construe equality by having access to and taking up the same kinds of choices, whereas subjects of unequal status take up choices of different kinds. Terms of address are one obvious exemplar in this area – do we address each other in the same way (say first name to first name), or is the naming skewed (you call me Professor, I call you by your first name). For solidarity Poynton suggests the realisation principles of 'proliferation' and 'contraction'. Proliferation refers to the idea that the closer you are to someone the more meanings you have available to exchange. One way of thinking about this is to imagine the process of getting to know someone and what you can talk about when you don't know them (very few things) and what you can talk about when you know them very well (almost anything). Contraction refers to the amount of work it takes to exchange meanings, and the idea that the better you know someone the less explicitness it takes. Poynton exemplifies this in part through naming, pointing out that knowing someone very well involves short names, whereas knowing them less well favours longer ones (e.g. Mike vs Professor Michael Alexander Kirkwood Halliday, FAHA). For foundational work on tenor in SFL see Poynton 1984, 1985, 1990a&b, 1993, 1996. Eggins & Slade 2005 develop this work focussing on casual conversation in the workplace and home. Martin & White 2005 look closely at evaluative language use, expanding on the appraisal framework introduced in Martin 2000 (see also Macken-Horarik & Martin 2003).

Next **field**: Field is concerned with the discourse patterns that realise the activity that is going on. Technically speaking a field consists of sequences of activities that are oriented to some global institutional purpose, whether this is a local domestic institution such as family or community, or a broader societal institution such as bureaucracy, industry or academia. Each such activity sequence involves people, things, processes, places and qualities, and each of these elements are organised into taxonomies – groupings of people, things and processes; these taxonomies in turn distinguish one field from another. From the perspective of field, the discourse patterns of texts vary in the degree to which they are organised as activity sequences, and whether they are about specific people and things, or about general classes of phenomena and their features. For example, on the specific side, text [1:3] recounted a sequence of Conal's personal activities in minute detail, whereas [1:5] described his dog Tammy. On the general side, text [1:11] explained processes in the evolution of life, whereas [1:4] classified crocodiles and enumerated their parts. These examples of variation in field are illustrated in Figure 1.5.

Figure 1.5 Dimensions of variation in field

We'll explore just a few fields from the perspective of genre in this volume, including history in Chapter 3, science and geography in Chapter 4, and science based industry in Chapter 5 – in each case focussing on Australian texts in order to bring some topical unity to the volume. For related SFL work on field, exploring everyday language, technicality and abstraction, on technology and bureaucracy, and on the discourses of humanities, social science and science see Halliday & Martin 1993, Hasan & Williams 1996, Christie & Martin 1997, Martin & Veel 1998, Christie 1999, Unsworth 2000, Hyland 2000, Martin & Wodak 2003, Christie & Martin 2007.

Next **mode**: Mode deals with the channelling of communication, and thus with the texture of information flow as we move from one modality of communication to another (speech, writing, phone, SMS messages, e-mail, chat rooms, web pages, letters, radio, CD, television, film, video, DVD etc.). One important variable is the amount of work language is doing in relation to what is going on. In some contexts language may have a small role to play since attendant modalities are heavily mediating what is going on (e.g. image, music, spatial design, action). In other contexts language may be by and large what is going on, sometimes to the point where its abstract phrasing is considerably removed from sensuous experience we might expect to touch, taste, feel, hear or see. This range of variation is sometimes characterised as a cline from language in action to language as reflection.

A second key variable is the complementary monologue through dialogue cline. This scale is sensitive to the effects of various technologies of communication on the kind of interactivity that is facilitated. The key material factors here have to do with whether interlocutors can hear and see one another (aural and visual feedback) and the imminence of a response (immediate or delayed). As with field, mode is not our main focus here. This dimension of register is further explored in Halliday 1985, Halliday & Martin 1993, Martin & Veel 1998, Martin & Wodak 2003. Examples of variations in mode are illustrated in Figure 1.6. Varieties of dialogue that accompany social action include intermittent exchanges while carrying out domestic or other activities, whereas dialogue that constitutes social activity includes casual conversations (e.g. at the dinner table, in the coffee shop), arguments and so on. Monologues that accompany activity include sports commentary or oral instructions for doing a task, whereas monologue that constitutes its own field includes story telling, oratory, and all forms of written texts.

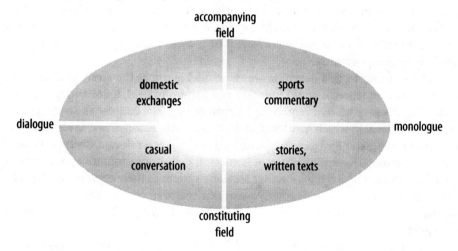

Figure 1.6 Dimensions of variation in mode

Looking beyond language, mode is the contextual variable that would have be developed to coordinate the distribution of meaning across modalities in multimodal discourse. While SFL work on the grammars of various non-linguistic modalities of communication has developed rapidly over the past decade, work towards a theory of inter-modality is just beginning. For foundational SFL work on non-verbal modalities see O'Toole 1994, Kress & van Leeuwen 2006 on images (Goodman 1996, Jewitt & Oyama 2001, Stenglin & Iedema 2001 provide useful introductions), van Leeuwen 1999 on music and sound, Martinec 1998, 2000a, b on action and Martin & Stenglin 2006 on spatial design. As a result of these studies multimodal discourse analysis has become a very exciting area of work in functional linguistics (Kress & van Leeuwen 2001, O'Halloran 2003, Royce 2006), inspired in part by the new electronic modalities of communication enabled by personal computing technologies (Baldry 1999).

1.3.2 Genre – variations in culture

This tenor, field and mode model was essentially the framework for studying social context we had to work with when we began looking at text types around 1980. And it left us with a puzzle – what to do with genre? Halliday (e.g. 1978) had treated genre as an aspect of mode; and Hasan (1977, 1985) derived her obligatory elements of text structure from field and so appeared to handle genre relations there. To our mind however each genre involved a particular configuration of tenor, field and mode variables, so we didn't feel comfortable making genre part of any one register variable on its own. Taking the genres in Figure 1.1 for example, procedures, protocols, descriptions, reports, observations, recounts and narratives could be about almost any field, they could be spoken or written, and their producers and audience could be close or distant, equal or unequal. Clearly genre and register could vary independently.

Our solution to this dilemma was to model genre at the stratum of culture, beyond register, where it could function as a pattern of field, tenor and mode patterns.[6] In this step we had remodelled language in social context as an integrated semiotic system, in which 'situation' and 'culture' were reconstrued as social semiotic strata – **register** and **genre**. Hjelmslev 1961 makes a relevant distinction here between connotative and denotative semiotics, defining connotative semiotics as semiotic systems which have another semiotic system as their expression plane. In these terms, language is a denotative semiotic realising social context, and social context is a connotative semiotic realised through language. This step is outlined in Figure 1.7.

The reasoning involved in this modelling decision is reviewed in some detail Martin 1992, 1999, 2001. Stratifying register and genre in this way allowed us to develop an integrated multi-functional perspective on genre, cutting across register variables. We can think of field, tenor and mode as resources for generalising across genres, from the differentiated perspectives of ideational, interpersonal and textual meaning. This made it easier for us to model relations among genres (as in

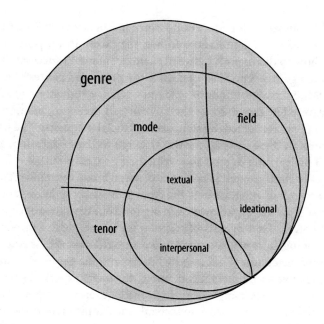

Figure 1.7 Genre as an additional stratum of analysis beyond tenor, field and mode

Figure 1.1 above) without being stuck in any one of tenor, field or mode. This was particularly important for our schools work, both in terms of mapping curriculum and building learner pathways (Martin 1999). It also made it easier to explore the range of field, tenor and mode configurations a culture enacts compared with those it doesn't – including configurations it has no more use for (extinct genres) and future possibilities. It seemed to us that tenor, field and mode choices in context combined nowhere near as freely as interpersonal, ideational and textual meanings did in grammar. That is to say, cultures seem to involve a large but potentially definable set of genres, that are recognisable to members of a culture, rather than an unpredictable jungle of social situations. To us cultures looked more like outer space than biospheres, with a few families of genres here and there, like far flung galaxies. We wanted a theory that accommodated all this empty room.

The potential emerging from this model, for mapping cultures from a semiotic perspective as systems of genres, together with variations in tenor, field and mode, also resonated with Bernstein's (1971, 1977, 1990, 1996) theory of socio-semantic codes. In this model, varieties of social subjectivities are distinguished by differing orientations to meaning, that Bernstein referred to as coding orientations, and these are manifested as 'relations between' and 'relations within' social contexts. Bernstein emphasised the primacy of relations between contexts; that is, individuals' coding orientations varied with their capacity for recognising one type of context from another, with what he called a 'sense of specialised interactional practices'. This obviously had implications for education – since teachers were failing to recognise distinctions between one genre and another, they were in no position to teach their students how to distinguish between them, let alone to successfully produce a range of written genres. Furthermore, since the privileged genres of modernism had evolved within the institutions of academia, science, industry and administration, that relatively few members of the culture had access to, relations between these and other genres reflected the structures of social inequality. The pathway for exercising control in these institutions was through tertiary education, and that in turn depended on learning to read and write their genres in school.

Members of cultural groupings gain control over a broad common set of genres as we mature – we learn to distinguish between types of everyday contexts, and to manage our interactions, apply our experiences, and organise our discourse effectively within each context. Control over the genres of everyday life is accumulated through repeated experience, including more or less explicit instruction from others. As young children, our experience of the culture is necessarily limited and the genres we can recognise and realise are relatively undifferentiated, but as our social experience broadens, the system of genres we control complexifies. In Bernstein's terms our coding orientation becomes more elaborated, as we learn to recognise and realise a more diverse range of contexts. We have illustrated a fragment of such a genre system, for written genres in primary schools, in Figure 1.1 above. But of course, differences in social experience will produce differences in access to the genre systems that have evolved in a culture.

1.3.3 Ideology – variations in access

Inequalities in access to the privileged genres of modern institutional fields is a concern for developing democratic pedagogies, but also more generally for understanding how symbolic control is maintained, distributed and challenged in contemporary societies. Bernstein's code theory has been expressly developed for exploring these issues. For Bernstein, differences in coding orientations are conditioned by one's relation to power and control within the division of labour in a society. In post-colonial societies five general factors are generally assumed to position us in relation to power and control: generation, gender, ethnicity, capacity and class. We use generation to refer to inequalities associated with maturation; gender covers sex and sexuality based difference; ethnicity is concerned with racial, religious and other 'cultural' divisions; capacity refers to abilities and disabilities of various kinds; class is based on the distribution of material resources and is arguably the most fundamental dimension since it is the division on which our post-colonial economic order ultimately depends. Our positioning begins at birth in the home, and all five factors condition access to the various hierarchies we encounter beyond domestic life – in education, religion, recreation and the workplace.

It is of course ideology that regulates social categories, of generation, gender, ethnicity, capacity and class, to differentially condition our access to power and control. It is ultimately ideology that differentially shapes our coding orientations, through our socialisation in the home and education systems. And it is ideology that differentially distributes control over the privileged genres of modernity, by means of differing educational outcomes. Bernstein refers to these effects of ideology as 'distributive rules', i.e. the patterns of distribution of material and semiotic resources in a society. The distribution of material resources is mediated by the distribution of semiotic resources, so that in industrialised societies power operates through control of both industrial capital and symbolic capital. For Bernstein this duality gives rise to tension between what he calls the old and new middle classes, whose occupations are associated with material and symbolic production respectively. He defines ideology as 'a way of making relations. It is not a content but a way in which relationships are made and realised' (1996:31). This marks an important distinction from other interpretations that construe ideology as a content of discourse, leading for example to the popular liberal view that social equity can be achieved by changing the ideological content of school curricula. In our emerging model of discourse in social context, ideology is understood more generally as relations that permeate every level of semiosis; there is no meaning outside of power.

Even in everyday contexts within our local kin and peer groups, our relative power and control in a context may be conditioned by age, gender and other status markers. In post-colonial societies the range of genres in a culture is further differentiated by institutions such as science, industry and administration, and as we have said, control over these genres depends on specialised educational pathways, and access to these pathways depends largely on our position in relation to socio-economic power (i.e. our socio-economic class position). In this kind of social complex, the scope of our control over genres of power in turn conditions our status ranking in social hierarchies, our claim to authority in institutional fields, and our prominence in public life. Within specific situations, these register variables translate into our options to dominate or defer, to assert or concede authority, and to command attention or pay attention to others. Ideology thus runs through the entire ensemble of language in social context, differentiating social subjects in hierarchies of power, control, status, authority and prominence, for which we have used the following proportions (from Martin 1992):

ideology (access)	*power*
genre (management)	control
tenor (social hierarchy)	status
field (expertise & rank)	authority
mode (attention)	prominence

1.3.4 Related approaches to genre – three traditions

Space precludes a scholarly review of alternative approaches to genre that have developed in parallel to our own. Our own approach has come to be referred to as the 'Sydney School', a term introduced by Green & Lee 1994.[7] Hyon's influential 1996 article on 'Genre in three traditions' designates New Rhetoric and ESP traditions as the main alternative perspectives; her framework also informs Hyland's 2002 review of genre theory and literacy teaching. Seminal publications associated with the New Rhetoric group include Miller 1984, Bazerman 1988 and Berkenkotter & Huckin 1995; Freedman & Medway 1994a, b and Coe et al. 2002 assemble inspiring collections of like-minded work. Seminal work grounding the ESP tradition would include Swales 1990, Bhatia 1993, Paltridge 1997 and Hyland 2000. Paltridge 2001, Johns 2002 and Hyland 2004 focus on a range of applications of ideas from all three schools to literacy teaching. Coppock 2001 and Colombi & Schleppergrell 2002 provide expansive windows on recent research.

From our own perspective the main thing that distinguishes our work is its development within SFL as a functional linguistic perspective on genre analysis. This means that our approach is:

- social rather than cognitive (or socio-cognitive as in say Berkenkotter & Huckin 1995)[8]
- social semiotic rather than ethnographic, with tenor, field and mode explored as patterns of meaning configured together as the social practices we call genres
- integrated within a functional theory of language rather than interdisciplinary; note however that our theory is multi-perspectival (i.e. including several complementary ways of looking at text, e.g. metafunction, strata)
- fractal rather than eclectic, with basic concepts such as metafunction redeployed across strata, and across modalities of communication (e.g. image, sound, action and spatial design)
- interventionist rather than critical[9] since following Halliday we see linguistics as an ideologically committed form of social action.

Our basic definition of genre as a configuration of meanings, realised through language and attendant modalities of communication, is designed to generalise across these distinguishing features. Among linguists, our approach is probably most closely related to the work of Biber and his colleagues on text types (e.g. Biber & Finnegan 1994, Biber 1995),[10] although their work has been far more quantitative than ours and far less informed by rich descriptions of meaning such as those we derive from SFL. So it is to this model of language, and the thinking it enabled, that we now turn.

1.4   Systemic functional linguistics

Systemic functional linguistics (hereafter SFL) is a big multi-perspective theory with more dimensions in its theory banks than might be required for any one job. So we're going to be selective here and introduce some of the basic ideas we need for the chapters which follow, setting aside some things to be introduced as they impinge on what we're doing later on. We'll begin with why SFL is systemic and why it's functional.

1.4.1 Axis – system and structure

SFL is called systemic because compared with other theories it foregrounds the organisation of language as options for meaning. In this view, the key relations between the elements of language are relationships of choice – basically between what you say and what you could have said instead if you hadn't decided on what you did say. Traditionally these relations are modelled in paradigms like those you find for inflecting verbs and nouns in language manuals. For example, Table 1.1 shows the choices that speakers of the Australian language Pitjantjatjara can make, for expressing the time of events in the tense system of verbs.

Table 1.1 Options in TENSE in Pitjantjatjara

time	verb inflection	translation
future	*tati-lku*	will climb
present	*tati-ni*	is climbing
past	*tati-nu*	did climb
past durative	*tati-ningi*	was climbing
habitual	*tati-lpai*	does climb

Such a paradigmatic perspective is often used in linguistics, but SFL privileges this perspective on language as sets of resources for making meaning, rather than rules for ordering structures. Furthermore, because the relations among options for making meaning are so complex, systemic linguists generally model paradigms as diagrams called system networks, rather than as tables. We used one of these networks in Fig. 1.1 above to show how the genres we were discussing were related to one another, shown again here.

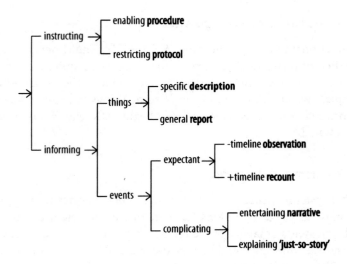

Figure 1.1 (repeated)

The horizontal arrows in the network lead to systems of choices in which you can choose one feature or another; and these choices lead on to other systems, in which you can choose another feature, until you get to the end of the feature path. So to get to the recount genre you have to choose **informing** (not instructing), and then **events** (not things) and then **expectant** (not complicating). The final choice for recount genre inherits meaning from each choice taken up along the path. As we can see, this is a relational theory of meaning, influenced by Saussure's notion of *valeur* – which means that the features don't refer to objects in the world or concepts in the mind (as is supposed in representational theories of meaning) but rather outline the significant contrasts that organise language or other semiotic systems as a meaning making resource.

Although paradigmatic relations are foregrounded in SFL, each feature in a system is realised as some kind of structure, or 'syntagm' (including of course structures consisting of a single element). Units of syntagmatic structure are given functional labels, that describe the contribution they make to the structure as a whole. We presented structures of this kind above, in relation to the staging of genres of service encounter, appointment making and narrative of personal experience. The structure of Mitchell's market auction can be represented as a tree diagram with four constituents (a constituency tree), as in Figure 1.8.

In SFL constituency diagrams of this kind, labels for classes of structures (such as 'market auction') are conventionally written in lower case, while functional elements of structure are written with an initial upper case letter. The class labels correspond with choices, or bundles of choices, from system networks, and each choice is realised as a functional element of structure, or **function structure**.

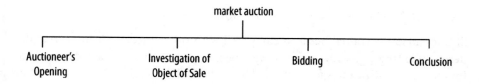

Figure 1.8 Schematic structure for Mitchell's market auction

The 'underlying' connection between paradigmatic choice and syntagmatic realisation is outlined in Figure 1.9, for the three kinds of Libyan service encounters
in Mitchell's description. The small arrows angled from top left to bottom right
symbolise this 'choice to chain' connection; the '+' sign indicates that the stage
is present; and parentheses indicate that the element is optional. To simplify the
presentation we haven't tried to specify in the network how elements are sequenced
in structures, although this is another important aspect of the realisation relationship
between system and structure.

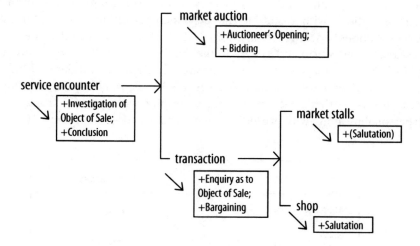

Figure 1.9 System network and realisation rules for Mitchell's analysis

The system network and realisation rules in Figure 1.9 help to clarify the sense
in which system is foregrounded over structure in SFL. Both are considered, but
structure is derived from system – syntagmatic relations are modelled as the consequence of paradigmatic choice. The complementary dimensions of system and
structure in SFL are referred to as **axis**.

1.4.2 Metafunction – enacting, construing, organising

SFL is called functional because compared with other theories it interprets the design of of language with respect to ways people use it to live. It is one of a family of functional linguistic theories (reviewed by Butler 2003) that share this goal. Within this family SFL stands out with respect to the emphasis it places on interpreting language as organised around three major strands of meaning that we introduced above as **metafunctions** – the ideational, interpersonal and textual metafunctions. Ideational resources are concerned with construing experience: what's going on, including who's doing what to whom, where, when, why and how and the logical relation of one going-on to another. Interpersonal resources are concerned with negotiating social relations: how people are interacting, including the feelings they try to share. Textual resources are concerned with information flow: the ways in which ideational and interpersonal meanings are distributed in waves of semiosis, including interconnections among waves and between language and attendant modalities (action, image, music etc.).

Metafunctions have implications for both paradigmatic and syntagmatic relations. Paradigmatically, they organise system networks into bundles of inter-dependent options, with lots of internal dependencies within metafunctions but fewer connections between metafunctions. Halliday & Matthiessen's 2004 networks for TRANSITIVITY, MOOD and THEME in the English clause reflect organisation of this kind. Syntagmatically, metafunctions are associated with different kinds of structure (Halliday 1979). In Martin's terms (1996, 2000), ideational meaning is associated with particulate structure, textual meaning with periodic structure and interpersonal meaning with prosodic structure, schematised in Figure 1.10.

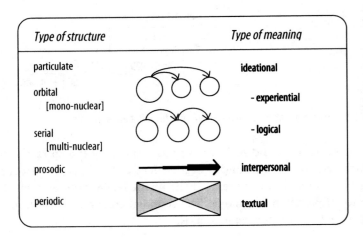

Figure 1.10 Kinds of meaning in relation to kinds of structure

Particulate structure is segmental, with segments organised into orbital or serial patterns. By orbital structure we mean structure with some kind of nucleus on which other segments depend – as with solar systems and atoms. For Mitchell's service encounters for example we might argue that examining the object for sale and deciding whether to buy it or not are nuclear; you can't have a service encounter without these steps. Then for market and shop transactions there are additional dependent stages – asking whether the goods are available or not, bargaining for them if they are present and desirable, and perhaps more peripherally an exchange of greetings between buyer and seller. This nucleus and satellite proposal is outlined in Figure 1.11.

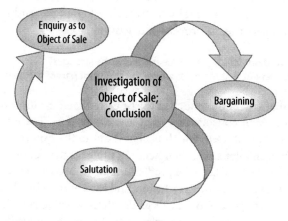

Figure 1.11 Orbital ideational structure (nucleus & satellites)

By serial structure we mean structure in which segments depend on one another but there is no nuclear element – as with links in a chain or a line of telephone poles. These might be thought of as multi-nuclear rather than mono-nuclear structures. The protocol text reviewed above is a canonical example of this genre. There we had a list of rules, with no one rule more important than the others. The sequence of events in recounts and procedures also displays serial structure of this kind. This relatively open ended iterative organisation is exemplified in Figure 1.12, drawing on the event sequence in text [1:2] above (Conal's trip to the Blue Mountains).

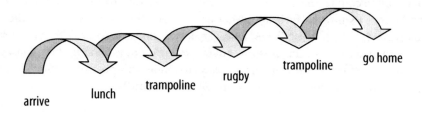

Figure 1.12 Serial ideational structure (segmental interdependency)

Periodic structure organises meaning into waves of information, with different wave lengths piled up one upon another. Linguists may be most familiar with this kind of pattern from phonology, where we can interpret a syllable as a wave of sonority (rising then falling), a foot as a wave of stressed and unstressed syllables, and a tone group as a wave of pre-tonic and tonic feet (Cleirigh 1998). To see how this works for genre let's go back to the magnet experiment, text [1:7]. This experimental procedure began with a title, 'The Strongest Parts of a Magnet', and continued with five headings: Aim, Equipment, Steps, Results, Conclusion. As far as layout is concerned, these headings were given equal status; but semantically speaking the first pairs off with the last. This is made clear through the complementarity of the headings (Aim and Conclusion) and by the wording *to find out* and *I found out* (a switch from an irrealis to a realis process of discovery):

Aim: **To find out** which part of the magnet is the strongest.
Conclusion: I **found out** that the poles where the strongest part of the magnet.

The Aim predicts what is to come (much as the title predicted the topic of the experiment) and the Conclusion consolidates what was discovered. These two segments thus bracket the experiment itself, which is played out in the Equipment, Steps and Results sections. On a smaller scale, each heading prefaces the details which follow.

Overall then we have three layers of prediction: the title to the rest of the text, the Aim to the rest of the text minus the Conclusion, and each of the 5 headings in relation to the clauses that spell them out (so 4 layers in all). Retrospectively on the other hand we have just two layers, the Conclusion in relation to the text that it distills. We've used indentation to display these layers of scaffolding for text [1:7] in Figure 1.13.

The wave metaphor suggests that each clause is a small pulse of information, that each of these combines with its heading to form a larger wave, that the Equipment, Steps and Results wave combine with Aim in one direction and Conclusion in the other to form a larger wave still, and that finally all of this combines with the title to form the tidal wave of information comprising the text as a whole. From this example we can see that periodic structure organises serial or orbital structure into pulses of information of different wave lengths so that the ideational meanings can be digested textually, byte by byte.

Prosodic structure involves continuous motifs of meaning colouring extended domains of discourse. In text [1:5] for example, Conal doesn't just describe his red setter, he tells us how he feels about her as well. For this he uses some explicitly evaluative lexis (*lovely, sweet, loving, cute, very loved*), and also some descriptive lexis that can be read as connoting positive qualities (*fluffy, furry, smooth, shiny, big, tall, very long*). The effect is cumulative, and relays to readers his positive feelings for his pet (attitudinal lexis <u>underlined</u>, descriptive lexis in **bold**).

The Strongest Parts of a Magnet

Aim:
To find out which part of the magnet is the strongest.

Equipment:
You will need a magnet, pins or some-thing . . . iron.

Steps:
1. Spread your pins out on the table.
2. Put your magnet over your pins.
3. See what happened/s.
4. Repet trying sides with pins.
5. See which side is the strongest by comparing.

Results:
The pins all went to the poles.

Conclusion:
I found out that the poles where the strongest part of the magnet.

Figure 1.13 Waves of periodic structure

[1:5']

My dog Tammy has a <u>lovly</u> reddy brown furr. Here eyes are brown too. Her shape is skinny. She has a **fluffy, furry, smooth and shinny texture**. She moves by wagging her tail and waving her body. The feelings that I feel of my dog is <u>sweat</u>, <u>loving</u> and <u>cute</u>. My dog is <u>very loved</u>. She smells <u>sweet</u>. My dog is **big, tall and very long**.

Conal's description reflects two strategies for mapping prosodic structure onto discourse – saturation and intensification. Saturation involves opportunistic realisation; you realise a meaning wherever you can (for Conal this means creating opportunities for attitudinal adjectives). Intensification involves amplifying the strength of your feeling so that it has more mass; turning up the volume as it were. This can be done through submodification (*very loved*) and iteration (*fluffy, furry, smooth and shiny; sweat, loving and cute*), illustrated in Figure 1.14.

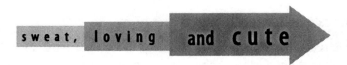

Figure 1.14 Prosodic intensification

Another way in which prosodic structure can map itself over a stretch of discourse is to associate itself with a dominant textual position – the peak of a higher level wave which previews or reviews smaller waves of information. Conal's trip to the park observation/comment and Blue Mountains recount use evaluation retrospectively in this way to project his positive feelings over the experience as a whole.

> **[1:1']**
>
> On Sunday the 9th of November Jesse my friend and me Conal, went to the park called Jonson park me and Jesse played on the playaquitmint and **it was very fun**…

> **[1:2']**
>
> Last Sunday me and My family went to the blue Mountains to go and see my dads friends. … I had **a great day**.

This kind of cumulative evaluation scoping back over stretches of text is illustrated in Figure 1.15.

Figure 1.15 Cumulative evaluation scoping back

From examples like these we can see that textual meaning packages interpersonal and well as ideational meaning, reconciling particulate and prosodic with periodic structure. The result is a metafunctionally composite texture integrating ideational, interpersonal and textual meaning with one another. It follows from this that the staging structures proposed by Mitchell, Hasan and Labov & Waletzky have to be read as provisional, since they in fact reduce three strands of meaning to a simple constituency tree. We'll unpick the limitations of this compromise at several points in Chapters 2 to 7 below.

1.4.3 Stratification – levels of language

Alongside axis and metafunction, we also need to look at stratification. We introduced this dimension of analysis above, in relation to the strata of social context, but within language itself the way in which SFL interprets levels of language is distinctive in important respects.

Basically what we are dealing with here is a hierarchy of abstraction, which for linguists is grounded in phonology.[11] But beyond phonology, the levels of language we recognise and what we call them gets very theory specific. Hjelmslev 1961 moves from 'expression form' to 'content form', arguing that language is a stratified semiotic system, not simply a system of signs. In mainstream American linguistics the most familiar hierarchy is probably phonology, morphology, syntax, semantics and pragmatics. SFL's approach to stratification is influenced by the fact that it is a functional theory not a formal one, and so is more concerned with language and social context than language and cognition; and as far as levels are concerned, axis and metafunction play a critical role.

The impact of axis and metafunction is the descriptive power they bring to a given level in the model. Both paradigmatic and syntagmatic relations are considered; and three complementary kinds of meaning and their distinctive structuring principles are brought into play.[12] The richness of the descriptions these complementarities afford is best exemplified in SFL's extravagant descriptions of lexicogrammar, in English (e.g. Halliday & Matthiessen 2004) and other languages (e.g. Caffarel et al. 2005, Rose 1993, 1996, 2001a, 2004a, 2005a&b). In these grammars a good deal of analysis that is relegated to semantics or pragmatics in formal models is managed at a less abstract level of interpretation, next to phonology. This makes room at the next level up for the discourse oriented semantics developed in Martin 1992 and Martin & Rose 2003/2007.

Levels of language, or strata, are conventionally modelled as nested co-tangential circles in SFL, as shown for language in context in Figures 1.2, 1.3 and 1.7 above, and here in Figure 1.16 for levels within language.

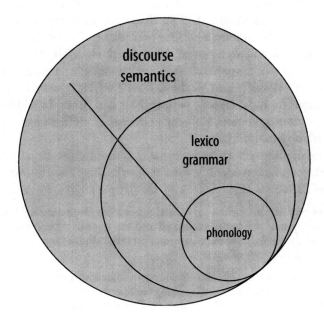

Figure 1.16 Levels within language

Layers of abstraction begin with expression form in the lower right hand corner of the diagram (here phonology). Phonological patterns are reinterpreted at a higher level of abstraction as grammar and lexis (or lexicogrammar as it is generally known). Lexicogrammatical patterns are in turn reinterpreted at the next stratum as discourse semantics. Strata are related through realisation and metaredundancy – patterns of patterns of patterns, as we discussed above. It is important to note that realisation is not directional – lexicogrammar for example construes, is construed by, and over time reconstrues and is reconstrued by discourse semantics. It's the same for all levels.

It is important to keep in mind at this point that axis, metafunction and stratification articulate a multi-dimensional theoretical space which is difficult to represent in two-dimensional diagrams on a printed page. The intersection of metafunction and stratification is configured in Figure 1.7 above; but behind this lies axis; and beyond this there is the alignment of axis with constituency hierarchy to worry about. For example, there are system and structure cycles for clauses, for their component groups and phrases, for their component words in turn, and ultimately in a language like English for their component morphemes. For the purposes of this book we don't need to probe further into this complexity here.

1.5   Tools for analysis: discourse semantics

Defining genre as a configuration of meanings means that we have to analyse those meanings. When analysing English genres the SFL descriptions we've relied on are Halliday 1967, 1970 for phonology, Halliday 1994 and Halliday & Matthiessen 2004 for lexicogrammar and Martin 1992 for discourse semantics. Obviously we can't introduce all of this description here. Our basic strategy in the chapters which follow will be to introduce analyses as we need them, especially for phonology and lexicogrammar. We will however at this point present a brief overview of discourse semantics as it is developed in Martin & Rose 2003/2007, since these are the resources which interface most directly with register and genre. In addition we'll include short notes on negotiation, Halliday's concept of grammatical metaphor and emerging work on multimodality.

Martin & Rose organise their discourse analysis around five major headings: appraisal, ideation, conjunction, identification and periodicity. They introduce these systems as follows (2003: 16–17):

> **Appraisal** is concerned with evaluation – the kinds of attitudes that are negotiated in a text, the strength of the feelings involved and the ways in which values are sourced and readers aligned. Appraisals are interpersonal kinds of meanings, that realise variations in the tenor of a text. ...

> **Ideation** focuses on the content of a discourse – what kinds of activities are undertaken, and how participants undertaking these activities are described and classified. These are ideational kinds of meaning, that realise the field of a text.

Conjunction looks at inter-connections between activities – reformulating them, adding to them, sequencing them, explaining them and so on. These are also ideational types of meanings, but of the subtype 'logical'. Logical meanings are used to form temporal, causal and other kinds of connectivity.

Identification is concerned with tracking participants – with introducing people, places and things into a discourse and keeping track of them once there. These are textual resources, concerned with how discourse makes sense to the reader by keeping track of identities.

Periodicity (as we've already seen) considers the rhythm of discourse – the layers of prediction that flag for readers what's to come, and the layers of consolidation that accumulate the meanings made. These are also textual kinds of meanings, concerned with organising discourse as pulses of information.

We'll now illustrate each of these with examples from the texts introduced above.

1.5.1 Appraisal – negotiating attitudes

The focus here is on attitude – the feelings and values that are negotiated with readers. The key resources here have to do with evaluating things, people's character and their feelings. In [1:10] for example Conal describes the feelings of the white people and the sparrow (affect), makes a judgement about the physical capacity of the sparrow when it was trying to escape the bullets (judgement) and comments on his own and the white people's reactions to the sparrow (appreciation).

[1:10']

Once when the white people came to Australia there was a little bird called a sparow. It was a very nice bird but the white people that first came to Australia they thoute that the sparrow as a very annoying bird because it slowly flew around them slowly. One time they got so annoyed that they got a gun out and tride to shote it so he got his gun out and shot his gun but it didn't hit the bird it was write behind the sparow the sparow's aims got so tiyard that he had to stop flapping its wings and it sort of glided just near the ground and he moved and the bullets went away and that is how the sparow's lernt how to glide. And they lived happily ever after.

Four of these evaluations are explicitly intensified, through submodification (*so*, *very*), reflecting the fact that attitude is a gradable system:

affect:	**so** annoyed; happily
judgement:	**so** tiyard
appreciation:	a **very** nice bird; a **very** annoying bird

It's also possible to scale the grading of a feeling down, as Conal did in [1:3] when describing how he felt riding on the ghost slide (*a bit scared*). Grading is also related to quantity, and distance in time and space:

heps of other rides [1:3]
you coldn't see **everything** [1:3]
they **finily** announced [1:3]
they lived happily **ever after** [1:10]
just near the ground [1:10]

In addition to grading of this kind, we find resources for blurring and sharpening categories. Conal uses these to blur one of his processes, and to approximate age and time:

it **sort of** glided [1:10]
about 19 or 18 years old [1:2]
about half an hour [1:2]

Alternatively, boundaries might have been strengthened (e.g. *true gliding, exactly half an hour*).

Alongside attitude and graduation, the other dimension of appraisal analysis we need to consider has to do with the sourcing of evaluation. Conal himself is the source of opinions in most of the writing introduced above, but he does use projection to assign feelings to others (he thinks the sparrow was a very nice bird but it was the white people who came to Australia who found it annoying):

It was a **very nice** bird
but
the white people… they thoute that the sparrow as a **very annoying** bird [1:10]

Projection (quoting and reporting) and related resources such as modality, polarity and concession bring voices other than the writer's own voice into a text. Together they are referred to as engagement, which we'll explore in more detail as analysis requires in Chapters 2–6 below (drawing on Martin & White 2005).

1.5.2 Ideation – construing experience

Here we're concerned with people and things, and the activities they're involved in. In Conal's recounts and procedure, there's lots of activity involved and it unfolds in sequences. Getting to Ottawa in [1:3] takes 10 steps (activities in **bold**):

Me my sister my Brother my dad and Sue our house mate all **got ready to go**
the taxi **came** at about 9:30
we **got on** the taxi
(we) **went** to the airport
(we) **waited** for the people to announe when our plain is going to come…
they finily **announced** that the plain is here
we **got strait on** the plain
it **left** at about 10:00 in the morning
it **took** a day and a harf **to get** there
we **got off** the plain
we **went** on a taxi to Autawa

Each step tells us who or what was involved (people, taxi, plane), what happened (come, go, wait etc.) and sometimes when and where it happened as well (at about 930, to the airport).

As well as sequences of activities, ideation is concerned with describing and classifying people and things. In [1:4] for example Conal classifies crocodiles as reptiles, decomposes them (four legs, scales, jaw, tail, eggs) and describes their parts (long, powerful, big).

1.5.3 Conjunction – inter-connections between processes

Conal uses a variety of these in his 'just so' story [1:10]. His favourite move is simply to add on clauses with *and*, leaving it to readers to construe implicit temporal or causal links as required. Next most common are his explicit causal connections (*because, so x that* and *so*). And there are two concessive links, countering expectations (*but*). Interestingly enough there is no explicit temporal succession at all, which underscores the importance of field specific activity sequencing (in this case a hunting sequence) in structuring recount and narrative genres.

Once **when** the white people came to Australia
there was a little bird called a sparow.
It was a very nice bird
but the white people … they thoute that the sparrow as a very annoying bird
because it slowly flew around them slowly.
One time they got **so** annoyed[13]
that they got a gun out
and tride to shote it
so he got his gun out
and shot his gun
but it didn't hit the bird
it was write behind the sparow
the sparow's aims got **so** tiyard
that he had to stop flapping its wings
and it sort of glided just near the ground
and he moved
and the bullets went away
and that is how the sparow's lernt how to glide.
And they lived happily ever after.

The system of conjunction described in Martin & Rose 2003/2007 is also closely related to the model of logicosemantic relations developed by Halliday 2004, summarised in Table 1.2. We use this model in *Genre Relations* to describe how text segments are linked to each other in series, including phases within stories (Chapter 2), images to verbal text (Chapter 4), and genres connected in series in textbooks (Chapter 5).

Table 1.2 Types of logicosemantic relations (from Halliday 2004: 220)

type	symbol	subtypes
elaborating	=	*restating in other words, specifying in greater detail, commenting or exemplifying*
extending	+	*adding some new element, giving an exception to it, or offering an alternative*
enhancing	x	*qualifying it with some circumstantial feature of time, place, cause or condition*
projecting	'	*a locution or an idea*

1.5.4 IDENTIFICATION – tracking people and things

Conal's 'just so' story for example has a sparrow as its main protagonist. This character is introduced indefinitely as *a little bird called a sparrow*, and then tracked through various forms of anaphoric reference – via the definite deictic *the* (*the sparrow, the bird*), and the pronouns *it, its* and *he*.

a little bird called a sparow
the sparow
it
it
the bird
the sparow
the sparow's [arms]
he
its [wings]
he

Note how Conal's reference switches from specific to generic in the last two lines (*the sparow's* <- *they*) as he generalises an explanation from his tale. The second last line also includes a good example of text reference, with his story as a whole consolidated as an anaphoric participant *that* (**that**'s *how the sparow's lernt to glide*). Text reference like this is an important resource for organising the global structure of genres.

1.5.5 Periodicity – the rhythm of discourse

Here we're concerned with information flow – the way in which meanings are organised so that readers can process phases of meaning. We looked at this from a top-down perspective when introducing periodic structure above. Moving down to information flow inside the clause we need to consider two complementary peaks of textual prominence. According to Halliday (e.g. 1994) in English the first of these occurs at the beginning of the clause and extends up to and including the first ideational element of structure. Halliday calls this peak of prominence **Theme**. In Conal's crocodile report [1:4] the ideational Theme is always *crocodiles* (realised lexically and pronominally), since this is his invariant angle on the field.

The second peak of prominence regularly falls towards the end of the clause, where English places the major pitch movement for each unit of information. According to Halliday (e.g. 1967, 1970, 1994) this pitch movement signals the culmination of **New** information, which can extend indefinitely to its left towards the beginning of the clause. For written texts we can usually assume an unmarked intonation structure, and treat the last ideational element of structure as minimal New. On the basis of this assumption we can analyse Theme and New in the crocodile report [1:4] as outlined below (Themes are underlined, New in **bold**).

<u>Crocodiles</u> are **from the reptile family**.
<u>Crocodiles</u> are **like snakes but with two legs on each side of the crocodiles body**.
<u>Crocodiles</u> have **four legs**
and <u>the crocodiles</u> have **scales all over its body**.[14]
<u>Crocodiles</u> have a **long gore**
and <u>they</u> have a **long powerful tail**
<u>so it</u> can nock its **enems into the water**
<u>so it</u> can **eat the animal**.
<u>Crocodiles</u> live on the **ege of a swamp or a river**.
<u>They</u> make there **nests out of mud and leaves**.
<u>Crocodiles</u> eat meat lke **chikens, cows and catle and other kinds of animals**.
<u>Crocdils</u> move by **there legs**.
<u>Crocodiles</u> can **walk on legs**.
<u>Crocodiles</u> have **four legs**.
<u>Crocodiles</u> also have **scals all over there body**
and <u>they</u> have a **powerfall tail**
[-][15] to swim **in the water**.
<u>Crocdils</u> have **eggs**
<u>they</u> do not have (live) **babys**.
<u>Crocodiles</u> can carry **there egg(s) in there big gore**.

Clearly choices for New are much more variable than for Theme. Conal uses them to elaborate his field, incorporating a range of information into his report. Although exaggerated here, this kind of complementarity between consistent selections for Theme and varied selections for New is quite typical.

In adult texts it is more common to find discontinuity in Theme selection. We'll deal with the meaning of such discontinuity as examples arise in Chapters 2–6 below. But we can note here in passing the way in which Conal manages the transition in his recount [1:3], from his trip to Ottawa to his day at Cascades water park. The trip to Ottawa features people as Theme (Conal and his family, and airport officials); the trip to Cascades on the other hand features the park and its rides. So Conal's angle on the field shifts from people to places. He also uses what Halliday 2004 calls a **marked Theme** to signal his move from one activity sequence to the next (*On that same day*). Because the most typical ideational Theme is Subject in

English, an ideational element coming before the Subject is a marked Theme (in declarative clauses). Marked Themes and shifts in thematic continuity of this kind are important realisations of global text organisation.

> …
> and we got strait on the plain
> and it left at about 10:00 in the morning
> it took a day and a harf to get there
> so when we got off the plain[16]
> we went on a taxi to Autawa,
> Autawa is where my grandma and granpa live.
> On that same day we went to a playce called cascads
> it was a water park.
> it was so big there was only about 10 or 11 water slides
> but they were so fun.
> My favorite water salide was the gost slide
> it was pitch black
> four or five peaple can go at a time
> because it was lick one of those small pools
> but it didn't have water in it
> …

Taking this clause perspective back to the discussion of periodic structure above, we can treat peaks of textual prominence which predict how a text will unfold as higher level Themes, and peaks which sum up what has unfolded as higher level News. Martin & Rose 2003/2007 use the terms hyperTheme and hyperNew for the first level up from clause Theme and New, and macroTheme and macroNew for further layers in a text's hierarchy of periodicity. We modelled this kind of hierarchy with the diagram in Figure 1.17.

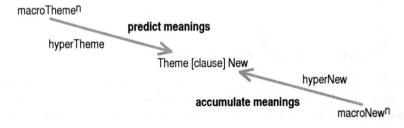

Figure 1.17 Layers of Theme and New in discourse

1.5.6 NEGOTIATION – enacting exchanges

These are discourse semantic resources for managing turn taking and speech functions in dialogue. In the 2nd edition of *Working with Discourse* Martin & Rose 2007 include a chapter on these resources, called negotiation. Since we're dealing mainly with written genres here we won't need to draw heavily on negotiation but can direct readers interested in work by the Sydney School on spoken genres to Ventola 1987 (service encounters), Eggins & Slade 2005 (casual conversation), Christie 2002 (classroom discourse) and Iedema 2003 (meetings).

However the interpersonal systems of mood and speech function, that enact negotiation, are relevant to both genre classification and genre staging. Halliday 2004 describes how selections in the mood of clauses typically realise speech functions in the following proportions:

MOOD	SPEECH FUNCTION
imperative	command
declarative	statement
interrogative	question

In terms of negotiation, the function of a command is to demand goods-&-services, the function of a question is to demand information, while a statement gives information. In Figure 1.1 we distinguished instructing from informing genres on the basis of the way they interact with readers through speech functions: procedures and protocols give commands, while the other genres make statements. And inside [1:7], the science experiment text, we find commands in imperative mood in the Steps section, but statements in declarative mood in the Results and Conclusion.

[1:7] The Strongest Parts of a Magnet

Aim:

To find out which part of the magnet is the strongest.

Equipment:

You will need a magnet, pins or some-thing that is mad out of iron.

Steps:

1   Spread your pins out on the table.

2   Put your magnet over your pins.

3   See what happened/s.

4   Repet trying sides with pins.

5   See which side is the strongest by comparing.

Results:

The pins all went to the poles.

Conclusion:

I found out that the poles where the strongest part of the magnet.

The Equipment section is arguably a command too, although the mood is declarative. The Aim is moodless (a non-finite clause) and so harder still to classify as statement or command. Perhaps like the title of the text, which is a nominal group rather than a clause, it would be better left alone as far as speech function analysis is concerned. We'll return to these issues of interpretation in our discussion of grammatical metaphor in a moment. Our point here is simply to illustrate that the way a text interacts with readers is an important interpersonal dimension of a genre.

We can also note that even though our sample texts are in one sense monologue, they do involve some repartee – since Conal's and Ben's teachers have responded to them. In this negotiation, Conal's narrative, text [1:9] functions as a kind of initiation, and his teacher's encouragement and query as a response (in this context an evaluation of his unconsummated narrative structure).

> **Initiation** – In the outback in vicktorya in 1918 there was three there names where isack, jane, and frank isack was 4, Jane was 7 and frank was 9. there mother told them to go to some brom bushes so there mother could mack a brom. They left on Friday and when they didn't come back!!!!!!
>
> **Response** – A good start, Conal. What next?

Ben's teacher was less understanding, using a range of moods to respond to his history of the planet:

> Where is your margin?   [interrogative]
> This is not a story.   [declarative]
> Finish please.   [imperative]

Despite their grammatical variety, these can all arguably be interpreted as commands, since each tells Ben to do something to his text and image (literally speaking she says '*Add a margin, switch genres and finish your picture*'). This brings us once again to the problem of grammatical metaphor, and the role it plays in interpreting genres as configurations of meaning.

1.6   Grammatical metaphor

This takes us back to the stratified model of language we presented in Fig. 1.16 above. Basically Halliday is suggesting that in models of this kind lexicogrammar can realise discourse semantics directly or not. Suppose for example it is the first day of school and Conal's teacher is asking him his name. The direct way of doing this is through a wh-interrogative clause:

> What's your name? [interrogative:wh mood]
> - Conal.

But there are alternatives. The teacher could use an imperative clause with a process naming what she wants him to do and a participant naming the information she wants:

> Tell me your name. [imperative mood]
> - Conal.

Or she could use a declarative, with rising intonation, and with an empty slot instead of New at the end:

> And you are… ? [declarative mood]
> - Conal.

From the perspective of discourse semantics each alternative has a comparable effect; as exemplified through Conal's compliant responses above the teacher does learn Conal's name – he gives her the information she demands. But Halliday's point is that they don't all mean the same thing since in the first example the grammar and semantics match whereas in the second and third examples they don't. The second example is an imperative standing for a question, just as the third is a declarative standing for one. For indirect realisations to work they have to dress themselves up as the meaning they imply, so listeners know not to take them at face value. The second example symbolises a question by combining the demanding function of imperative with naming what the teachers wants done (*tell* and *name*). The third example symbolises a question by using rising intonation to signal a demand and leaving a hole at the end to be filled with the new information she wants.

Halliday refers to realisations of this kind as grammatical metaphors because:

- there are two meanings involved (the lexicogrammatical and the discourse semantic one)

- the meanings are layered, with the grammar as figure and semantics as ground (grammar the 'literal' meaning and semantics the meaning it is 'transferred' to)

- one layer resembles the other, with grammar symbolising semantics.

- Technically speaking there is inter-stratal tension, and the meaning of the metaphor is more than the sum of its parts. This makes it possible for grammatical metaphors to be misunderstood or deliberately ignored. In the opening scene of the film *Educating Rita* for example Frank (Michael Caine) asks Rita (Julie Walters) indirectly for her name, but she misunderstands the move completely:

> Frank: And you are …?
>
> Rita: I'm a what?

And a close colleague of ours once walked into a bakeshop and asked politely for his favorite bun, only to have the server parry his indirectness with some blunt repartee:

> Client: I wonder if I could have one of those…
>
> Server: Why do you wonder? It's right here in front of you.

Failed metaphors are of course the exception to the rule. In general people deploy them to expand their resources for making meaning. A language with grammatical metaphor is not grammar squared, since the grammar has to symbolise semantics and this acts as a constraint on indirectness. But a system with interpersonal grammatical metaphor has an indefinitely larger repertoire of meanings for negotiating social relations than one without – as any parent knows from their interactions with pre-pubescent offspring who are largely limited to managing family life with direct commands working in tandem when required with emotional and physical outbursts.

So far we've looked at interpersonal metaphors of mood. Interpersonal metaphors of modality are also possible, and will be explored in more detail as required in the chapters below. Basically what is involved here are alternatives to direct realisations through modal verbs and adverbs. This can involve making the modality more subjective, by symbolising it with a first person present tense mental process:

direct: That's <u>probably</u> Conal's.

subjective metaphor: <u>I suppose</u> that's Conal's.

Or it can involve making the modality more objective, by nominalising it as an adjective or noun:

direct: You <u>must</u> finish it.

objective metaphor: It's <u>necessary</u> for you to finish it.

As with metaphors of mood, there are possibilities for misunderstanding and for resistance – at times enabling verbal play, as Doyle's long suffering Dr Watson knows very well:

'**I'm inclined to think**--' said I.

'**I should do so**,' Sherlock Holmes remarked impatiently. [Doyle 1981: 769]

Watson's metaphorical modality is taken literally by Holmes, who dismisses Watson's subjectively modalised conjecture before he gets it out of his mouth.

A comparable process of inter-stratal tension is found in the ideational realm. In English grammar, Halliday divides ideational meaning into logical and experiential resources. Logical resources expand segments in serial chains, as we described above, whereas experiential resources arrange segments in orbital configurations. Logical grammatical metaphors involve indirect realisations of conjunction, several examples of which are used to scaffold Conal's magnet experiment: Aim, Steps, Results, Conclusion.[17] Each of these headings is a noun and nominalises a temporal or causal meaning. We can explore this by re-writing these sections of [1.7] as a recount, turning these logical metaphors back into direct realisations as conjunctions linking clauses to one another.

> **[1.7']**
> We did an experiment
> **in order to** find out which part of the magnet is strongest.
> **First** we spread the pins out on the table.
> **Then** we put our magnet over our pins.
> **Then** we saw what happened.
> **Then** we tried the sides with pins.
> **Then** we saw which side was strongest by comparing.
> **Because** we did this,
> we saw that the pins all went to the poles.
> **So** we found out that the poles were the strongest part of the magnet.

Thus the heading Aim corresponds with the purpose linker *in order to*; Steps 1, 2, 3, 4 and 5 are reworked as successive connectors (*first, then*); and Results and Conclusion are rewritten as causal conjunctions (*because, so*). The proportions are as follows:

[1:7]	[1.7']
Aim	in order to
1	First
2	Then
3	Then
4	Then
5	Then
Results	Because
Conclusion	So

The nominalised realisations are used as scaffolding for stages in [1.7]; but as nouns they could have been deployed to realise logical connections inside the clause. So we can rewrite [1.7] again, expressing logical relations inside the clause this time, as [1.7"]:

> **[1.7"]**
>
> **The aim** of our experiment was to find out which part of the magnet is the strongest. **The steps** involved spreading our pins out on the table, putting our magnet over our pins, seeing what happened, repeating trying the sides with pins and seeing which side was the strongest by comparing. **The result** was that the pins all went to the poles. **Our conclusion** is that the poles are the strongest part of the magnet.

This text reconstructs what happened through a series of relational clauses in which the aim, steps, results and conclusion are identified with respect to what went on. The overall effect is to make things more abstract than [1.7] rather than more concrete.

Conjunctive relations can also be realised through verbs and prepositions:

verbal realisation: Careful experimentation **led to** our results.
prepositional realisation: We reached our conclusion **through** experimentation.

Logical metaphors of this kind depend on nominalising what happened as well, so that the prepositions and verbs have something to hang on to. Nominalisation of goings on is referred to by Halliday as experiential grammatical metaphor. Put simply, this involves realising processes and information dependent on them as nominal groups. To explore this process let's go back to Conal's crocodile report and look at some of the scaffolding his teacher used to help him organise his information when he was doing research as part of a unit of work on Kakadu National Park. At the top of a 2 page worksheet she outlined his task as follows:

> Pick one of the animals mentioned in the book Kakadu and write a report on it. You will need to find the information and take notes in point form first. Then you need to write the report using full sentences, a new paragraph for each heading and don't forget capital letter and full stops.

And she then provided a list of seven headings with room next to each for Conal to record his information. He undertook this task as follows:

Classification: crocodiles are in the reptile family. Crocodiles are like snakes but with legs.

Appearance: crocodiles have legs and have scalies and they have a long gore and It as a long and powerful tail to nock down its enemy in the water so it can eat it.

Habitat: crocdiles live on the ege of a swamp or a river. They make there nests out of mud and some leaves.

Food: crocodiles eat meat like chickens and cows and catle and other animals.

Movement: Crocodiles can walk on land and they swim with there powerfall tail.

Reproduction: Crocodiles have egge they don't have babyies.

Interesting Information: Crocodiles cary eggs in there moth.

This scaffolding involves several nominalisations, alongside the general terms *habitat* and *food* (comparable to *equipment* in the science experiment). Each is derived from a process, and so can be rewritten in a non-metaphorical way:

experiential metaphor	direct realisation
classification	classify
appearance	appear
movement	move
reproduction	reproduce
interesting information[18]	interest (as in *that interests me*)

As with the logical metaphors scaffolding the experiment, none of this metaphorical language appears in Conal's notes, nor in his report. At age 8, he's too young a writer to manage ideational metaphor on his own. Watching his struggles with this phenomenon reflects one of the most fascinating aspects of language and literacy development (Derewianka 2003, Painter 2003). For his description of Tammy, for example, his teacher provided him with comparable scaffolding (although in the shape of a pie with wedges for each heading this time and with more general terms than genuine metaphors); Conal compiled his notes as follows:

Size: big tall long

Colour: reddy, brown brown eyes

Shape: skinny

Texture: fluffy furry smoth shinny

Movement: waggy wavy

Feelings: sweat loving cute

Uses: loving

Smell: sweet

He then wrote a first draft of his description, in which he tried to incorporate a number of the headings (something he didn't attempt at all for the crocodile report):

[1.5′]

My dog Tammy has a lovly reddy browny furr. her eyes are brown too. The shape of my dog is skinny. The texture of Tammy my dog is fluffy, furry, smoth and shinny. The movement of my dog is she has a wagging tail and waving body. The feelings that I feel of my dog is sweat, loving and cute. My dog is used for loving. My dog smells like sweet. The size of my dog. My dog is big, tall and very long.

This works out fine as far as general terms like shape and texture are concerned. But his language doesn't unfold maturely once experiential metaphors are involved. He simply doesn't have the nominalisations to finish off his relational clauses, and so ends them as best he can. We know what he means, but it's not written English (this is a native speaker keep in mind). His teacher steps in and edits the *movement* clause (producing the version in [1.5] above):

The movement of my dog is she has a wagging tail and waving body.
[**edited as**: She moves by wagging her tail and waving her body.]

But she leaves the feeling clause, which isn't quite so easy to fix up:

The feelings that I feel of my dog is sweat, loving and cute.

This seems to frustrate Conal too, who verbalises *uses* in the following clause, with rather amusing results (needless to say his teacher does edit this one).[19]

> My dog is used for loving.
> [**edited as**: My dog is very loved.]

As a final step, Conal decides to avoid integrating headings in his sentences completely, writing down the heading and then starting a new sentence about the size of his dog:

> The size of my dog. My dog is big, tall and very long.

What these struggles underscore is the immense and generally overlooked watershed constituted by processes of grammatical metaphor for literacy development. We'll return to this theme at various points in our discussion, and try and address it explicitly in our presentation of a learner pathway for history genres (Chapter 3). As Conal's description suggests, certain kinds of abstraction are fine in primary school; general terms like *equipment, habitat, food, size, shape, colour, texture* and *smell* are not an issue. But experiential and logical metaphors are not under productive control; that control is the mission of secondary schooling, although few teachers there have any linguistic awareness at all of what they are meant to achieve.

That said, the abstract and grammatically metaphorical scaffolding Conal's teachers are providing seems to be working very well as an organising tool for his research and writing. It functions in a sense as a surrogate hierarchy of periodicity for his texts, and in doing so it anticipates the uses he will make of this kind of language to construct his own layers of prediction and summary as he develops his writing in secondary school. As may be apparent, the scaffolding is derived from the generic staging proposed for various genres by ourselves and various colleagues. So it is also introducing a degree of metalinguistic awareness into schools, at least with respect to genres (grammar is another matter). In this regard it is useful to keep in mind as genre analysts that the names we use for genre and genre stages are just that – names. As such they compartmentalise complex linguistic processes as things, and misconceive texts as compositions made of parts in wholes. It's hard to hang on to a dynamic conception of genres as ongoing expansions of instantial meaning; but we should try.

1.7   A note on multimodality

Having defined genres as configurations of meaning, our ultimate goal has always been to map cultures as systems of genre. This is an ambitious project, that we are nowhere near achieving. It's important to stress at this point however that the project depends on multimodal discourse analysis, since genres are typically realised through more than one modality of communication (i.e. some combination of language, image, sound, action, spatial design etc.). Multimodal analysis is not the focus of this book, although we will deal with intermodality issues as they arise, especially in Chapters 4 and 5. For ongoing social semiotic work on this frontier see Iedema 2001, 2003b, Jewitt 2002, Lemke 1998, 2002, Macken-Horarik 2003, 2004, Martin & Stenlin 2004, O'Halloran 1999a, b, 2000, Ravelli 2000, Royce 1998, Unsworth 2001, van Leeuwen & Humphrey 1996.

The first multimodal text we presented here was Ben's history of the planet, text [1:11]. The image from is text is presented as Figure 1.18 – a drawing of the planet earth with what appear to be continents sketched in. In Kress & van Leeuwen's 2006 terms, the image is a conceptual rather than a narrative representation, analytical (involving a part-whole structure), and has a scientific coding orientation. As such, it is an appropriate image to accompany Ben's geological discourse. Taken together, the verbiage and image certainly interact to construct [1:11] as a scientific explanation, not a narrative. Their multimodal synergy makes the teacher's response even less compliant than it might be had she evaluated either modality on its own.

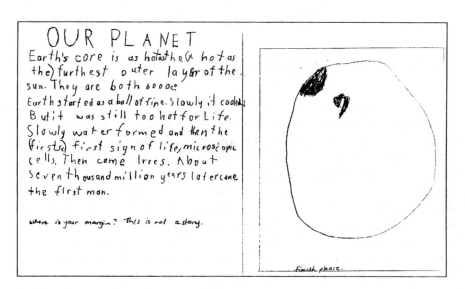

Figure 1.18 Ben's drawing of the planet earth (from Martin 1990)

The other multimodal text we noted in passing was Conal's pie chart scaffolding for his description of his dog, shown here as Figure 1.19. Once again this involves a conceptual, analytical image, but this time with a centre and margin textual organisation (and with a ring of section headings mediating nucleus and periphery). The verbiage, including both the teacher's scaffolding and Conal's notes, is part of this image.

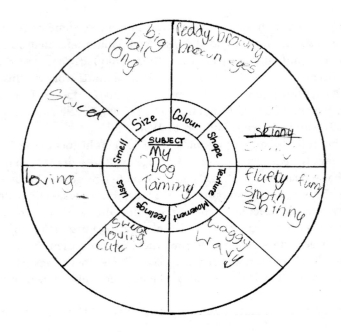

Figure 1.19 Conal's pie chart scaffolding for text [1:5]

This kind of integrated multimodal text makes us wonder whether pie charts (and tables in general) should be treated as extensions of English graphology, or as images in their own right. This reminds us that writing systems have evolved from images, and that electronic texts seem to be in the process of reinvigorating this imagic potential through the use of elaborated fonts, formatting, colour, layout, emoticons, symbols and the like. The graphology in other words is making meaning, in ways reminiscent of the wonderful illuminated manuscripts that constituted writing before the domination of the printing presses dulled things down.

Conal's handwriting and spelling underscore the contribution that graphology can make to the meaning of a genre. They mark his texts as immature, and to some readers perhaps shockingly illiterate. In his defence we perhaps need to explain that one of the legacies of process writing and whole language programs in Australia has been the idea that when students write they need to concentrate on lexicogrammatical and discourse semantic meaning (although the advocates of process writing had no such technical model of language) and not get bogged down in the finer points of spelling and punctuation. Errors are corrected (or not) by teachers as part of an editing, evaluation and 'publishing' process, and students are expected to move towards adult literacy over time. The idea here is that spelling and punctuation will mature 'naturally' in writing, just like pronunciation does for spoken language.

This is not the place to intervene too strongly in this debate. Obviously from the perspective on genre we are developing here, the focus on developing whole texts is important and children are indeed managing meaning on several strata and in several metafunctions at the same time. There is no doubt that for young writers worrying too much about spelling first time round can get in the way. At the same time, invented spelling brands these writers as illiterate, and that's not part of the configuration of meanings they are trying to weave together in their genres. So traditional drilling, memorisation and spelling rules do have a role to play. The challenge is getting the balance right, when so many dimensions of meaning are being brought into play.

1.8 This book

Based on these foundations, we'll develop the rest of the book around families of genres. We begin in Chapter 2 with the story family, extending the discussion of recounts, narratives and 'just so' stories we began above. Then in Chapter 3 we turn to history, and look at the family of genres which have evolved to make sense of the past. In Chapter 4 we move into the fields of geography and science to look at reports and explanations. From there we move to the workplace, and consider the role of procedural and associated genres in science based industry. Finally in Chapter 6 we look briefly at some additional families in order to broaden our perspective on mapping culture as a system of genres.

Alongside concentrating on genre families, each chapter has a special theoretical focus. In Chapters 2 and 3 we focus on paradigmatic relations among genres; we consider this from the point of view of typology in Chapter 2, and topology in Chapter 3. In Chapter 4 we develop our notion of macro-genres – the nature of texts composed of more than one genre and how they unfold. In Chapter 5 we expand on the multimodal perspective introduced above, attending to verbiage/image relations. In Chapter 6 we canvass a range of issues, including ways in which different types of structure can be recognised in genres. Our aim throughout these chapters is to give analysts more tools for thinking about genres and genre relations than have been generally deployed in the past.

No single book can be the final word on genre, especially if mapping culture as a system of genres is the game we want to play. Even within our own SFL framework, we're cheating badly here, skipping over register to discuss genre in relation to discourse semantics (and the other levels of language only as required). This means we're not doing justice to genre as a configuration of field, tenor and mode variables. For reasons of space and clarity of presentation this can't be helped here. But it is a big gap for future work to fill.

Our basic goal has been to document to some extent the explorations of genre undertaken by the so-called Sydney School – both theoretically and descriptively.

The many references to our colleagues work we hope pay tribute to their individual and collective contributions. In particular we are indebted to two action research projects undertaken in collaboration with the Sydney Metropolitan East Region of the New South Wales Disadvantaged School Program – the Language and Social Power project in the late 80s and the Write it Right project in the early 90s. We are trying here to voice their vision of the kind of genre theory they needed to get on with literacy work in disadvantaged schools.

2 Stories

2.0 Variation in stories

Stories are central genres in all cultures, in some form in almost every imaginable situation and stage of life. They are intimately woven into the minutiae of everyday life, whenever we come together. They are told in all social groupings to interpret life's chaos and rhythms, to evaluate each other's behaviour, and to educate and entertain our children. There is something miraculous about the way a child's attention is instantly drawn by a story, as their imagination is ignited and held. And the power of stories to grip the imagination of adults is no less mysterious, either as origin myths so potent they have moulded the destinies of nations and continents for millennia, or as literary fiction that can absorb and excite the most rational minds of the modern era.

Stories are also the most widely studied family of genres; there is a very large narrative literature in many contemporary fields, not to mention classical traditions of story exegesis in literature, philosophy and religion. Contemporary narrative studies are often traced to Propp's (1958) 'morphology' of episode types in Russian folktales, and Levi-Strauss' (1960) 'semantic fields' in indigenous American myths, both of which influenced Barthes' (1966) *Introduction to Structural Analysis of Narratives,* and in turn Labov & Waletsky's (1967) *Narrative Analysis: oral versions of personal experience.* These are widely cited as founding texts, in the European and North American traditions of narratology and sociolinguistics respectively. Other influential work on narrative structure includes, among many others, van Dijk (1977) on semantic 'macrostructures' and 'macrorules', Chafe (1980), Hymes (1981) or Scollon & Scollon (1981) on variation in narrative across languages and cultures, and others who find narrative-type structures across various forms of discourse such as Hoey (1983) and Jordan (1984). In addition, narrative analysis has been applied extensively in psychology, sociology and related fields, such as Bruner's (1986) interest in the role of stories in shaping cultural identities, along with feminist, psychotherapeutic and other interpretations. Our work on stories from the late 1970s (Martin 1981) initially took Labov & Waletsky as point of departure, but expanded to explore variation in types of stories, their social roles, and their linguistic realisation.

Labov & Waletsky (1967, reprinted in Bamberg 1997) proposed a generalised structure potential for narratives of personal experience, unfolding through stages of Orientation, Complication, Evaluation, Resolution and Coda, with Complication and Resolution the obligatory stages, and other stages optional. In other words, they saw their oral stories as centrally concerned with a disruption to an expected course of events, resolved by a return to order. A simple example they present includes three steps, which we have labelled to the right:

Well this person has a little too much to drink	**Orientation**
and he attacked me	**Complication**
and the friend came in	**Resolution**
and she stopped it	
(1997:12).	

And they also found an evaluation stage to be a key narrative component, 'defined by us as that part of the narrative that reveals the attitude of the narrator towards the narrative by emphasising the relative importance of some narrative units' (1997:32).

Labov & Waletsky's analysis is a useful starting point but also needs problema-tising from three perspectives. Firstly their attempt to account linguistically for narrative staging founders on what Bruner (1997:65) calls a 'failed clausal analysis', a consequence of the formalist grammatics of the time. Indeed, Bruner takes this shortcoming as an object lesson to advocate a more discourse oriented approach to narrative analysis, suggesting that 'what one should look for as the constituents of narrative is not an underlying clausal structure, but the processes of linguistic construction by which prototype narratives are adapted to different and varying situations' (ibid). Secondly, while they recognise the importance of evaluation, a formalist bias towards constituency structure and experiential meaning leads them to subordinate its interpersonal function by using evaluation to define segmental structure (the boundary between complication and resolution):

It is necessary for the narrator to delineate the structure of the narrative by emphasising the point where the complication has reached a maximum: the break between the complication and the result. Most narratives contain an evaluation section that carries out this function (1997:30).

Thirdly the reductive inclination of formal structuralism leads them to disregard significant variations in the staging of stories, using various rationales. For exam-ple they recognise that stories frequently terminate with an evaluation, but they maintain a universal complication-resolution rule with the artifice that 'in many narratives, the evaluation is fused with the result' (1997:35). In the story cited to support this, a life-threatening incident is not explicitly resolved, but is simply commented on: 'And the doctor just says, 'Just about this much more,' he says, 'and you'd a been dead.'' (1997:7). They also exclude stories which they characterise as not 'well-formed', for example 'in narratives without a point it is difficult to distinguish the complicating action from the result' (1997:30), and 'unevaluated narratives lack structural definition' (1997:34). Ultimately, Labov & Waletsky construe story variation in terms of individually based language deficit – as deviance from what they term a 'normal form', which they believe is 'told by speakers with greater overall verbal ability' (1997:37).[1]

With the advantages of a stratified model of text in context, that can motivate both text staging and relations between interpersonal meanings and social functions, SFL based research has been able to systematically identify and account for variation in types of stories, expanding and refining the models initiated by Labov & Waletsky and others. Working with a large corpus of oral stories Plum (1988/1998) identified four other major story types, in addition to narratives, that display varying staging (cf. Martin & Plum 1997), varieties also found by Rothery (1990) in her corpus of children's written stories (cf. Rothery & Stenglin 1997), in casual conversation (Eggins & Slade 2005), in literary fiction (Macken-Horarik 1999, 2003, Martin 1996), in stories of illness and treatment (Jordens 2002, 2003), and in traditional stories across language families (Rose 2001a&b, 2005b, to appear a). Each story type typically (but optionally) begins with an Orientation stage that presents an expectant activity sequence, but varies in how this expectancy is disrupted and how the disruption is responded to. Indeed Plum (1988/1998) found that the Complication-Resolution narrative structure accounted for only 15% of the 134 stories he recorded. For these reasons we refer to these genres as the 'story family', of which narrative is one member.

Alongside narratives, Plum recognised the recounts of personal experience introduced in Chapter 1, which record a sequence of events without significant disruption. Rather than a distinct evaluation stage, the events are typically appraised prosodically as the recount unfolds. Far from being 'pointless', recounts function in a wide variety of social contexts to share experiences and attitudes of all kinds.

Secondly, there were anecdotes, which involve some remarkable disruption to usuality, which is not resolved, but simply reacted to. The remarkable event may be tragic or comic, engaging or revolting, so the ensuing reaction may be either positive or negative affect.

Thirdly, exemplums, which also involve a disruption, but this is interpreted rather than reacted to, and the type of attitude expressed in the interpretation tends to be judgement of people's character or behaviour. Again the incident may involve behaviour that is either admirable or damnable, so the ensuing judgement may either admire or criticise, praise or condemn.

Fourthly, observations, which involve a description of a significant event, followed by a personal comment appreciating an aspect of it, again with either positive or negative value (as in the doctor's comment in Labov & Waletsky's example). Jordens (2002:68) succinctly summarises the rhetorical functions of these latter three story types:

> Each of these terminate in an evaluative stage, and they are differentiated according to the 'point' of the story: the 'point' of an Anecdote is to share a reaction with the audience, the 'point' of an Exemplum is to share a moral judgement, and the 'point' of an Observation is to share a personal response to things or events.

Finally, we reserve the term 'narrative' specifically for the generic pattern that resolves a complication. Evaluation of narrative complications can vary between affect, judgement of people, or appreciation of things and events. The evaluation is often deployed to suspend the action, increasing the narrative tension, and so intensifying the release when tension is resolved. The options in staging in the story genre family, and tendencies in their appraisal, are set out in Table 2.1. These are the obligatory stages for each genre, each of which may also open with an Orientation stage, and close with a Coda.

Table 2.1 Family of story genres

staging:	experience	response	experience	attitude
recount	Record	[prosodic]	–	variable
anecdote	Remarkable Event	Reaction	–	affect
exemplum	Incident	Interpretation	–	judgement
observation	Event Description	Comment		appreciation
narrative	Complication	Evaluation	Resolution	variable

We have chosen to illustrate each of these types of stories with examples by or about Indigenous Australians, for several reasons. They allow us to introduce the Australian theme of this book through the voices of Indigenous speakers, they serve to illustrate the trans-cultural phenomena of story genres, and the stories themselves are intrinsically interesting and provide a window on the history, culture and politics of the country.

Several of the stories we present were told to the *National Inquiry on the Separation of Aboriginal and Torres Strait Islander Children from their Families* (1995–7), by Indigenous people who were removed their families as children. These stories of forced separation, and its long-term consequences, are published in the report of the inquiry, *Bringing Them Home: The 'Stolen Children' report*, by the Human Rights and Equal Opportunity Commission (HREOC). Australian social commentator Robert Manne describes the policy of Indigenous child removal as follows:

> *Bringing Them Home* suggests that between one in three and one in ten Aboriginal children were separated from their mothers... All one can say for certain is that in the seventy or so years in question tens of thousands of babies and children were removed. Yet there is an even more extraordinary fact than this. Until the last year or so most non-Aboriginal Australians either did not know or were at best dimly aware that for some seventy years Australian governments had been involved in a more or less routine practice of part-Aboriginal child removal. This was something almost every Aborigine understood (1998: 53).[2]

2.1 Recount: recording personal experience

Two recounts are presented here, to display variations in the way that appraisal can be distributed through recounts. The first story [2:1] is from an Indigenous woman identified in *Bringing Theme Home* as 'Fiona', who lived with her family in northern South Australia in the 1930s. Her European great-uncle ran a sheep station at Ernabella, on the margin of Australia's vast Western Desert, whose Indigenous people at that time still lived a traditional life of nomadic hunting and gathering. Fiona was one of many children born of Indigenous mothers and white fathers in the region, most of whom were removed from their families. Locations in Fiona's story are shown in Map 2.1. In the following story transcripts, headings are given for each stage and appraisals are highlighted in bold.

Map 2.1 Places in Fiona's story

[2:1] Fiona's story

Orientation

1936 it was. I would have been five. We went visiting Ernabella the day the police came. Our great-uncle Sid was leasing Ernabella from the government at that time so we went there.

Record

We had been playing all together, **just a happy community** and the **air was filled with screams** because the police came and mothers tried to hide their children and blacken their children's faces and tried to hide them in caves.

We three, Essie, Brenda and me together with our three cousins ... the six of us were put on an old truck and taken to Oodnadatta which was hundreds of miles away and then we got there in the darkness.

My mother had to come with us. She had already lost her eldest daughter down to the Children's Hospital because she had infantile paralysis, polio, and now there was the prospect of losing her three other children, all the children she had. I remember that she came in the truck with us **curled up in the foetal position**. Who can understand that, the **trauma** of knowing that you're going to lose all your children? We talk about it from the point of view of our **trauma** but – our mother – to understand what she went through, I **don't think anyone can really understand that**.

It was 1936 and we went to the United Aborigines Mission in Oodnadatta. We got there in the dark and then we didn't see our mother again. She just kind of disappeared into the darkness.

Reorientation

I've since found out in the intervening years that there was a place they called the natives' camp and obviously my mother would have been whisked to the natives' camp. There was no time given to us to say goodbye to our mothers.

HREOC 1997:129

As far as time is concerned, the story records a series of events that unfolded the day Fiona's family went visiting Ernabella. There is no resolution to the awful events, nor is there a terminating evaluative stage, rather evaluations of various kinds are dispersed through the events.

Firstly *playing altogether* is appraised with positive affect as *just a happy community*, and this contrasts with the next event *the police came*, which is appraised negatively by the metaphorical *air was filled with screams*. The children themselves do not explicitly react to being taken to the distant railhead town of Oodnadatta, but their mother's intense unhappiness is evoked by her behaviour *curled up in the foetal position*. Rather than intensifying the feelings here, Fiona reconstrues them as an abstract 'thing' – *the **trauma** of knowing that you're going to lose all your children*, which she appreciates as beyond understanding. Following this appreciation, the recount returns to the events without explicit appraisal. Rather the children's experience is recounted as arriving at Oodnadatta in the dark, and their mother disappearing. This Record of events is then followed by a Reorientation stage that addresses events in hindsight, events from the perspective of adult knowledge. Note that although the reader may draw a moral conclusion about the children's and mother's treatment, there is no explicit judgement made in this final stage.

Map 2.2   Places in Greg's story

The next story [2:2] is from an Indigenous man identified as 'Greg', who was removed from the Tasmanian island of Cape Barren (see Map 2.2) as a 12 year old. Greg's island community are descendants of Indigenous Tasmanian women who survived the British genocide against their people in the mid-19th century and were married to European seal hunters.

While the events in this story are harrowing, they are recounted relatively dispassionately. The Orientation stage establishes the context of family and community, and the stability of Greg and his siblings' home and family. The Record stage begins

> **[2:2] Greg's story**
>
> *Orientation*
> I was born on Cape Barren. At the time I was taken the family comprised mum, my sister and my two brothers. And of course there was my grandmother and all the other various relatives. We were only a **fairly small isolated community** and we all grew up there in what I considered to be a **very peaceful loving community**. I recall spending most of my growing up on the Island actually living in the home of my grandmother and grandfather. The other children were living with mum in other places. Until the time I was taken I had not been away from the Island, other than our annual trips from Cape Barren across to Lady Baron during the mutton bird season.
>
> *Record*
> The circumstances of my being taken, as I recollect, were that I went off to school in the morning and I was sitting in the classroom and there was only one room where all the children were assembled and there was a knock at the door, which the schoolmaster answered. After a conversation he had with somebody at the door, he came to get me. He took me by the hand and took me to the door. I was physically grabbed by a male person at the door, I was taken to a motor bike and held by the officer and driven to the airstrip and flown off the Island.
>
> *Reorientation*
> I was taken from Cape Barren in October 1959 aged 12. I had no knowledge I was going to be taken. I was not even able to see my grandmother and I had just the clothes I had on my back, such as they were. I never saw mum again.
>
> HREOC 1997:99

with the specific setting of his removal from the school, followed by the events in rapid succession. Note that the shift from Orientation to Record stages is explicitly signalled here as *The circumstances of my being taken*. Such explicit signalling of stage shifts is a common feature of story genres. In Chapter 1 we noted how Conal used a marked Theme to signal such a transition in his trip to Ottawa [1:3]. Finally the story concludes by re-orienting the events in relation to the place and time, his age and circumstances, and finally a consequence of separation. The pattern of event sequence is illustrated in Figure 2.1.

Appraisals in Greg's story are limited to appreciating his community as *fairly small isolated* and *very peaceful loving*, and suggestions that the circumstances of his removal and its outcome were unreasonable, using negatives and counterexpectant continuity (***no** knowledge, **not even** able to see my grandmother, **just** the clothes I had on my back, **never** saw Mum **again***). These resources suggest that Greg might reasonably have expected to have been warned, been allowed to see his grandmother, gotten his clothes and seen his mum again, but as with Fiona's story this is merely implied; there is no explicit affect or moral judgement. This type of recount with minimal attitude is a common choice in legal testimony, exemplified again with text [3:15] in the next chapter. The genre's significant 'point' in this context is the record of events, that are allowed to speak for themselves – as witnessing justice or truth.

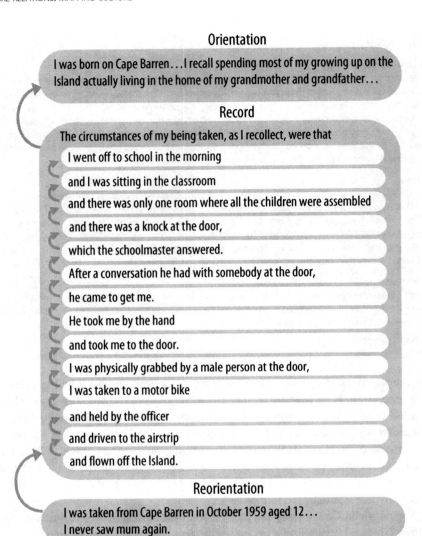

Orientation

I was born on Cape Barren...I recall spending most of my growing up on the Island actually living in the home of my grandmother and grandfather...

Record

The circumstances of my being taken, as I recollect, were that

I went off to school in the morning

and I was sitting in the classroom

and there was only one room where all the children were assembled

and there was a knock at the door,

which the schoolmaster answered.

After a conversation he had with somebody at the door,

he came to get me.

He took me by the hand

and took me to the door.

I was physically grabbed by a male person at the door,

I was taken to a motor bike

and held by the officer

and driven to the airstrip

and flown off the Island.

Reorientation

I was taken from Cape Barren in October 1959 aged 12...
I never saw mum again.

Figure 2.1 Event sequence in recount

2.2 Anecdotes – reacting to events

As quoted from Jordens above, the point of an anecdote is to share an emotional reaction. To this end, anecdotes present a sequence of events that is out of the ordinary, and conclude with the protagonists' reaction to the events. Here we present three examples; the first is again a story of personal experience from the *Bringing Them Home* report, the second is an extract from a novel (to illustrate how story genres are included and expanded in literature), and the third is a humorous story to illustrate the potential relationship between anecdotes and humour.

[2:3] Millicent's story

Orientation

My name is Millicent D. I was born at Wonthella WA in 1945. My parents were CD and MP, both 'half-caste' Aborigines. I was one of seven children, our family lived in the sandhills at the back of the Geraldton Hospital. There was a lot of families living there **happy and harmonious**. It was like we were all part of **one big happy family**.

Remarkable Event

In 1949 the Protector of Aborigines with the Native Welfare Department visited the sandhill camps. All the families living there were to be moved to other campsites or to the Moore River Aboriginal Settlement. Because my parents were fair in complexion, the authorities decided us kids could pass as whitefellas. I was four years old and that was the last time I was to see my parents again. Because my sisters were older than me they were taken to the Government receiving home at Mount Lawley. My brother Kevin was taken to the boys home in Kenwick. Colin and I were taken to the Sister Kate's Home. We were put in separate accommodation and hardly ever saw each other.

Reaction

I was **so afraid and unhappy** and **didn't understand** what was happening

HREOC 1996:115

The first anecdote of personal experience [2:3] from Millicent D. illustrates the policy of separating children on the basis of gradations in skin colour. As the intent of the policy was to 'assimilate' Indigenous people into the colonising race, children with lighter skin were sent to institutions such as the notorious 'Sister Kate's Home' in Perth, and then if possible to white families as foster children or domestic servants. Map 2.3 shows the location of Millicent's home area Wonthella, Moore River Native Settlement and Perth, to where her siblings were taken.

Map 2.3   Places in Millicent's story

The anecdote structure is distinct in [2:3], with the of Orientation establishing a happy normalcy, disrupted by a Remarkable Event that is signalled by a temporal Theme *In 1949*, and terminating with a Reaction which appraises the events from the narrator's perspective as a child, of her feelings of fear, unhappiness and confusion. Of course as a child she could not have known that the colonisers' theory of race classified both her parents as 'half' Aboriginal, and therefore herself as 'quarter' Aboriginal, and an ideal candidate for assimilation. We should note that 1949 was the year after Australia ratified the UN Charter on Human Rights, which expressly forbade such policies.

[2:4] Follow the Rabbit Proof Fence p43

Orientation

Molly and Gracie finished their breakfast and decided to take all their dirty clothes and wash them in the soak further down the river. They returned to the camp looking clean and refreshed and joined the rest of the family in the shade for lunch of tinned corned beef, damper and tea.

Remarkable Event

The family had just finished eating when all the camp dogs began barking, making a **terrible din**. 'Shut up,' **yelled** their owners, throwing stones at them. The dogs **whined and skulked away.** Then all eyes turned to the cause of the commotion. A tall, rugged white man stood on the bank above them. He could easily have been mistaken for a pastoralist or a grazier with his tanned complexion except that he was wearing khaki clothing.

Fear and anxiety swept over them when they realised that the **fateful day** they had been **dreading** had come at last. They always knew that it would only be a matter of time before the government would track them down.

When Constable Riggs, Protector of Aborigines, finally spoke his voice was full of **authority and purpose**. They **knew without a doubt** that he was the one who took children in broad daylight – not like the evil spirits who came into their camps at night. 'I've come to take Molly, Gracie and Daisy, the three half-caste girls, with me to Moore River Native Settlement,' he informed the family.

The old man nodded to show that he understood what Riggs was saying. The rest of the family just **hung their heads**, refusing to face the man who was taking their daughters away from them. **Silent tears welled** in their eyes and trickled down their cheeks.

'Come on, you girls,' he ordered. 'Don't worry about taking anything. We'll pick up what you need later.' ... 'Hurry up then, I want to get started. We've got a long way to go yet. You girls can ride this horse back to the depot,' he said, handing the reins over to Molly. Riggs was **annoyed** that he had to go miles out of his way to find these girls.

Reaction

Molly and Gracie sat silently on the horse, **tears streaming down their cheeks** as Constable Riggs turned the big bay stallion and led the way back to the depot. A **high pitched wail** broke out. The **cries of agonised** mothers and the women, and the **deep sobs** of grandfathers, uncles and cousins filled the air. Molly and Gracie looked back just once before they disappeared through the river gums. Behind them, those remaining in the camp found sharp objects and **gashed** themselves and **inflicted deep wounds** to their heads and bodies as an expression of their **sorrow**.

The two **frightened and miserable girls began to cry**, silently at first, then **uncontrollably**; their **grief made worse by the lamentations** of their loved ones and the visions of them sitting on the ground in their camp letting their **tears mix with the red blood** that flowed from the cuts on their heads.

Coda

This reaction to their children's abduction showed that the family were now in **mourning**. They were **grieving** for their abducted children and their **relief** would come only when the **tears ceased to fall**, and that will be a long time yet.

Pilkington 1996:43

In the next story [2:4], the structure of anecdote is used by Indigenous author Doris Pilkington (also known as Nugi Garimara), to present the experience of child removal from the family's perspective, and invite the reader to empathise with their feelings. This anecdote is an extract from Pilkington's novel *Follow the Rabbit-Proof Fence*, about the epic journey of three girls who had been removed from their families, to return to their home at Jigalong in the Western Australian desert (see Map 2.4). In this extract, the policeman charged with removing the girls appears at the family campsite, and announces his intention.

Map 2.4   Places in *Follow the Rabbit-Proof Fence*

In this written story, Pilkington sets a scene of tranquil normalcy, then signals a disruption with a shift in time, as in the oral stories above, but here using a whole clause *The family had just finished eating*, when the tranquillity is shattered by the dogs barking. The Reaction stage is highly developed with a prosody of intense affect, realised by an intensifying series of behaviours including *tears, wail, cries, sobs, gashed themselves, lamentations, letting tears mix with blood*, and qualities *frightened, miserable, grief made worse*. This stage is also presaged by two lesser reactions: initially the Remarkable Event could be either good or bad, but the family's *fear and anxiety* establishes its negative character; and their initial reaction of *silent tears* to Constable Rigg's announcement foreshadows their intense grief when the girls are taken. There is a subtle contrast here between the family's feelings and the white man merely feeling *annoyed*. The author also provides a Coda interpreting the family's behaviours as 'now in mourning', and re-orienting the story from the past to the present, with the final shift in tense from potential past *would only come when the tears ceased to fall* to unfulfilled future *that will be a long time yet*.

So from one stage to the next there is a shift in field and tenor, from the normality of the girls washing and family lunch, disrupted by the dogs and the appearance of Riggs, at first reacted to anxiously but silently, and then intensely as Riggs takes the girls. But the stages are also distinguished by the participants presented first, as the Theme of the opening sentence in each stage. In the Orientation this is *Molly and Gracie*. The Remarkable Event then opens with *The family*, who continue as thematic participants through this stage, along with Riggs. The Reaction then returns to *Molly and Gracie... The two frightened and miserable girls*, while the Coda begins with *This reaction* that the author explains for us.

The serial event structure we saw for the recounts is developed here at a larger scale, in a sequence of intensifying problems and reactions. The first is the appearance of the white man and the reaction of *fear and anxiety*; the next is Riggs' announcement and the reaction of *silent tears*; and the next is his taking the girls and the intense grief of the Reaction stage.

These patterns are illustrated in Figure 2.2. The affect of the reactions scopes back over the events, indicated by shading.

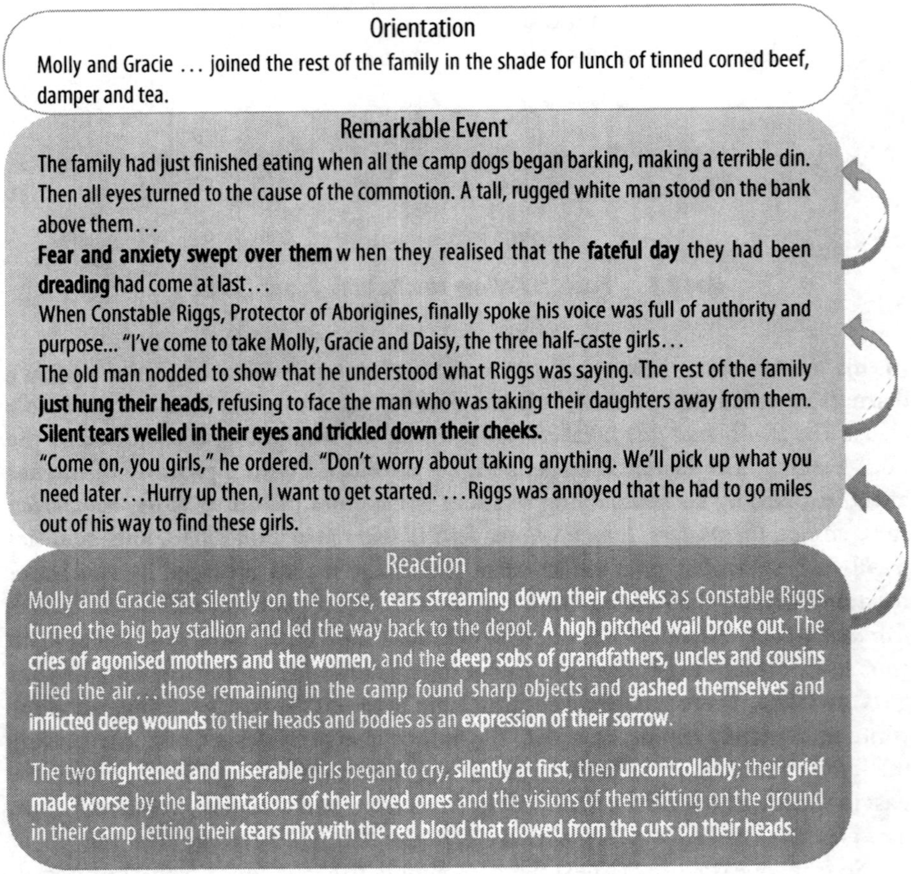

Orientation

Molly and Gracie ... joined the rest of the family in the shade for lunch of tinned corned beef, damper and tea.

Remarkable Event

The family had just finished eating when all the camp dogs began barking, making a terrible din. Then all eyes turned to the cause of the commotion. A tall, rugged white man stood on the bank above them...

Fear and anxiety swept over them when they realised that the **fateful day** they had been **dreading** had come at last...

When Constable Riggs, Protector of Aborigines, finally spoke his voice was full of authority and purpose... "I've come to take Molly, Gracie and Daisy, the three half-caste girls...

The old man nodded to show that he understood what Riggs was saying. The rest of the family **just hung their heads**, refusing to face the man who was taking their daughters away from them. **Silent tears welled in their eyes and trickled down their cheeks.**

"Come on, you girls," he ordered. "Don't worry about taking anything. We'll pick up what you need later...Hurry up then, I want to get started. ...Riggs was annoyed that he had to go miles out of his way to find these girls.

Reaction

Molly and Gracie sat silently on the horse, **tears streaming down their cheeks** as Constable Riggs turned the big bay stallion and led the way back to the depot. **A high pitched wail broke out.** The **cries of agonised mothers and the women,** and the **deep sobs of grandfathers, uncles and cousins** filled the air...those remaining in the camp found sharp objects and **gashed themselves** and **inflicted deep wounds** to their heads and bodies as an **expression of their sorrow.**

The two **frightened and miserable** girls began to cry, **silently at first,** then **uncontrollably; their grief made worse** by the **lamentations of their loved ones** and the visions of them sitting on the ground in their camp letting their **tears mix with the red blood that flowed from the cuts on their heads.**

Figure 2.2   Affect scoping back over events in anecdote

Beyond this extract, *Follow the Rabbit-Proof Fence* is a long story whose overall purpose is to applaud the girls' tenacity at returning to their family against all odds. But like novels in general, it is constructed as a series of smaller stories which function to engage the reader in sharing the protagonists' feelings, admiring the girls and their helpers and condemning their captors and pursuers, and appreciating the events and the land through which they travelled. One way this is achieved is by building and releasing tension, through series of problems and responses on the various scales of events, story stages, and whole chapters. These kinds of story patterns will be discussed further in section 2.8 below.

An anecdote may be comic rather than tragic; indeed anecdotes are a popular genre for humorous stories and jokes, as the following example [2:5] illustrates. This anecdote was originally told by an Indigenous elder at a gathering called by the Narrandera Koori Community, NSW, to deal with emotional problems arising from continual deaths in the community and cultural loss. (The word *Koori* denotes the Indigenous people of south-eastern Australia.) A distinctive theme of Indigenous humour is linguistic or cultural misunderstanding, that may be intertwined in the same story.[3] A favoured object of mirth is cultural naïvete, of either Indigenous or non-Indigenous individuals or both. In this story, the narrator makes fun of his own naïvete. It was retold in the written report of the gathering. Again staging is shown and attitude is highlighted.

[2:5] Uncle Mick's story

Orientation

Most of the churches in town are Church of England, so to go to the Catholic Church was pretty unusual.

Remarkable Event

During the service there was a **huge** thunder and lightning storm. Every time the priest said something about the woman who had died, a **huge** clap of thunder would shake the building and Uncle Mick would think – whatever he just said about her couldn't have been **true**! This kept happening every time the priest said something about the woman who had died. Even when she was placed into the grave the same thing happened – **huge** thunder and lightning. But as soon as the earth was put over her, the storm finished, the sky cleared up, and the sun came out.

Reaction

Uncle Michael remembered thinking at the time that when he died he'd **like** to have his funeral at the Catholic Church because they put on a **very impressive** show there!

from Narrandera Koori Community Gathering 2002

This example contrasts with the previous anecdote in its understated reaction, a strategy of 'deadpan' humour. Uncle Mick's mild desire (*he'd **like** to have his funeral at the Catholic Church*) is built upon much stronger repeated appreciation of the storm (***huge** thunder and lightning storm, **very impressive** show*). Again there is a lesser reaction within the Event stage (*Uncle Mick would think – whatever he just said about her couldn't have been true!*), foreshadowing the joke on his naïvete.[4] Again the Remarkable Event is signalled by time *During the service...*

2.3 Exemplum – interpreting incidents

The point of an exemplum is to share a moral judgement, illustrated here with one story that praises the protagonists and another that condemns them. The first is a story from *Lighting the Way: reconciliation stories*, a collection of stories about individual and community acts of reconciliation between Indigenous and non-Indigenous Australians. The story here [2:6] relates what now seems an extraordinary incident from colonial days at Butheroe in central NSW, shown in Map 2.5, when a group of Aboriginal men lit the way home in the dark for a young European couple, by throwing returning boomerangs which they had set alight, above the couple's heads.

Map 2.5   Location of Lighting the Way story

[2:6] Lighting the way

Orientation

When my parents were married in 1863, they lived across the creek at Butheroe, from the original home, where the Joseph Nevells lived then. My mother was **always nervous** of the Aborigines.

Incident

One dark night, my parents had been at tea at the Joseph Nevells' home and as they were going home, some Aborigines were sitting around a fire, about half way between the house and the old well, going down to the creek. Father said, '**don't be afraid**, they will not hurt us', and he spoke to one of the group as they passed by. A few minutes later, boomerangs were lighted at one end, came overhead and of course, went back to the Aborigines, then came a series of these lighted boomerangs showing a light to father and mother until they reached the front door.

Interpretation

It was a **kindly action** from the natives.[5]

Miss F. May Nevell in Johnson 2002:iii

While the behaviour of the 'the natives' is eventually praised as *a kindly action* in [2:6], the rhetorical effect of this emerges from the tension that is created and released in the preceding events. The mother's insecurity described in the Orientation (*always nervous*), creates an expectancy for an ensuing problem. The Incident is then signalled by the temporal circumstance *One dark night*, that strongly expects a frightening event. However this expectancy is countered by Father's reassurance (*don't be afraid, will not hurt*) and the tension is released by the *lighted boomerangs showing a light to father and mother*. This sequence of stages and attitudes is diagrammed in Figure 2.3. Here the affect in the Orientation scopes forward over the following events, expecting a problem. The judgement on the other hand scopes backwards over the preceding event, evaluating the behaviour (indicated by shading).

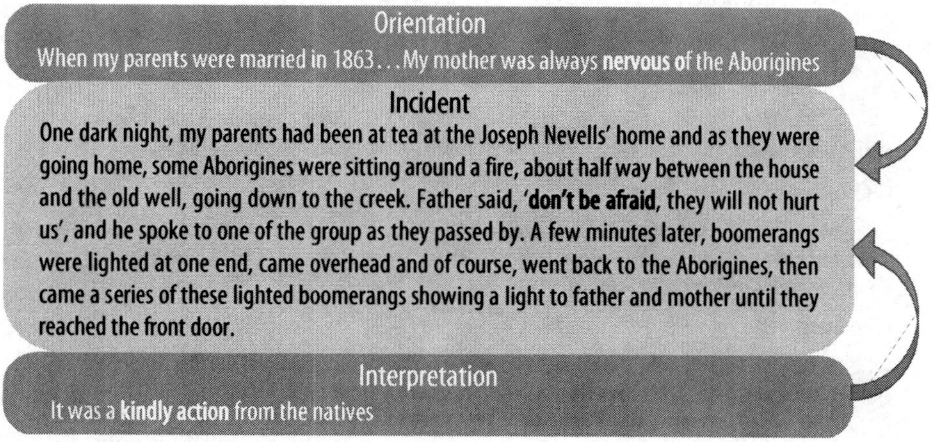

Orientation
When my parents were married in 1863…My mother was always **nervous of** the Aborigines

Incident
One dark night, my parents had been at tea at the Joseph Nevells' home and as they were going home, some Aborigines were sitting around a fire, about half way between the house and the old well, going down to the creek. Father said, '**don't be afraid**, they will not hurt us', and he spoke to one of the group as they passed by. A few minutes later, boomerangs were lighted at one end, came overhead and of course, went back to the Aborigines, then came a series of these lighted boomerangs showing a light to father and mother until they reached the front door.

Interpretation
It was a **kindly action** from the natives

Figure 2.3 Attitude scoping forward and back

Perhaps because the mother's expectation of a problem with the Aboriginal men was countered by their 'kindly act', Miss Nevell's exemplum serves as the introduction and title for this collection of reconciliation stories. It is a token both for (unexpected) empathy between black and white, and for Indigenous people showing other Australians how to achieve it. Reconciliation between Indigenous and non-Indigenous Australians became a major national movement in the 1990s, with hundreds of thousands participating in symbolic walks across city bridges and legal recognition of Indigenous land title. Unfortunately it subsequently retreated from the centre of public life, discouraged by the neo-conservative government of Prime Minster John Howard, that successfully distracted voters with a debilitating politics of fear focused on racial and religious difference.

A more negative judgement is made in the following exemplum by 'Evie' [2:7], from the *Bringing Theme Home* report. Evie's grandmother had been removed from her family in the Northern Territory, she had two children to a white Aboriginal Protection Officer, including Evie's mother who was also removed; Evie herself was removed from her mother as a baby in 1950, and her own children were removed from her as infants in 1977, so her story is a long one, involving a series of shorter stories of various types. The excerpt here begins with an observation about growing up in a church institution on Garden Point island in Darwin, on which Evie comments *I was **actually relieved** to leave the Island* (the observation genre is discussed in the next section). Locations in Evie's story are shown in Map 2.5, including Garden Point on Melville Island, the towns of Darwin and Tennant Creek, and the Aboriginal community of Hermannsburg near Alice Springs.

As the observation involves mention of sexual abuse, the interviewer asks Evie
if any girls got pregnant and then who was responsible, which prompts Evie to relate
an Incident and then judge the man responsible.

[2:7] Evie's story

Part 1: observation

Orientation

I was taken away in 1950 when I was 6 hours old from hospital and put into Retta Dixon until I was
2 months old and then sent to Garden Point. I lived in Garden Point until 1964. And from Garden
Point, Tennant Creek, Hermannsburg.

Event Described

While in Garden Point I always say that some of it was the happiest time of my life; others it was the
saddest time of my life. The happiest time was, 'Yippee! all these other kids there'. You know, you
got to play with them every day. The saddest times were the abuse. Not only the physical abuse,
the sexual abuse by the priests over there. And they were the saddest because if you were to tell
anyone, well, the priests threatened that they would actually come and get you.

Everyone could see what they were doing but were told to keep quiet. And just every day you used
to get hidings with the stock-whip. Doesn't matter what you did wrong, you'd get a hiding with the
stock-whip. If you didn't want to go to church, well you got slapped about the head. We had to go
to church three times a day.

Comment

I was actually relieved to leave the Island.

Q: Did any girls get pregnant at Garden Point when you were there?

Part 2: exemplum

Orientation

I remember one and they actually took her off the Island. And when I ask everyone, like even now
when I ask people about her, they don't know what happened to her. All they remember is her
being put on the helicopter and flown out and I've never heard her, about her name or anything
about her anymore. They remember her but don't know what happened to her.

Q: Who was the Father?

The Priest. The same bastards who ...

Q: How do people know that?

Incident

Well, the reason they know is, Sister A, poor thing, who's dead – I know she was upset because that
priest had that young girl living in his place. He used to come and get her out of the dormitory
every night. He used to sneak in about half past twelve, one o'clock in the morning and take her.
We'd get up in the morning and she'd be just coming in the door.

All the girls slept in one dormitory. All the boys slept in the other. And we couldn't lock the
dormitory from the inside – it had a chain through and padlock outside, so there was only the nuns
or priest could get in there. I know he used to come and get her because I was three beds up from
her.

> *Interpretation*
>
> There was another priest, but he's dead. The rest of the mob that were on the Island are all dead. He's the only one that's kicking and **he should have been the one that's bloody dead for what he did.**
>
> He not only did it to girls, he did it to boys as well. There was six of 'em involved. Nuns were assaulting the young fellas as well as the priest assaulting the young fellas and the girls. There was four priests and two nuns involved. We were in their care.
>
> *Coda*
>
> That fella's still walking around. He's now got charge of other kids. He's got charge of other kids in D.
>
> HREOC 1997:147

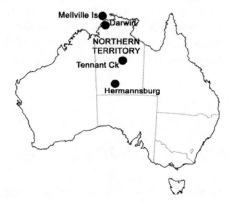

Map 2.6   Places in Evie's story

Stories of personal experience are commonly prompted by the listener like this. To support her moral judgement of the priest that *he should have been the one that's bloody dead for what he did*, Evie first mentions how *Sister A* was upset about his behaviour. The judgement is then elaborated by the extent of his crimes against boys and girls, and the crimes of the other priests and nuns, and the judgement of criminality is reinforced by pointing out that *We were in their care*. The Coda then recontextualises the Interpretation in the present.

2.4 Observations – commenting on events

As Jordens explains, the point of an observation is to share a personal response to things or events. Rather than unfolding in a sequence, as in other stories, the events described in observations tend to be collapsed into what Rothery and Stenglin (1997) call 'a snapshot frozen in time', followed by the narrator's comment. This is evident in Evie's observation about growing up at Garden Point above [2:7], in which she groups the events and generalises them as playing, abuse and the stockwhip. In a brief form, observations are probably very common in everyday discourse, as the following story [2:8] from 'Jennifer' illustrates.

[2:8] Jennifer's story

Event

When I was thirteen years old Mrs S. called this middle-aged male doctor to the house and said she wanted an internal examination of me.

Comment

That was terribly shameful for me, I will not say anymore.

HREOC 1997:52

In the next example from 'William' [2:9], the Event is described briefly, but the Comment stage is much longer, as it appreciates the consequences on his life of repeated sexual abuse in a series of foster homes. This extract from his life story follows two anecdotes, about being removed and separated from his siblings after his mother's death, and about repeated sexual abuse as a young child in a foster home.

[2:9] William's story

Orientation

They shifted us again and that was into town again.

Event

And then they put us in with this bloke ... They've got records of what he did to me. That man abused me. He made us do dirty things that we never wanted to do.

Comment

Where was the counselling? Where was the help I needed? They knew about it. The guy went to court. He went to court but they did nothing for me, nothing. They sent us off to the Child Psychology Unit. I remember the child psychologist saying, 'He's an Aboriginal kid, he'll never improve. He's got behavioural problems'. I mean, why did I have behavioural problems? Why didn't they do anything? Why did I have behavioural problems? I hit the streets of Adelaide. I drank myself stupid. I drank to take the pain, the misery out of my life. I couldn't stop. I smoked dope, got drugs. I tried everything. I did everything. I just couldn't cope with life. I lived under cardboard boxes. I used to eat out of rubbish bins. I'm so ashamed of what I've done.

I suffer today. I still suffer. I can't go to sleep at night. It's been on for years. I just feel that pain. Oh God, I wake up in the middle of the night, same time. My kids have asked me why I get up in the middle of the night and I can't explain it, I can't tell them – shamed. I can't sleep too well with it. I can't go to bed. I leave it 'til 12 o'clock sometimes before I go to bed. I lay there awake, knowing I'm gonna wake up at that time of the morning, night after night. I often wish I was dead. I often wish I was gone. But I can't because of my children. You can't explain this to your kids. Why did this happen? I had nobody. I've had my secret all my life. I tried to tell but I couldn't. I can't even talk to my own brothers. I can't even talk to my sister. I fear people. I fear 'em all the time. I don't go out. I stay home. It's rarely I've got friends.

HREOC 1997:371

So observations differ from other story genres, both in the brevity with which the events are described, and in the type of attitude that evaluates the events. The narrator may express strong feelings (*ashamed, suffer, pain, wish I was dead*), and imply judgements of people (such as the racist child psychologist), but the primary point is to appreciate the effect of the events on the narrator. Jordens (2003:107) expands on this function as follows:

> Observations concern the appraisal of 'states of affairs' rather than the choices and actions of purposive moral agents. They are also a symbolising genre: the 'snapshot frozen in time' gathers up preceding meanings into a symbolic image, and in doing so creates a critical distance that is somehow useful in the process of making one's experience meaningful to one's self and to others.

2.5 Narratives – resolving complications

As with anecdote, exemplum and observation, narrative genres involve a disrupting event that is evaluated, but they differ in that the disruption is then resolved by the protagonists, returning the story to equilibrium, as Labov & Waletsky described. So the 'point' of a narrative is how the protagonists resolve a complication in their lives, once they have evaluated the complicating action with some type of attitude.

To this point we have illustrated story genres with oral stories of personal experience, and with an extract from written literature. Here we will expand our examples to show how story genres may occur as traditional stories told in Australian and other cultures. However we will begin with an oral narrative of personal experience [2:10], again from *Bringing Theme Home*. In this story 'Karen' relates and evaluates how her Aboriginality became a problem as she grew up in a white family, and how she attempted to resolve some issues by finding her birth parents.

[2:10] Karen's story

Orientation

I am a part Aboriginal woman, who was adopted out at birth. I was adopted by a white Australian family and came to live in New Zealand at the age of 6 months.

Complication

I grew up not knowing about my natural Mother and father. The only information my adoptive parents had about my birth, was the surname of my birth Mother. I guess I had quite a good relationship with my adoptive Mum, Dad, and sisters. Though my adopted Mother said I kept to myself a lot, while I was growing up. As I got older I noticed my skin colouring was different to that of my family. My Mother told me I was adopted from Australia and part Aboriginal.

Evaluation

I **felt quite lonely** especially as I approached my teens. I got teased often about being Aboriginal and became **very withdrawn and mixed up, I really did not know where I belonged.** As a result of this I started having **psychiatric problems. I seem to cope** and **muddle along.**

[2:10] Karen's story (Contd)

Resolution

I eventually got married to a New Zealander, we have two boys, who are now teenagers. One of our boys is dark like myself, and was interested in his heritage. I was unable to tell him anything, as I didn't know about it myself.

My husband, boys and myself had the opportunity to go to Melbourne about 7 years ago on a working holiday for 10 weeks. While in Melbourne I went to the Aboriginal Health Centre and spoke to a social worker, as I had a copy of my birth certificate with my birth Mother's name on it. The social worker recognized my Mother's surname 'Graham', and got in touch with my aunty, who gave me my Mother's phone number.

I got in touch with my birth Mother and made arrangements to meet her. I have a half brother and sister. My birth Mother and Father never married, though my Father knew my Mother was pregnant with me. My Mother did not know where my Father was, as they parted before I was born. My sister decided to call a local Melbourne paper and put our story in the paper on how I had found them after 29 years.

My Father who was in Melbourne at the time, saw the article and a photo of my Mother and myself in the paper. He recognized my Mother and got in touch with her. My Mother and I had been corresponding, after we returned to New Zealand. For her own reasons, she would not give my Father my address, so my Father went through the social service agency and got in touch with me two and a half years ago. I have met my birth Father, as I had a family wedding in Melbourne shortly after he made contact with me, so I made arrangements to meet him.

Coda

We kept in contact with one another, but I feel we will never be able to make up for lost time, as my birth parents live in Australia and myself in New Zealand.

HREOC 1997:244

Karen's story follows the canonical narrative pattern, beginning with an Orientation stage that 'sets the scene' of her family situation, which is appraised positively as *quite a good relationship*. This is the context which the Complication then disrupts, with problems arising from her skin colour, signalled by a time shift *As I got older…*, which is then evaluated in an intense series of her feelings and judgements on herself. The Resolution stage is signalled by a time shift *I eventually got married*, followed by a series of partial solutions to problems: marriage and children, finding her mother, and then her father finding her. However Karen's Coda returns us to the reality of the present, the damage to relationships that cannot be repaired.

The scope of the Evaluation in a narrative is both backwards, evaluating the preceding events as a Complication, and forward, expecting the following events to be a Resolution. This scoping of evaluation was recognised by Labov & Waletsky and diagrammed as an evaluation stage dominating the other stages (reproduced in Martin 1992). The pattern is illustrated here in Figure 2.4.

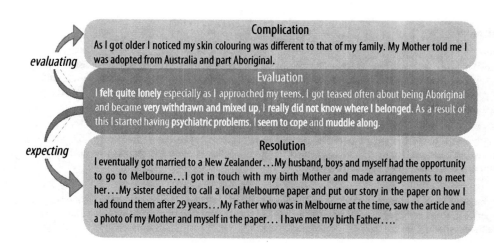

Complication
As I got older I noticed my skin colouring was different to that of my family. My Mother told me I was adopted from Australia and part Aboriginal.

evaluating

Evaluation
I felt quite lonely especially as I approached my teens. I got teased often about being Aboriginal and became very withdrawn and mixed up, I really did not know where I belonged. As a result of this I started having psychiatric problems. I seem to cope and muddle along.

expecting

Resolution
I eventually got married to a New Zealander...My husband, boys and myself had the opportunity to go to Melbourne...I got in touch with my birth Mother and made arrangements to meet her...My sister decided to call a local Melbourne paper and put our story in the paper on how I had found them after 29 years...My Father who was in Melbourne at the time, saw the article and a photo of my Mother and myself in the paper... I have met my birth Father....

Figure 2.4   Scope of Evaluation in narrative

Long before the 'Stolen Children' inquiry, Indigenous Australians had been organising means to put people, who had been removed as children, in contact with their families, by word of mouth and by formal networks such as the *Linkup* organisation. It was through such a network that Karen was able to find her mother. For deeply moving perspectives on the process of reunion, see the *Bringing Them Home* report, or the song *Took the Children Away* by the great Indigenous Australian singer Archie Roach. This song is also a narrative, in which the Resolution begins with the line *One sweet day all the children came back...*

It is sometimes assumed that the narrative pattern of resolving a complication is an artefact of the western cult of heroic individualism, and that very different cultures must tell very different kinds of stories. In our experience however, narrative is an important part of many cultures, although of course what constitutes complicating events and their resolution may differ. The following two mythic narratives illustrate this for Indigenous Australian and classical European cultures. The first [2:11] is from the Pitjantjatjara people of Australia's Western Desert (the people from whom 'Fiona' was taken in story [2:1]). This story was told by Nganyintja, the adoptive mother of David (who translated it),[6] and is about the origin of giant mythic serpents known as *wanampi*. These beings are common to all Australian cultures, often known as 'rainbow serpents' (and perhaps analogous with mythic serpents and dragons the world over). In this complex narrative, the first Complication is temporarily resolved, which is followed by a second Complication, before the final Resolution.

[2:11] Piltati myth

Orientation

There were two men, it's said, who were brothers. Two young women were married to them, who were sisters. Those two men went hunting for kangaroos. For wallabies, that is, they climbed up in the hills, and they brought back wallaby meat. And the other two went down for vegetable foods, and were collecting wild figs. Exactly at that place [Piltati] they were living.

Complication 1

Then one day as all the game finished, a drought began. Unable to dig anything up, the women kept walking. They travelled far away, it's said, and camped away overnight. Then after sleeping, hunting and camping out further, they reached another place. There they continued digging.

Evaluation

Meanwhile the other two were unable to find them. They searched and searched, 'The women should've arrived. What's happened to them, eh? They must've gone far away.' Then they thought, 'They're probably alright. So now if we can't see them, what will we do?'

Resolution (temporary)

At that they put their spears in a cave, they thought some more, and then they rose up into the sky, twisting around each other. As those two climbed up, they transformed into wanampi serpents. Then they saw the women, 'Oh, there they are, at that place far away.' And then they descended and entered the earth.

Complication 2

Meanwhile those two sisters were still digging, heedlessly, the two women were digging, digging and digging. And one said "Hey, get me a long stick!"

So the other one went, and going she saw 'What's this? It's like a wanampi!' She mistakenly thought it was a desert python. A burrow mouth is what she saw, this was the mouth of a burrow. That wanampi crawled back inside the burrow and was lying close inside. And seeing its tail, the woman thought 'Ah, I'll catch it on my own!' But as she pulled its tail, trying to catch it, it nearly pulled her into the burrow. The woman jumped up and ran, and coming up to her sister she said "Get up and come here! Sister, will I tell you what happened?"

And her sister said "What did you see? What? What? Tell me quickly! What are you talking about?"

"Hey, come and look! A really huge python went into a burrow! It nearly dragged me in. It's really huge!"

They came and looked. They stopped digging for mitika (small marsupials) and came to that burrow. Then they saw it, "Something really big has gone in here!"

And the women started digging, digging and digging. And then they came out for a little while. They ate and slept, and waking up, they looked again. As the hole got bigger the Wanampi would keep going in. Crawling along it would now go further in. As they dug it out, the women kept killing and eating little snakes. They'd see this big thing and keep killing little ones. They kept doing this, kept on digging on and on. They'd keep on killing little ones and the big one would go further in. Digging, digging, they created the creek, *Piltati* creek they created, digging digging. Those two men were racing away from them. At last they reached the hills and could go no further. The elder brother said, 'Coil up underneath and I will lie on top.'

The women were digging and digging. And seeing the wanampi lying there they were horrified, 'Aah, it's huge!' And the elder sister picked up her digging stick and stabbed the wanampi.

Resolution

At that the two wanampi reared up. And seeing them the sisters ran; they threw away their head rings and ran. One ran up towards the hills, and the other ran down. But the wanampi chased them and caught them. The two sisters were in the mouths of the wanampi and were laughing. Then the men swallowed them and inside their husbands they also transformed into wanampi.

Nganyintja in Rose 2001a

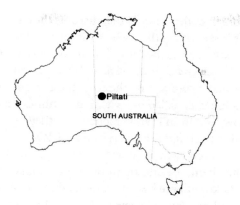

Map 2.7   Location of the Piltati story

The Orientation presents two brothers married to two sisters, camping at a place called *Piltati*, in the Mann Ranges of South Australia (Map 2.7), with the men hunting game and the women gathering vegetable foods. The first Complication begins as a drought sets in, forcing the women to travel further each day, until they fail to return, leaving their husbands to wonder what has befallen them. The men imagine their wives have transformed into mythic beings, so their Resolution is to transform themselves into *wanampi* serpents, twisting around each others' bodies as they rise into the sky, before diving back into the earth. The second Complication begins as the women return, find the wanampi burrow and, mistaking them for a large edible desert python, try to dig them out. When at last they see them, in horror the elder sister stabs her *wanampi* husband with her digging stick, triggering the final Resolution. The English translation here maintains the textual, interpersonal and experiential patterns of the Pitjantjatjara original as closely as possible.[7]

While getting swallowed by giant serpents may not seem to be a Resolution to many modern Europeans, for the Pitjantjatjara it signifies the transformation of the women into members of their husbands' estate group at marriage, so that their children will also be members. The positive value of this outcome is signalled by the women laughing in the wanampis' mouths before being swallowed, perhaps also an oblique sexual image. It's said the wanampi still reside in the deep pool at the head of Piltati creek, and that they recognise and assist members of the families that belong to the Piltati area, who are considered to be their spiritual descendants, and therefore landowners and custodians of the area.

The narrative structure of the story unfolds as follows. Firstly the Orientation presents the men and women, their activities and locations, encoding the normative division of labour in Pitjantjatjara society between men who hunt game and women who gather vegetable foods and return each day. The first Complication is signalled by a shift in time (*Then one day…*), and a switch in thematic identity from the men and women to the drought that disrupts the daily routine. In the first Evaluation, the men's insecurity at their wives' disappearance is realised by repetitions of uncertainty, expressed as modality (*should've, must've, probably*), inability (*can't*), and questions (*What's happened?, what will we do?*), and in the spoken telling, the men's feelings are also expressed by the narrator as a querulous voice quality. The second Complication is signalled by switching identities back to the two sisters, and the events are now seen from their perspective as they react to their discovery of the 'python' in dialogue (*What did you see? What? What? Tell me quickly!... It's really huge...*). However their excitement is frustrated by the wanampi continually burrowing away from them, leaving them only little snakes to eat. The second Complication is not followed here by a discrete Evaluation, but simply concludes with the women's fearful reaction. However, the final Resolution is signalled by a marked Theme and identity switch (*At that the two wanampi...*).

Lest we imagine that stories of giant serpents and shaping landmarks are peculiar to Australian cultures that Europeans may see as remote from their own, the following narrative [2:12] is a European origin myth about a giant serpentine creature named Typhon. In this story the hero is not the serpent but the god Zeus who slays it. The story's locations around the Mediterranean are shown in Map 2.8.

Map 2.8   Places in the Typhon story

This narrative pattern is comparable in several respects to that of the *Piltati* story, except that the Resolution is to kill the serpent instead of becoming one (a common trope in Indo-European and Semitic mythology). The *Typhon* myth is also a serial narrative with a temporary Resolution and second Complication. Again the attitudinal reactions of the protagonists evaluate the Complications and expect Resolutions. First the gods' terror evaluates *Typhon's* horrible description and aggressive action, but *Athena's* call to courage expects a victorious solution. Then the gods' dismay evaluates *Zeus'* temporary defeat and compounds our desire for his victory. As with the *Piltati* myth, material evidence of *Zeus'* victory is manifested in the landscape, in the bloody colours of Mt Haemus and the fiery character of Mt Aetna.

[2:12] Typhon myth

Orientation
In revenge for the destruction of the giants, Mother Earth lay with Tartarus, and brought forth her youngest child, Typhon.

Complication 1
Typhon was the largest monster ever born. From the thighs downwards he was nothing but coiled serpents, and his arms had countless serpents' heads instead of hands. His ass-head touched the sky, his vast wings darkened the sun, fire flashed from his eyes, and flaming rocks hurtled from his mouth. He came rushing towards Olympus.

Evaluation
As he rushed towards them, the gods fled in terror to Egypt, where they disguised themselves as animals, Zeus becoming a ram,... Athene alone stood her ground, and taunted Zeus with cowardice.

Resolution (temporary)
Resuming his true form, Zeus threw a thunderbolt at Typhon, and followed this with a sweep of the same flint sickle that had served to castrate his grandfather Uranus. Wounded and shouting, Typhon fled to Mt Casius, which looms over Syria to the north.

Complication 2
There the two grappled. Typhon wound his myriad coils around Zeus, disarmed him of his sickle, and after severing the sinews of his hands and feet with it, dragged him into the Corycian Cave. Zeus is immortal but now he could not move a finger, and Typhon had hidden the sinews in a bear-skin, over which Delphyne [a serpent-tailed sister monster] stood ground.

Evaluation
The news of Zeus' defeat spread dismay amongst the gods.

Resolution
But Hermes and Pan went secretly to the cave, where Pan frightened Delphyne with a sudden horrible shout, while Hermes skilfully abstracted the sinews and replaced them on Zeus' limbs. Zeus returned to Olympus, and mounted upon a chariot drawn by winged horses, once more pursued Typhon with thunderbolts. Typhon reached Mount Haemus in Thrace and picking up whole mountains hurled them at Zeus. But Zeus interposed thunderbolts, so that they rebounded on the monster, wounding him frightfully. The streams of Typhon's blood gave Mt Haemus its name. He fled towards Sicily where Zeus ended the running fight by hurling Mt Aetna upon him, and the fire belches from its core to this day.

Graves 1955:133

It is surely interesting that traditional stories from widely divergent cultures can share so much of their generic organisation and their fields, along with their social functions to encode certain ideological principles, such as the gendered mode of production in Pitjantjatjara society, or the military expansionism of Hellenic Greece.[8] But despite their similarities the myths differ markedly in the value they are afforded in contemporary European culture, in Australia and elsewhere: the Greek myths are treasured as artefacts of classical European civilisation, studied for their archetypal insights into human nature, while Indigenous Australian myths are generally regarded as childish explanations of physical phenomena – 'just-so-stories'. This attitude certainly has its roots in imperial propaganda, that infantilised the peoples and cultures conquered by the European empires. It was in this climate that Kipling invented the just-so-story genre which is still the dominant template for interpreting Australian mythology,[9] evidenced in the school writing task to which Conal responded in his story *How the sparow could glide* [1:10].

The reason for this misinterpretation also lies to some extent in the way the myths themselves work as layered texts. At first glance they are partly about ordinary activites and emotions of people, partly about transformations into metaphysical creatures, and partly about creation of the landscape. This is the level accessible to children and the uninitiated, but to those in the know what is more significant are the abstract principles of social and natural order that such stories encode. In the Piltati myth these including marital and economic relations between the genders, and the spiritual basis of patrilineal land ownership (the present Piltati clan descends from the wanampi brothers). These levels of interpretation are revealed as individuals grow older, but are only meaningful in relation to the whole system of social principles encoded in the culture's mythological system, and its associated religious songs and ceremonies. Every landform in the entire Australian continent was once associated with such a sacred story, interconnected in complex networks of 'Dreaming tracks' or 'songlines', where the ancestor beings travelled over the country in creation times.

These 'inner' levels of interpretation are well known to scholars of the Greek myths, which would consequently never be regarded as simply just-so-stories. But they are not available to the average European on hearing apparently bizarre stories of other peoples, and unfortunately the surface interpretation often resonates with the widely held if unconscious view that other cultures lack the sophistication of European civilisation. If it were possible to treat Indigenous mythologies as part of our national heritage, as much as ancient Greek or Hebrew myths, it could perhaps help our transplanted European culture to find its place in the Australian landscape. The power of origin myths in shaping and holding group identities is well known. But story genres in general are clearly very powerful resources for cultural reproduction, which may have been a key factor in their evolution in human societies, and the reason for their extraordinary persistence across time and space.

2.6   News stories – new kinds of stories

To this point we have explored types of stories, and their social functions in sharing a record of events, an emotional reaction, a moral judgement, a personal response or the resolution of a problem. We have found that these story types may be realised in various modes, including oral storytelling, written literature and song, and we have found them in various cultural contexts, including contemporary and pre-modern cultures of Indigenous Australia and Europe. In a preliminary survey of stories across fifteen language families (Rose 2005b), we have also found that traditional stories seem to be dominated by the generic patterns of narrative and exemplum, with some anecdotes. This suggests to us that these members of the story family persist because they are highly functional across diverse cultural formations, including the hunting-gathering, pastoralist, farming, and urban cultures surveyed in that study. The work of Labov & Waletzky and many others has also shown how stories tend to follow comparable patterns in contemporary industrial communities.

On the other hand, the rise of modernity has undoubtedly sparked significant changes in patterns of stories, as it has led to the development of other genres in the new social institutions of science, industry and bureaucracy. A very recent expansion in story genres is the evolution of the modern news story around the turn of the 19th century, described by Iedema, Feez & White 1994. Until this point, newspapers had tended to appeal to sectional readerships, and reporting consisted of sequential recounts written for specific audiences. However when broadsheets appeared for mass audiences from the 1890s, the nature of the stories began to change. The need for a sensational lead to attract readers meant that a story might begin at any point in the sequence, and jump about in time as it presented different aspects of the events. Furthermore, a multiplicity of sources for a story and varying interests of readers met a shift from a single point of view on an event, to multiple points of view, each elaborating the event anew as the news story unfolded. The development of these patterns over a century is described in Iedema 1997.

These patterns are illustrated here with two news stories: the first reports the reaction of the neo-conservative government of Prime Minister John Howard to the *Bringing Them Home* report, showing how news stories are presented from various perspectives; the second reports the response of the Howard government to the crisis of refugees attempting to enter Australia, showing how news stories jump around in time.

When the *Bringing them Home* report was released in May 1997, newly elected Prime Minister Howard had his ministers attack the Human Rights and Equal Opportunity Commission (HREOC) and its chairman, Sir Ronald Wilson, over the report, which found that the policy of Indigenous child removal constituted genocide under the UN definition of the term, and recommended a national apology and compensation for the suffering it caused. Howard also allowed the extreme views of Pauline Hanson to be aired in parliament without rebuttal, and later echoed them himself. As more and more state governments, churches and other organisations said sorry, Howard offered a 'personal apology' but refused to apologise on behalf of the nation, claiming that: 'My view was that this generation can't be held accountable for the mistakes of past generations' (Gordon & Harvey 1997). The following story [2:13] from *The Australian* newspaper records the government's and Hanson's first reactions. The story's paragraphs have been numbered for discussion.

[2:13] Government rejects genocide finding, compensation

1   THE Federal Government yesterday rejected the Human Rights and Equal Opportunity Commission finding that the forced removal of 100,000 Aboriginal children from their parents was genocide, as federal Independent MP Ms Pauline Hanson said many Aborigines "were only alive today" because of the policy of assimilation between 1910 and 1970.

2   In the Federal Government's first response to the commission's report into "the stolen children", the Attorney-General, Mr Williams, rejected the genocide finding as "flawed and wrong", and reiterated Canberra's opposition to compensation.

3   Ms Hanson said the victims should not receive an apology or compensation. "Many of the children that were taken away are only alive today because they were taken. They more than likely lived a better lifestyle and are healthier and better educated than they otherwise would have been," she said. "I don't believe there is a need for an apology, these policies were well-meaning in their day. As with land rights, we can not continue to try and make Australians today feel guilty about the policies of the past. Society still removed children from families which do not look after their welfare", she said.

4   In a statement, Mr Williams said the Government "understands and appreciates the emotional and social significance" of the report for Aborigines and is committed to giving it "careful and proper consideration". He said the report would be tabled in Parliament next week.

5   In rejecting the commission's finding of genocide, Mr Williams said the UN convention on genocide defined it as an act intended "to destroy, in whole or in part" a racial group. "Adopting this view of the aim of removal is hard to reconcile with its (the commission's) own finding that child removal policies `were often concerned to protect and preserve' individual children," Mr Williams said.

6   The 689-page HREOC report has concluded the forced removal policies which continued until 1970 constituted a "crime against humanity", with many children emotionally, physically and sexually abused while in care. It has called for a national "sorry day" and a national victims compensation fund.

7   Mr Williams republished extracts from the Government's initial submission to the commission in which the Commonwealth stated it could see "no equitable or practical way" of paying compensation to stolen children. The Government had already voiced its opposition to the "notion of extravagant or divisive compensation claims", said Mr Williams, refusing to be drawn on the issue of an apology. He said the Government could not necessarily "condemn" those responsible for the events of the past.

8   Denying he was attempting to "bury" the report he received on April 5, Mr Williams said it would have been "inappropriate" to table it during Budget week and he did not have enough copies to table it earlier. He has attacked the HREOC's pre-tabling release of the report to the media on Tuesday.

9   The Opposition spokesman on Aboriginal Affairs, Mr Daryl Melham, demanded the report be tabled, saying discussion in a "vacuum" was "not conducive to a good debate on the issue" (Sutherland & Windsor 1997:3).

The lead paragraph gives the nucleus of the story, expanding the headline, with the government's strategic attack on the report's genocide finding, and Hanson's defence of the assimilation policy. The story then oscillates between and expands these elements, and brings in other positions. Paragraph 2 introduces the voice of Howard's Attorney-General Williams to further attack the finding of genocide and recommendation for compensation. Paragraph 3 then switches to Pauline Hanson's voice rejecting the apology recommendation and expanding her defence of assimilation policies. Paragraph 4 returns to Williams introducing a new element of the story – the official tabling of the report in parliament. Paragraph 5 then continues with Williams, here echoing Hanson's defence of assimilation policies. Paragraph 6 introduces the voice of the HREOC report itself, to explain the genocide finding and introduce another recommendation for a national 'sorry day'. Paragraph 7 returns again to Williams reiterating his government's rejection of compensation and now echoing Hanson's rejection of an apology (for similar reasons). Paragraphs 8 and 9 return to the issue of the report's tabling, first with William's lame excuse for withholding it, and his attack on HREOC for forcing the government's hand, and then introducing the voice of the Opposition demanding it be tabled.

The pattern of alternation between voices and issues as the news story unfolds is diagrammed in Figure 2.5. The speakers are represented as projecting the issues (as speech bubbles), of which there are five: genocide, apology, compensation, past policies and tabling the report. The first mention of each issue is in bold, and further mentions are linked by vertical lines.

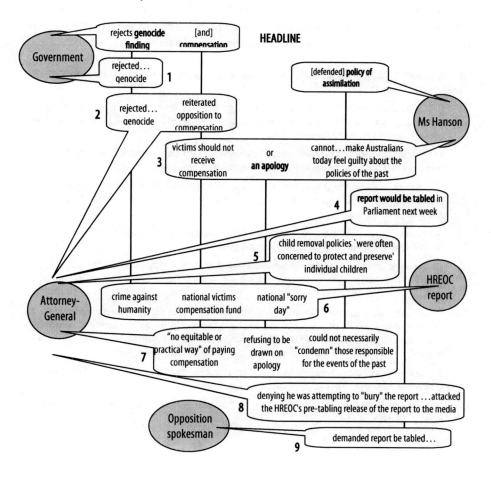

Figure 2.5 News story structured by alternating voices and issues

This switching from voice to voice differs from the representation of dialogue in stories, such as we saw in the novel *Follow the Rabbit-Proof Fence* [2:4] and the Pitjantjatjara myth *Piltati* [2:11], which present one speaker then another in temporal sequence. Rather the sequence of speaking is chopped about in news stories to present various speakers and issues; the sequence of unfolding of the news story genre replaces the sequence of unfolding of the events it reports. We refer to this tendency of organisation in written texts as 'text time vs field time'.

What we have not discussed here are the patterns of appraisal used by the speakers and journalists in [2:13] to engage and manipulate the reader. For a rich analysis of appraisal in new stories, see White 1997. The second news story [2:14] we have chosen is from *The Daily Telegraph* in August 2001. It reports an incident that brought international shame to Australia at the time, when the Howard government refused to allow the Norwegian container ship *MV Tampa*, that had rescued 438 refugees from a boat sinking in the Indian Ocean, to enter Australian waters at Christmas Island, off Western Australia. This text illustrates the way that action oriented news stories jump around in time. Here we have numbered each paragraph, and highlighted the wordings indicating the time of each event.

[2:14] TURNED AWAY – `We have a lot of sick people on board. These people are in really bad shape'

1   DRIFTING 22km off Christmas Island and with food and supplies running low, Captain Arne Rinnan was **last night** trying to maintain order on his besieged ship **after being turned away** by Australia and warned off by Indonesia.

2   The Norwegian captain of the MS Tampa **last night** told The Daily Telegraph by satellite phone many of the 438 men, women and children on his ship were ill **after their 11th day at sea.**

3   ``We have a lot of sick people on board. They are vomiting, have diarrhoea. These people are in really bad shape,'' Capt Rinnan said. ``I have tried to explain that situation to Australian authorities.''

4   But Prime Minister John Howard said **after a cabinet meeting yesterday afternoon** that the ship **would not be allowed to enter** Australian waters.

5   ``It is our view that as a matter of international law, this matter is something that **must be resolved** between the Government of Indonesia and the Government of Norway,'' Mr Howard said.

6   **Hours later**, the Indonesian Government responded by saying the boat people – who are believed to be **from Pakistan, Sri Lanka, Afghanistan and Indonesia – could not return to Indonesia**. Capt Rinnan told The Daily Telegraph he had not yet informed the boat people **last night** that Australia had refused them permission to land at Christmas Island.

7   Asked if he was afraid of violence, he said: ``Not **at the moment**, but we **were** and we **will be** if they are turned away. They are starting to get frustrated.''

8   The 26 women, 43 children and 369 men were in quarters below deck, and extra toilets had been installed.

[2:14 Contd]

9 The 262m long ship, which is fully loaded with mixed cargo headed for Singapore, has facilities intended only for the 27 Norwegian officers and Filipino crew. The captain said he and the crew **had done** the best they could for the boat people, but the situation was uncomfortable.

10 Some asylum seekers were dehydrated, two were unconscious, one had a broken leg, and two women were pregnant – one in her third trimester.

11 Although Mr Howard said Australia had finished with the issue, **by late yesterday** no-one had told Capt Rinnan.

12 He said he was still hopeful Australian authorities **would allow him to enter** the waters off Christmas Island.

13 ``If we are not allowed to go to Christmas Island, it **will be** very difficult for us,'' he said.

14 ``This **might turn into a situation** where ... well, I don't know **what will happen**.''

15 Capt Rinnan said he feared many **would carry out** their threat to jump overboard if they were not permitted to land at Christmas Island.

16 When he picked up the distress call **24 hours earlier**, he believed he would be carrying out a rescue operation, delivering the boat people to the nearest Indonesian port.

17 **After reaching** the stricken 20m wooden vessel, KM Palapa 1, the crew helped the boat people on board.

18 With the strong south-easterly winds which buffet the area at this time of year, it took the Tampa crew **three hours** to get them all on board.

19 ``We helped them up the gangway, and they were running. It wasn't very orderly, they were running to get on the ship,'' said Capt Rinnan.

20 They were given basic food and the women and children were provided with blankets.

21 Capt Rinnan said the boat people had become distressed when told they might have to return to Indonesia **earlier in the day**, with some threatening to jump overboard.

22 ``I said we are heading towards Indonesia and they said `No, you must head to Australia.'''

23 Capt Rinnan said they were ``just hanging around'' **late yesterday**, waiting for Australian officials to come on board

(Tsavdaridis 2001:1).

Figure 2.6 diagrams the disjunction in [2:14] between the text time of the news story, and the field time of the events it reports (modelled on an analysis developed by Iedema 1997). Six general time periods are indicated for the events: **11 days ago** when the refugees first set sail, **24 hours ago** when the Tampa picked them up, **early yesterday** when they were refused permission to enter Australia or return to Indonesia, **late yesterday** when Howard announced it was a matter for Norway and Indonesia, but had not informed the captain of the Tampa, **last night** when Captain Rinnan spoke to the press but had not told the refugees, and **possible future** events, when Rinnan was still hopeful Australia would allow him into Australian waters.

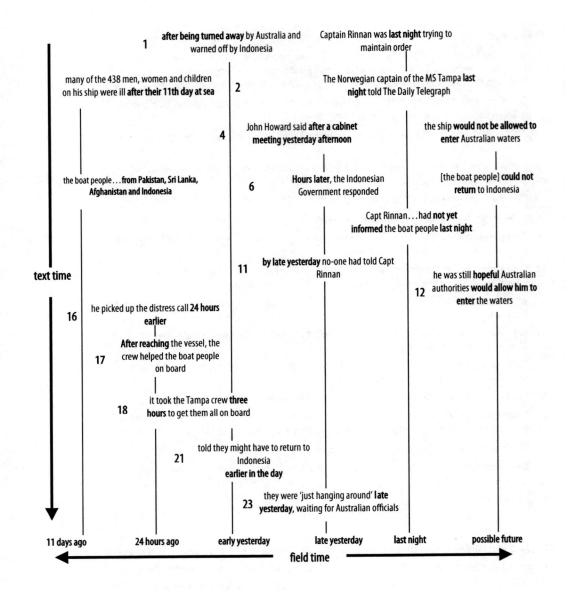

Figure 2.6 Text time reorders field time in news stories

Figure 2.6 shows how the first twelve paragraphs jump forward and back, and forward again, between time periods. Paragraphs 16–23 then go back in time to tell the story of the refugees rescue in three temporal steps, and conclude with their 'hanging around' on the ship late yesterday. Paragraphs without explicit temporal markers are not included here.

As it turned out, Captain Rinnan eventually defied the Howard government and entered the waters of Christmas Island, forcing the government to take the refugees off the Tampa, and becoming an international hero in the process. Nevertheless, Howard shamelessly manipulated the event to foster racial fears in the midst of an election campaign which he went on to win. We return to these events from the perspective of history genres in Chapter 3 below.

2.7   A system of story genres

We are now in a position to sum up the types of stories we have surveyed, as a system network in Figure 2.7. Firstly, in the previous section we saw that news stories are opposed to other types, in that they privilege textual organisation over temporal sequence; we might say they are text structured rather than time structured. Within the other time structured stories, recounts are then opposed to other types which involve a disruption to an expected course of events; that is recounts record an expectant sequence of events, while the others involve a counterexpectant stage. Within counterexpectant stories, narratives are then opposed to those that terminate with an attitudinal response (whereas counterexpectancy is resolved in narratives, following its evaluation). Finally, stories that terminate with a response are distinguished by the type of evaluation: anecdotes involve an emotional reaction, exemplums involve a moral interpretation, and observations involve a personal comment appreciating the events.

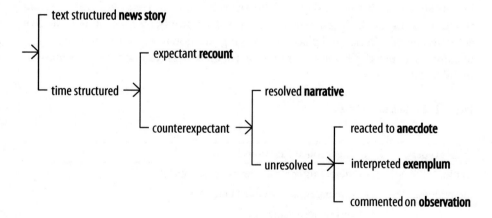

Figure 2.7   System of story genres

2.8 Story phases – another perspective

We have been focusing so far on patterns that distinguish types of stories, including their generic staging, their evaluations, and their broad social functions. Here we will adjust our focus to show how the story family shares a common set of resources for moving sequences forward and engaging readers, which we'll refer to as phases. From a segmental perspective, phases consist of one or more messages,[10] and one or more phases constitute a generic stage. While the stages of a genre are relatively stable components of its organisation, that we can recognise in some form in text after text of the genre, phases within each stage are much more variable, and may be unique to the particular text. Stages unfold in highly predictable sequences, but phases may or may not occur within any stage, and in variable sequences.

Related work on discourse phases includes Gregory & Malcolm (1981), for whom phases 'characterize stretches of discourse in which there is a significant measure of consistency and congruity', Hoey (1983) who describes patterns of problem-solution phases in stories, Jordan (1984) who extends problem-solution phases to all manner of texts, and Macken-Horarik (1996, 1998, 2003) and Martin (1996) on phases in literary narrative. Our perspective on story phases here goes beyond Gregory & Malcolm's work on criteria for delineating phases in general, by identifying specific types of phases characteristic of stories. And it extends Hoey's and Jordan's work which is centred on problem-solution patterns.

Here we describe some common types of phases that are used to construct the stages of stories. We have found these phase types in a wide range of oral and literate stories in English and other languages. Each phase type performs a certain function to engage the listener/reader as the story unfolds, by construing its field of activities, people, things and places, by evoking emotional responses, or by linking it to common experiences and interpretations of life. These functions are summarised in Table 2.2.

Table 2.2: Common story phases

phase types	engagement functions
setting	presenting context (identities, activities, locations)
description	evoking context (sensual imagery)
events	succeeding events
effect	material outcome
reaction	behavioural/attitudinal outcome
problem	counterexpectant creating tension
solution	counterexpectant releasing tension
comment	intruding narrator's comments
reflection	intruding participants' thoughts

While some of the terms for story phases resemble those used to denote genre stages, we denote stages with Initial Capitals and denote phases with lower case. Importantly, these are general terms for phase types, but any phase may be labelled more specifically according to its function in a particular story sequence, and there are undoubtedly other general phase types we have not covered here.

In terms of Halliday's 2004 model of logicosemantic relations, setting and description phases elaborate the story line, by presenting or describing identities, locations or activities. Event phases involve successive events ('then'), without the implication of consequence or concession. Effects and reactions are consequences of preceding phases ('so'): effects are material outcomes; reactions are participants' behaviour or attitudes in response to preceding phases. Problems and solutions are counterexpectant ('but'): problems create tension by countering a positive expectancy; solutions release tension by countering the negative expectancy created by problems. The relation of comment and reflection phases to the story is more like projection, much as saying projects locutions and thinking projects ideas. Comments suspend the flow of activity to intrude the narrator's comments, while reflections intrude the thoughts of participants.

Shifts from one phase to the next are typically signalled to the listener by a significant change in the starting point of a clause, its Theme. This most commonly includes a switch in the major identity presented as Theme, and sometimes involves a shift in time or other circumstance, as in the marked Themes we have noted above, and conjunctions can also help to signal phase shifts, particularly concessive 'but'. These thematic variations are indicative of shifts in field and tenor from one phase to the next. But these register shifts themselves are realised by lexical changes, in the activity, the people, places and so on, and also by appraisals in the case of evaluative phases (reactions, comments, reflections). In the presentations below, Themes are underlined up to the first participant, to show their roles in signalling transitions from phase to phase.

These patterns are illustrated in [2:15], the opening narrative from the Indian epic, the *Mahabharata*, in which King Shantenu falls in love with a woman who marries him but then throws all their children into a river.[11] The story is translated from an oral version in the south Indian language Kodava (see Rose 2005b for more detailed analysis). As for the Pitjantjatjara story [2:11] above, the original discourse patterns are maintained as closely as possible in this translation.

The narrative staging is quite clear in [2:15]: the story genre is signalled by the marked Theme *Once upon a time*, and the Complication is signalled by the concessive conjunction *However*. As illustrated in Figure 2.4 above, Shantenu's intense sadness both evaluates the Complication and expects the Resolution, which is signalled by the time Theme *One day...* The key organising principle in this narrative sequence is **expectancy**: falling in love, marrying and having a child expect an ongoing series of happy events. Countering this expectancy with shocking behaviour, such as throwing the children in a river, creates tension that engages the listener. However the Complication is not entirely unexpected: the listener already knows that the

[2:15] Shantenu Raaje

Orientation

setting	Once upon a time, the king of Hastinapura, called Shantenu, went to the riverside to hunt. While hunting, he saw a very beautiful woman.
reaction	Having seen that woman, he fell in love. It was her he wished to make a wife.
problem	But she said 'I will become your woman, but you may never ask me any question.'
solution	He then married her, and to him a child was born.

Complication

problem	However the child she threw into the river. In the same way, his next six children she threw into the river, and the seventh child she also threw into the river.
reaction	When she was going to throw the eighth child into the river, he asked why she was throwing the child.
problem	Then she said 'Because you have put the word to me after all, 'I am going to leave you, and that child I will also take.'

Evaluation

reaction	Shantenu the king was very sad in the palace.

Resolution

setting	One day he went hunting again.
problem	There he caught sight of a small boy. That boy knew who the king was but the king didn't know that it was his son.
solution	Just then his wife arrived there. She said 'That is your son and you may take him to the palace.' Having said this she disappeared.

Baumgartner in Ebert 1996

story will involve countexpectancy, because the genre is flagged from the opening phrase *Once upon a time*, so that concessive *However* signals to us that a disruption is imminent. What we don't initially know is what form the disruption will take, and what kind of counterexpectant story to expect: the complicating problems create a trajectory of bad news that may or may not be resolved. A Resolution must thus counter this gloomy expectancy. But like the Complication, it is not entirely unexpected; a Resolution is flagged by the Evaluation, so that the marked Theme *One day* signals it for us. This sequence is diagrammed as pulses of expectancy in Figure 2.8. *Once upon a time* expects the genre, which together with *However* expects the Complication. The Evaluation both appraises the Complication, and together with *One day* expects the Resolution.

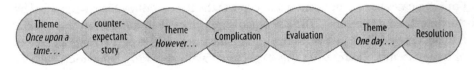

Figure 2.8 Pulses of expectancy in narrative

This pattern of expectancy is repeated at the smaller scale of phases within each stage. Minimally each generic stage consists of just one phase, so that *Shantenu Raaje* would still be a narrative as follows:

[2:15'] Shantenu Raaje

Orientation	Once upon a time the king of Hastinapura, called Shantenu, saw a very beautiful woman, fell in love, then married her, and a child was born.
Complication	However she said 'I am going to leave you, and that child I will also take.'
Evaluation	Shantenu the king was very sad in the palace.
Resolution	One day he caught sight of a small boy. His wife arrived and said 'That is your son and you may take him to the palace.'

However such a narrative is hardly engaging. Instead the narrator manipulates expectancy more subtly through a series of phases in each stage. As we said above, the shift from one phase to another is often signalled by a switch in identity, and sometimes also by conjunctions or marked Themes. But these are merely signals; the narrative is carried forward by swings in expectancy from phase to phase. The Orientation begins with a setting phase involving Shantenu in two activities, hunting by the river and seeing a woman. This setting already expects a probable range of events, which Shantenu's reaction of falling in love narrows and intensifies. This happy expectancy is momentarily countered by a problem, signalled by counterexpectant *But*, the woman's odd proviso to never ask any question. This cannot be the story's Complication as the potential disruption is immediately countered by marrying and have a child. By mildly disrupting the happy course of events, the overall effect is to intensify expectancy for an idyllic outcome, while paradoxically encouraging the seed of doubt. These pulses of expectancy are illustrated in Figure 2.9. The setting expects Shantenu's reaction, which expects marriage, but this is countered by the problem of the woman's proviso, signalled by *But*. This negative trajectory is then countered by the solution of marriage and child.

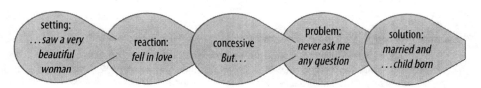

Figure 2.9 Phases as pulses of expectancy

Likewise, the Complication involves two problems, and Shantenu's reaction to the first problem, by asking his wife the prohibited question, gives rise to the second problem of her leaving him. This chain of events invites us to identify with Shantenu's predicament and empathise with his *very sad* reaction. The listener thus expects and desires a Resolution, but tension is further strung out in the Resolution stage, by the problem of not recognising his son, making the final solution an even more satisfying release. There is thus a kind of fractal relation between narrative stages and phases, each a mirror of the other at different scales, in both form and function. As [2:15] shows, settings, problems, reactions and solutions may occur in any stage.

Within Complications, problem-reaction patterns are commonly repeated, with the problems getting worse, and the reactions more intense, building up tension in a story. These patterns are illustrated in [2:16], from a short story by Australian children's author Paul Jennings. At this point in the story, two boys are trapped in a rubbish tip at midnight, which they have heard is haunted by a ghost.

[2:16] A Good Tip for Ghosts

...

Complication

problem1   A little way off behind some old rusting car bodies, I thought I heard a noise. Pete was looking in the same direction.

reaction   I was too terrified to move. I wanted to run but my legs just wouldn't work. I opened my mouth to scream but nothing came out. Pete stood staring as if he was bolted to the ground.

problem2   It was a rustling tapping noise. It sounded like someone digging around in the junk, turning things over. It was coming in our direction.

reaction   I just stood there pretending to be a dead tree or post. I wished the moon would go in and stop shining on my white face.

problem3   The tapping grew louder. It was coming closer.

description And then we saw it. Or him. Or whatever it was. An old man, with a battered hat. He was poking the ground with a bent stick. He was rustling in the rubbish. He came on slowly. He was limping. He was bent and seemed to be holding his old, dirty trousers up with one hand. He came towards us. With a terrible shuffle.

problem4   Pete and I both noticed it at the same time. His feet weren't touching the ground. He was moving across the rubbish about 30 centimetres above the surface.

It was the ghost of Old Man Chompers.

Evaluation

reaction   We both screeched the same word at exactly the same moment. 'Run!'

And did we run. We tore through the waist-high rubbish. Scrambling. Screaming. Scrabbling. Not noticing the waves of silent rats slithering out of our way. Not feeling the scratches of dumped junk. Not daring to turn and snatch a stare at the horrible spectre who hobbled behind us.

Resolution

solution   Finally, with bursting lungs, we crawled into the back of an old car.

problem   It had no doors or windows

reaction   so we crouched low, not breathing, not looking, not even hoping.

Jennings 1997:53

In this extract the Complication and Resolution stages are strongly signalled by marked Themes (*A little way off behind some old rusting car bodies ... Finally, with bursting lungs ...*). But within the Complication, Jennings expertly manipulates a series of worsening problems and intensifying reactions, to build tension that reaches a crescendo in the Evaluation, before release in the Resolution. While the sequence of problems and reactions carries the action forwards, Jennings also uses a description phase here, suspending the action and so contributing to the build up of tension. Description phases are common in longer stories; like settings, they elaborate the story line by evoking images of people, things or locations. This pattern of mounting tension is illustrated in Figure 2.10.

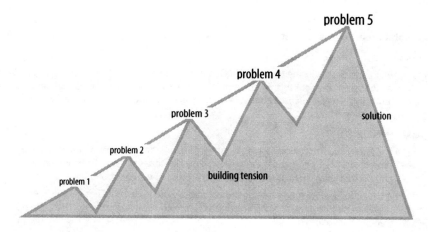

Figure 2.10 Building tension within a Complication

We can reiterate here that shifts from one story phase to another are realised by lexical changes, in the activity, the people, places and so on, and often by appraisals in evaluative phases; but types of phases are not determined by grammatical categories. For example, reactions may take many forms, including attitudinal attributes: *I was too terrified to move*, by ideas and locutions: *I wished the moon would go in, we both screeched... 'Run!'*, or by actions involving intensified processes: *We tore through the waist-high rubbish*. Likewise, settings, problems and solutions may be realised by actions: *Pete was looking, we crawled into the back*, by saying or sensing: *Pete and I both noticed it*, or by attributes *It was a rustling tapping noise*. Dialogue may be pressed into the service of any type of story phase, as [2:15] illustrates; indeed long sequences of activity may be carried forward in the form of dialogue, realising one phase after another.

The problem-reaction series in [2:16] also further illustrates the potential for fractal relations between patterns of phases and genre stages. The short story of which this is an extract is a serial narrative with five Complications that build in intensity, and as the intensity builds, so too do the Evaluations, as do the problems and reactions in this extract, which is the fourth of these Complications. Resolutions release the tension following each Complication, but like the one here they are only temporary until the last. Series of Complications and temporary Resolutions were illustrated above in the myths [2:11] and [2:12], and are typical of literary narratives, described by Rothery and Stenglin 1997. This phenomenon may also be found on the larger scale of whole novels, as we suggested above for the novel *Follow the Rabbit-Proof Fence*. The term **macro-genre** is used to refer to such large scale texts, further discussed in Chapter 4. Here we will briefly return to *Rabbit-Proof Fence* to illustrate how series of problems, descriptions and reactions can be subtly deployed in literary fiction.

[2:4'] Rabbit-Proof Fence anecdote

Orientation

events	Molly and Gracie finished their breakfast and decided to take all their dirty clothes and wash them in the soak further down the river. They returned to the camp looking clean and refreshed and joined the rest of the family in the shade for lunch of tinned corned beef, damper and tea.

Remarkable Event

problem	The family had just finished eating when all the camp dogs began barking, making a terrible din. 'Shut up,' yelled their owners, throwing stones at them. The dogs whined and skulked away. Then all eyes turned to the cause of the commotion.
description	A tall, rugged white man stood on the bank above them. He could easily have been mistaken for a pastoralist or a grazier with his tanned complexion except that he was wearing khaki clothing.
reaction	Fear and anxiety swept over them when they realised that the fateful day they had been dreading had come at last. They always knew that it would only be a matter of time before the government would track them down.
description	When Constable Riggs, Protector of Aborigines, finally spoke his voice was full of authority and purpose.
reaction	They knew without a doubt that he was the one who took children in broad daylight – not like the evil spirits who came into their camps at night.
problem	'I've come to take Molly, Gracie and Daisy, the three half-caste girls, with me to Moore Rive Native Settlement,' he informed the family.
reaction	The old man nodded to show that he understood what Riggs was saying. The rest of the family just hung their heads, refusing to face the man who was taking their daughters away from them. Silent tears welled in their eyes and trickled down their cheeks.

The Orientation here consists not of a setting phase, but a series of events. The peace of the Orientation is disrupted by the ominous portent of dogs barking, so that the following description of an anonymous white man expects the family's reaction of *fear and anxiety*. The description of Constable Riggs' identity and authority expects their reaction of certainty *without a doubt*, and then his intention to take the girls expects their reaction of *silent tears*. The author manages appraisal through these phases to account for the family's resignation to the abduction of their children. First there is a surge of attitude at the dogs barking, which then pauses to appreciate the white man as *tall* and *rugged*, but affect surges again in the family's reaction to recognising him. The next description is strongly marked by the circumstantial Theme *When Constable Riggs, Protector of Aborigines, finally spoke.* The judgement of his voice with *authority and purpose* thus serves as a pivot, from the family's fearful reaction, to resigned acceptance. Their next reactions go from certainty *without a doubt*, to resignation *just hung their heads*, to passive sorrow in *silent tears*. The appraisals chart a parabolic rise to the first reaction and descent to the last, diagrammed in Figure 2.11.

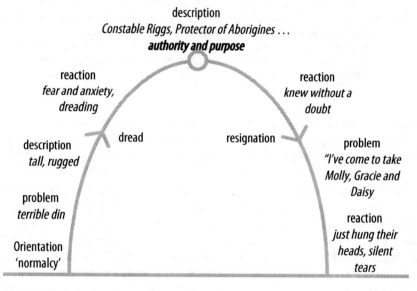

Figure 2.11 Patterns of appraisal and phases in [2:4]

Within the overall anecdote pattern of Event ^ Reaction, the author thus leads the reader's emotions through a seesaw of problems and reactions, to induce us to identify with the feelings of the family, and so to empathise with their resignation to the invader's final act of barbarity.

While the phases discussed so far elaborate or enhance the sequence of activities in a story, the relation of comment and reflection phases to the story is more like projection. In comments, the narrator intrudes their views into the activity sequence to comment on the events or participants.

In contrast to comments, reflections intrude the participants' thoughts, either as dialogue, or as 'inner speech'; they are a pervasive feature of literary fiction, but are less common in oral stories and children's fiction.

The following example [2:17] is from a short story that has been used for school examination in Australia and elsewhere.

[2:17] The Weapon (extract)	
Orientation	
setting	The room was quiet in the dimness of early evening. Dr James Graham, key scientist of a very important project, sat in his favorite chair, thinking. It was so still that he could hear the turning of pages in the next room as his son leafed through a picture book.
comment	Often Graham did his best work, his most creative thinking, under these circumstances, sitting alone in an unlighted room in his own apartment after the day's regular work.
problem	But tonight his mind would not work constructively. Mostly he thought about his mentally arrested son – his only son – in the next room.
reflection	The thoughts were loving thoughts, not the bitter anguish he had felt years ago when he had first learned of the boy's condition. The boy was happy; wasn't that the main thing? And to how many men is given a child who will always be a child, who will not grow up to leave him? Certainly that was a rationalization, but what is wrong with rationalization when it...

This example displays the contrast between a narrator's comments on a field of activity, and a protagonist's reflection on its meaning. This story is used in Martin 1996 to illustrate another level of phase analysis, in which two or more fields are woven into a literary narrative (see also Macken-Horarik 1999, 2003, Rothery & Macken 1991, Rothery & Stenglin 1997). While the phase types we have described here are used, as in other stories, to carry the story forward and engage the reader, they also realise multiple fields in the story that are continually interrupted to manipulate expectancy. In the above example these include the field of Dr Graham's academic work, which is interrupted by the domestic field of reflections on his son, a disruption that is explicitly signalled by concessive *But*. As we noted at the beginning of this section, phases may be specific to the field of a particular story, and this is illustrated by the shifts in field in this literary narrative. Extract [2.17'] below shows both levels of phase analysis, along with narrative staging. Each expected course, that is frustrated by the interruption, is also given in brackets.

This extract also illustrates a contrast between reflections on an activity's meaning, and reactions that entail a change in participants' disposition (realised by attitude, thought, locution or action). But the larger phases labelled in boxes here are significant shifts in field. Martin 1996 describes how appraisals are woven through each such shift in field to realise the underlying 'theme' of the story, so that successful students are able to read this modernist narrative as a token for an ideological message. This is a more elaborate critical literary analysis than we have attempted in this chapter, but see Macken-Horarik 1999, 2003.

[2:17′] The Weapon (extract)

Orientation

work activity	
setting	The room was quiet in the dimness of early evening. Dr James Graham, key scientist of a very important project, sat in his favorite chair, thinking. It was so still that he could hear the turning of pages in the next room as his son leafed through a picture book.
comment	Often Graham did his best work, his most creative thinking, under these circumstances, sitting alone in an unlighted room in his own apartment after the day's regular work.
[EXPECTING:	and tonight he was working on a particularly interesting problem...]

interrupted by domestic activity	
problem	But tonight his mind would not work constructively. Mostly he thought about his mentally arrested son – his only son – in the next room.
reflection	The thoughts were loving thoughts, not the bitter anguish he had felt years ago when he had first learned of the boy's condition. The boy was happy; wasn't that the main thing? And to how many men is given a child who will always be a child, who will not grow up to leave him? Certainly that was a rationalization, but what is wrong with rationalization when it...
[EXPECTING:	...makes it possible to live with something that would be otherwise unbearable...]

Complication

interrupted by service activity	
events	- The doorbell rang. Graham rose and turned on lights in the almost-dark room before he went through the hallway to the door.
reaction	He was not annoyed; tonight, at this moment, almost any interruption to his thoughts was welcome.
events	He opened the door. A stranger stood there: he said, 'Dr Graham? My name is Niemand; I'd like to talk to you. May I come in a moment?'
description	Graham looked at him. He was a small man, nondescript, obviously harmless – possibly a reporter or an insurance agent.
reaction	But it didn't matter what he was. Graham found himself saying, 'Of course. Come in, Mr Niemand.' A few minutes of conversation, he justified himself by thinking, might divert his thoughts and clear his mind.
events	'Sit down,' he said, in the living room. 'Care for a drink?'
	Niemand said, 'No. thank you.' He sat in the chair; Graham sat on the sofa.
	The small man interlocked his fingers; he leaned forward. He said, …
[EXPECTING:	'Dr Graham, it's a pleasure to be here this evening. Thank-you very much for agreeing to talk with me...]

interrupted by political activity	
problem	…'Dr Graham, you are the man whose scientific work is more likely than that of any other man to end the human race's chance for survival.'
reaction	A crackpot, Graham thought. Too late now he realized that he should have asked the man's business before admitting him. It would be an embarrassing interview – he disliked being rude, yet only rudeness was effective…

Brown 1984

These are a few brief examples of the application of story phase analysis, although many more are possible. The types of story phases we have described are set out in Figure 2.12. They are grouped according to their logical relation to the preceding phase in the story sequence, using the logicosemantic categories of expansion and projection. They are distinguished firstly on whether they expand the activity sequence or are projected by it, secondly whether the type of expansion is enhancing or elaborating, and thirdly whether the type of enhancement is time or consequence. Within these groupings, each phase type is specified by its particular function.

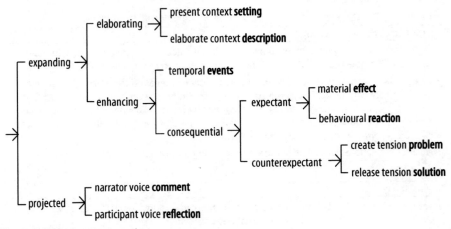

Figure 2.12 Options in story phases

Elaborating phases establish and expand contexts and characters, while enhancing phases carry the story forward in time. Events phases do so without an implication of consequence or concession. On the other hand, reactions are behavioural/ attitudinal consequences that are expected by preceding phases, and effect phases are material consequences (less common in stories and not exemplified above). Problems counter positive expectancy, while solutions counter negative expectancy created by problems.[12] In contrast to these expansions on the story line, projecting phases intrude into the sequence of activities, interrupting its flow to comment or reflect. While most story phases are equally common in oral and written stories, reflection often dominates in literary fiction, where the focus is on inner development of characters. These include 'thematic narratives', which embed an underlying 'message' or 'theme' in the story (Macken-Horarik 1999, 2003, Rothery & Macken 1991, Rothery & Stenglin 1997).

2.9 Response genres – evaluating stories

A major demand of the English curriculum in Australian schools is for students to evaluate the stories they read or view in 'text responses'. Four general types of response genre are described by Rothery & Stenglin 1997: **personal response**, **review, interpretation** and **critical response**. We will illustrate these genres here with responses from the media to the movie adaptation *Follow the Rabbit-Proof Fence*. Firstly, personal responses express one's feelings about a text. The following [2:18] is from a movie chat site on the internet, with attitudes highlighted:

[2:18] Personal response to Rabbit-Proof Fence

i **felt so much pain** for Gracie when she was taken again. I **felt like** rescuing her. I **felt like bursting into tears** when she **cried** 'i **wanna** take the train to mummy!' The whole situation is **hard to take in**... but the fact that no matter what they did they were driven back to that **horrible** moore river place. It **broke my heart** when she had the disagreement with molly because she was **desperate** to see her mother again. It was **so hard for her**, having a different mother to both the other girls, knowing she was only a while away.

'Come on, we've got to go'

'But Molly, Mummy at wiluna. I **want** mummy.'

In the real event, Gracie fields did get to Wiluna, but was discovered and taken the next day. she never made it to Jigalong

it **just teared me apart**... does anyone else **feel that**???

sweetprincess 2004

Although students are often encouraged in class to say and even write how they feel about a text, personal responses are actually the least valued response type in formal examinations, a cruel if unintentional duplicity that denies many students the keys to success in subject English (Rothery & Macken 1991, Macken-Horarik 1996, 1998, 2002). More highly valued in school English are reviews and interpretations, which are also common genres in entertainment pages of the media, while critical responses are associated with literacy criticism. Reviews typically summarise selected features of a story, such as its key incidents, characters and relationships, and evaluate these. According to Rothery & Stenglin their staging begins with the Context of the story, followed by a text Description and finally a Judgement, exemplified in [2:19] with a web review of the book:

[2:19] Review of Rabbit-Proof Fence

Context

This book is about one of the dark chapters of Aboriginal Australian history: The "Stolen Generations". The "Aboriginal Protection Act" of 1897 allowed the authorities "to cause every Aboriginal within any district [...] to be removed to, and kept within the limits of, any reserve". In addition, article 31 allowed them to provide "for the care, custody, and education of the children of Aboriginals" and prescribed "the conditions".

[2:19] Review of Rabbit-Proof Fence (Contd)

Description
This is the political background, the setting which must be comprehended before the story's full tragedy can be understood. Three girls, Molly, Gracie and Daisy, are "half-caste" Aboriginal youngsters living together with their family of the Mardu people at Jigalong, Western Australia. One day a constable, a "Protector" in the sense of the Act, comes to take the three girls with him. They are placed in the Moore River Native Settlement north of Perth, some 1,600 kilometres away. Most children this was done to never saw their parents again. Thousands are still trying to find them. This story is different. The three girls manage to escape from the torturing and authoritarian rule of the settlement's head. Guided by the rabbit-proof fence, which, at that time ran from north to south through Western Australia, they walk the long distance back to their family.

Judgement
The authors are not professional writers which you'll notice while you read. But despite occasional stylistic flaws, the book has one advantage over novels: it's authentic. And this makes the story even more remarkable and the reader more and more concerned and shocked about the circumstances of that time. In the end you'll be as happy as the Mardu people when the girls come home, but your understanding of Australian history may have changed.

Korff 2004

Mastery of the interpretation genre demonstrates "that one is able to 'read' the message of the text and hence is able to respond to the cultural values presented in the narrative" (Rothery & Stenglin 1997:156). Staging of interpretations include text Evaluation which presents the 'message' of the text, a Synopsis that selects certain elements of the story to illustrate the message, and Reaffirmation of the evaluation, elaborating the message. These stages are illustrated in [2:20] with an interpretation of the book *Rabbit Proof Fence*, from a review on the website of the ABC Indigenous program *Message Stick*:

[2:20] Interpretation of Rabbit-Proof Fence

Evaluation
It's intriguing how a simple story (originally released in 1996 with the title Follow The Rabbit-Proof Fence) could become such a huge international success. Aunty Doris had an amazing mother who undertook the most incredible journey of her life against every single adversity - both natural and man-made - and still ended up losing her own precious children to the same government policy she thought she had conquered. It could only happen in Australia really.

For those on another planet for the last 12 months (or in denial of Australia's terrible history of abuse against Aboriginal people), Rabbit Proof Fence is the true story of Molly, born near Jigalong in the remote Pilbara region of Western Australia. Forcibly stolen as a child from her mother, along with her two sisters she is taken to the penal like Moore River Settlement near Perth - a long way from home and virtually another world for the trio.

The policy makers of the time were adamant about the "rescue of the native" in Western Australia - that by integrating them into white society and breeding them out they could be saved from their own "primitive savagery". Moore River was a testament to these scruples in that it was responsible for training these half-caste children to be servants for white families, mainly in regional areas.

> **[2:20] Interpretation of Rabbit-Proof Fence (Contd)**
>
> Treated harshly at Moore River, Molly sees only one option for her and her siblings - to commence the journey back home to her mother and extended family on foot. Escaping from their captors, the girls had no maps to guide them on the 1600 kilometre journey, just a long standing landmark to man's battle against nature - a north/south running rabbit-proof fence that stretched the length of the country to lead them home.
>
> *Reaffirmation*
> It's gripping stuff really, full of adventure, tragedy and rejoices - prime material for a feature length movie. It took the bravery of Australian director Phillip Noyce to see the inner triumph of this novel and turn it into a much lauded and almost definitive visual record of this country's treatment of Aboriginal people. And every single word is based on truth.
>
> Aunty Doris has followed up this story with her recent release Under the Windmarra Tree. She writes with real passion and dignity that could only be conducted by the daughter of the main character. Needless to say, Rabbit-Proof Fence is one of the greatest Australian stories ever told. A milestone of an experience that still remains tragically silent in this country.
>
> K. Martin 2005

The film's twin messages as interpreted by this writer involve on the one hand the truth of 'this country's treatment of Aboriginal people…that still remains tragically silent', and on the other the 'inner triumph' of Aboriginal people like Aunty Doris Pilkington and her 'amazing mother' Molly. In contrast, critical responses go beyond interpreting, to challenge the message of a text. Following an outline by Rothery 1994, their staging may begin with a text Evaluation that suggests the possibility of challenge, followed by text Deconstruction that reveals how the message is constructed, and finally the Challenge which denaturalises the message. The following critical response [2:21] reveals how Noyce's film absolves Australian audiences by treating the story as a triumphal narrative, leaving out the unresolved realities, and deflecting our guilt onto the very English villain.

> **[2:21] Critical response to Rabbit Proof Fence**
>
> *Evaluation*
> *Rabbit Proof Fence*, directed by Philip Noyce, is a moving film about three young Aboriginal girls, aged 8, 11 and 14, who are stolen from their families at Jigalong and taken to a native settlement north of Perth. The girls, Daisy, Gracie and Molly escape from the settlement and begin a 1600 kilometre trek along a rabbit proof fence they know will lead them back home. Daisy and Molly make it home, with Gracie falling back into the hands of white authorities along the way. Noyce's narrative is a familiar one, with unjustly treated Aussie battlers drawing on mateship and courage to overcome adversity, embodied here by A O Neville (a wicked English overlord played by Kenneth Branagh), Chief Protector of Aborigines in Western Australia at the time. The effect of the narrative is to position viewers to sympathise with the brave girls and celebrate their eventual liberation from white authorities. However, the actual contribution made by a modernist narrative of this kind to reconciliation is open to question.

[2:21] Critical response to Rabbit-Proof Fence (Contd)

Deconstruction

Early on the film sets us up to sympathise with the girls by showing them being dragged from their family's arms, a horrifying scenario to say the least. Noyce then introduces us to the sterility of institutional life at Moore River Native Settlement, including the genocidal practice of sorting the children for adoption by the lightness of the colour of their skin. As the girls trek home we can't help cheering for them every step of the way, mesmerised by their courage and resourcefulness, and fearful of the challenges along the way. Viewers not in tears of joy by the time Molly leads Daisy home to their family will surely be so when Noyce introduces the real Molly and Daisy at the end of his film, as elders at home in Jigalong – surviving still.

However the absences from Noyce's film are more important than the things he does include. Noyce doesn't film what happened to Daisy and Molly after they reached home; or what happened to Gracie who was left along the way (not to mention the dozens of children they left behind at Moore Rover, and the tens of thousands of Aboriginal children like them). Molly for example married, had two daughters, and ended up incarcerated in Moore Rover Native Settlement with them again in 1940. Learning of the death of relatives in Jigalong, she undertook her long trek home once more, this time carrying her 18 month old daughter, Annabelle. Three years later Annabelle was removed and sent to Sister Kate's Children's Home; Molly never saw her again. So much for battlers overcoming adversity! Molly indeed survived, as did her daughter Doris who lived to tell this tale; but would we have cheered quite so loudly in the film had we known the fate that awaited Molly and Annabelle, who suffered the remorseless cruelty of our fellow white Australians?

Noyce's characterisation of Neville, the Chief Protector, is also open to question. Noyce portrays Neville as a personification of evil; a one dimensional character, his motives are not explored, nor do we end up with a deeper understanding of how the white authorities could have behaved this way. Even more troubling is the potential deflection of responsibility for what is going on onto his Englishness, thereby absolving the Australians involved in these crimes against humanity (a familiar motif of blame in Australian cinema, from movies such as Gallipoli and Breaker Morant). We know however that stealing indigenous children from their parents was not the triumph of evil over goodness, but rather a widespread institutional practice enjoying considerable political support – and Noyce's film tells us next to nothing about how Australians came to believe that forced removal was in the best interests of the stolen children.

Challenge

Noyce's message seems to be that the traditional Australian values of courage, perseverance and mateship will triumph over evil. But Indigenous history in Australia tells us this is wrong, however accomplished the modernist narratives assuring us it's true. Is Noyce's film any more in fact than a feel-good film for middle class liberals, who feel guilty about the past, and enjoy seeing two young Indigenous Australians win out against the odds? Will they simply use Noyce's film to feel they've made a contribution to reconciliation, when all they've done is cheer two exceptional Aussie battlers on? Will they take anything at all away from the film which will help them deal productively with Indigenous Australians in post-colonial Australia, in the face of a federal government hostile to reconciliation which gets re-elected over and over again? Perhaps not, but as they say in Hollywood, that's entertainment. Australia needed more from Noyce; perhaps he's been in Hollywood too long.

Jim wrote this critical response [2:21] based on a model designed by Rothery 1994, in order to make the functions and strategies of the genre explicit. Its purpose is explicitly political, to challenge the ideology promoted in a text; and its strategy is to deconstruct the narrative devices used to influence an audience. Although a critical response is often touted as the ideal response genre in secondary school English curricula, Rothery & Macken (1991) and Macken-Horarik (1996, 1998, in press) report that, even by the mid-nineties, it was rarely produced by students. It can be difficult enough to recognise and interpret the messages layered into literary stories, but it requires considerably more sophistication to challenge such artfully constructed messages. Recent changes to the NSW secondary school English curriculum make it more likely that a significant body of critical responses informed by cultural studies and focusing on texts from popular culture will be produced; but we have not yet had the opportunity to study this genre as it emerges in students' examination writing in the noughts.

Comparable sophistication is displayed in a critical response to the film by Evan Williams, film reviewer with *The Australian* newspaper [2:22]. Williams' deconstruction and challenge have a very different political purpose to ours in [2:21]; he also deconstructs Noyce's 'manipulative' positioning of the audience, but he finds the story itself hard to believe. His technique is to first woo the liberal reader by praising the film, before critiquing its narrative ploys.

[2:22] Conservative critique of Rabbit Proof Fence

Evaluation

IMPORTANCE is not something filmmakers should strive for. But some films – a very few – have importance thrust upon them. When Peter Watkins made The War Game, his horrific mock-documentary about a nuclear attack on Britain, Kenneth Tynan called it 'the most important film ever made'. Who knows? I think The Grapes of Wrath was important (as well as a masterpiece); like Marcel Ophuls' great documentary about the French resistance, The Sorrow and the Pity, it told us things, or reminded us of things, we didn't want to know or would rather forget. It's possible that Phillip Noyce's Rabbit-Proof Fence belongs in this precious company. This is the first film about the stolen generations and it's important in the best sense of the word. That doesn't mean that it's a very good film, still less a complete success. I wish it were. But it carries an overwhelming sense of conviction. And what makes much of it compelling is its lack of self-important flourishes. The story is slight, the direction understated, the cast largely untried. In one respect it reminded me of Schindler's List. At the end of that film, Spielberg tacked on a little epilogue in which the characters appeared as themselves, old and worn, but somehow recognisable. Noyce uses the same device. Molly and Daisy, two of the girls in the story, are seen at the end as elderly women. And after all they have endured the effect is oddly comforting. Here, it seems, is proof of their survival, proof that their story is real, proof, if you like, that their spirit lives on.

At the risk of being misunderstood, I should say that I still find the story difficult to believe. It's not that I doubt anyone's good faith. The screenplay was written by Doris Pilkington, whose mother Molly was one of three Aboriginal children forcibly separated from their families on the orders of O.A. Neville, Western Australia's protector of Aborigines, in 1931. Transported to the Moore River Native Settlement, the girls found their way back home to Jigalong, 2400km to the south, by following a rabbit-proof fence. It's an amazing tale, though sceptics may prefer to see it as a fabric of childhood memories, embellished by repeated embroidering. But even if it were wholly invented it would have the power to stir us: Rabbit-Proof Fence has been made with such transparent humanity and idealism it scarcely seems to matter whether the story is true or not.

Deconstruction

The early scenes with the girls – Molly (Everlyn Sampi), her little sister Daisy (Tianna Sansbury) and their cousin Gracie (Laura Monaghan) – were for me the least successful. For a start, I would have liked more of them. When Neville's functionaries arrive to take the children away we have seen so little of the girls with their families that the wrenching horror of their separation is blunted for us.

[2:22] Conservative critique of Rabbit Proof Fence

Many, I know, disagree: Who could be unmoved by the sight of screaming children being dragged from the arms of their loved ones and bundled into cars? But the scene would be more moving, and less manipulative, if we knew the characters better. And the thumping, doom-struck music on the soundtrack at this point might not have been needed to sharpen our responses.

Neville is played with flinty bureaucratic rectitude by Kenneth Branagh. His objective is to rid the Aboriginal population of so-called half-castes and their fairer-skinned variants by selective breeding. Children are paraded before him to have their skin colour solemnly assessed: the paler ones will go to school, the rest will find work as labourers or servants.

It's not so much a brutal regime, more one of numbing and demeaning helplessness, more chilling for the air of self-satisfied benevolence exuded by Neville and his staff. In this world of dusty dormitories, well-meaning matrons and unfamiliar religious teaching, hints of serious abuse are played down. Is this lonely, sobbing boy merely homesick or has he suffered something worse? No wonder the girls run away.

Perhaps it's because we're so used to car and helicopter chases that the scenes of pursuit feel less gripping than they should. Or is it that the police, led by a prickly Roy Billing as Chief Inspector Sellinger, and the ageing tracker (David Gulpilil) seem strangely half-hearted in their efforts to recapture the absconders? The children, we notice, seemed unscathed by their ordeal. Old clothes and food are scrounged along the way – miraculously, it sometimes seems – and the weather is remarkably benign. I kept wishing in these scenes that Noyce had let the children speak their own language, especially since their subtitled speech (heard at the start) sounds so lovely, and something is made of Neville's insistence on the use of English at the settlement. 'None of that jabber here!' the girls are told: in some ways it's the worst indignity they suffer.

The children perform with artless grace and candour. They are the film's luminous heart. But their reunion at the end, like their separation, seems strangely flat: the waiting mother and the grandmother are little more than patient faces, characters waiting to be drawn.

Challenge
Neville seems real enough – every story needs a villain – though anyone who has read Pat Jacobs's scrupulously fair and sensitive biography of this unhappy man, published in 1990, will know that villains can have honourable and compassionate motives. I hope Noyce will read this book, just as I hope people will see his film. It tells us something of the beauty and tragedy of the Aboriginal story; and, for all its faults, it tells it more eloquently than any film before it.
Williams 2002

It seems unlikely that Williams would describe his craft in terms such as critical deconstructionism, but he is keenly aware of the manipulative potential of narrative devices, and artfully persuades us that Noyce uses them to position his audience. After deconstructing and depreciating instance after instance, he contrasts Noyce's narrative trick of exaggerating Neville's villainy with a 'scrupulously fair and sensitive biography'. To avoid alienating liberal readers he leaves his challenge largely implied: that just as *Rabbit-Proof Fence* is 'difficult to believe', so too the whole story of the stolen generations may be little more than 'a fabric of childhood memories', or at the very least it unfairly ignores the 'honourable and compassionate motives' of its alleged perpetrators. Whereas our critique in [2:21] complains that Noyce's film lets us off the hook, Williams' complains that it hangs us too high, a sentiment that would certainly be endorsed by the Howard conservatives. Despite the left liberal ideals of much critical theory, its favoured genre of critical response may be pressed into the service of any ideology.

3 Histories

3.0 From stories to histories

In the previous chapter we looked at the family of story genres, which reconstruct real or imagined events and evaluate them in terms which enact bonds of solidarity among participating interlocutors. We suggested that key social functions of stories include maintaining and shaping social relationships, particularly at the level of local communities and kin, through evaluation of events and behaviour. In this chapter we turn to another family of event-oriented genres that have evolved to construct and maintain social order on the wider scale of peoples and their institutions, that is historical genres. We begin with biographical genres, which are closely related to the personal recounts reviewed in Chapter 2, but which move beyond the series of events that we have seen in stories, to a series of episodes that make up a person's life history. Then we explore history genres which manage time, cause and value in complementary ways, to recount historical episodes and to explain the reasons they occurred, from one or more angles. And finally we examine genres that explicitly argue for or against interpretations of history.

In terms of the SFL model of register and genre we introduced in Chapter 1, our focus of organisation will now shift from genre towards field. Whereas the subject matter of story genres is wide open, we are now considering relations among genres from the perspective of one of our academic disciplines – as constituting discourses of history. That is, we consider this family of genres to have evolved within the institutional contexts of recording, explaining and debating the past. While our criteria for distinguishing story genres was first and foremost their staging, our focus on history genres is on how time is manipulated to order past events, how cause is used to explain them, and how appraisal is used to value one or another interpretation. Ultimately, from a theoretical perspective we will also shift our strategy for relating genres to one another from typology, as a hierarchy of groupings, to topology, as regions of commonality between genres. This then enables us to propose a learner pathway for students apprenticing into this family of genres, particularly oriented to secondary school curricula.

As far as the subject matter of our texts is concerned, we will continue our interest in Indigenous concerns and points of view on Australian history (cf Rose to appear a), but we will also introduce another topic of deep current concern to many Australians, the movement of refugees from conflicts to our north, and the responses of Australian governments.

3.1   Biographical recounts – telling life histories

We'll begin with an autobiographical recount ([3:1]), in this case a spoken recount from Lavina Gray, who is a senior Aboriginal child care worker in Sydney. In this recount Lavina begins by introducing herself and her family and telling us where they are from. She then moves on to recount some of the significant stages of her life, from the central NSW town of Wellington, to the Aboriginal child care centre of Murrawina in Redfern, Sydney, up to her graduation as a teacher.[1] To scaffold these life stages for the listener, Lavina has mostly used temporal conjunctions (*then, first*), supported by the ordinal modifier *first* (*my* first *job*). These features are highlighted in the text in bold.

Phases of biographical recounts tend to be whole episodes in a person's life, although they may be signalled by similar means as the phases of story genres, such as temporal conjunctions. In addition a key episode, when Lavina's education begins, is signalled by a switch in thematic identity from the narrator's *I* to *The College of Advanced Education*. We could also note that cause and effect is already beginning to emerge as a feature of history telling, even in this spoken recount, to explain some events (*so I had to help my mother*, *so three of us applied*, *so graduating as an Aboriginal teacher was really a big boost for me*).

Lavina's recount features an ongoing prosody of evaluation through three phases of her life, first contrasting the racism in her home town with the fun-filled chaos of a large family, followed by the tightrope of possibilities and obligations which shaped her personal and professional life, and culminating with her pride in graduating as an Aboriginal teacher.

> ... There was **a lot of racism** there as well, in the school... It was **a bit chaotic** then as a child. But it was **fun.** It was a big family, so it was **good.**

> ... I **had to** leave school because there were **too many** children in the family so I had to help my mother.

> ... I then worked in factories wherever I **could**.

> ... I **needed to be near** my mother. Every girl **needs to be near** their mother with their first child. A **very dramatic** thing.

> ... An AEA job allows you to work in **any schools** where there's Aboriginal children or Aboriginal students. It can be primary, pre-school, long day or high school. **It doesn't really matter**.

[3:1] Lavina Gray's autobiography

My name is Lavina Gray. I grew up in Wellington NSW. My tribal area is the Wiradjuri tribe, which goes from Wellington around to the Riverina area. I went to school at Wellington Public School. There was a lot of racism there as well, in the school. I come from a family of 15 children, 9 boys and 6 girls. It was a bit chaotic then as a child. But it was fun. It was a big family, so it was good.

I went to Wellington High. I left school at 14. I had to leave school because there were too many children in the family so I had to help my mother. I **then** came to Sydney and stayed with my brother and sister-in-law and their children.

I **then** worked in factories wherever I could.

Then I became a defacto at 17. I was with him until the birth of my first child.

I **then** went back home to Wellington to my mother, cause I needed to be near my mother. Every girl needs to be near their mother with their first child. A very dramatic thing.

My first job in the education sector was AEA. AEA stands for Aboriginal Educated Assistant. I went to Sydney University for that course. An AEA job allows you to work in any schools where there's Aboriginal children or Aboriginal students. It can be primary, pre-school, long day or high school. It doesn't really matter.

I **then** stayed at Murrawina after graduation. Murrawina means 'black women' because black women started Murrawina. It was, it's a long day-care centre that caters for Aboriginal children.

The College of Advanced Education came to Murrawina and asked if any of us would like to go to do the course – the teaching course. So three of us applied.

I first began the course, there was thirteen of us. I'm the only one that graduated in that course. So graduating as an Aboriginal teacher was really a big boost for me. I got the biggest applause. I was nearly in tears. And I was wearing my Aboriginal sash down here, the black, yellow and red sash that represented my country, my culture. ...

[AMES Wanyarri (video) 1977]

The College of Advanced Education came to Murrawina and asked if **any of us would like** to go to do the course –

> ... I'm the **only** one that graduated in that course. So graduating as an Aboriginal teacher was **really a big boost** for me. I got **the biggest applause**. I was **nearly in tears**. And I was wearing my Aboriginal sash down here, the black, yellow and red sash that represented my country, my culture. ...

Where Lavina Grey tells her own history (virtually face to face for those with access to the video recording), the next biography is of Nganyintja, the Pitjantjatjara elder who narrated the *Piltati* narrative in Chapter 2. It was written by David in order to record and celebrate her life achievements, and is published for the first time here.[2] At this point we shift modes, from spoken to written, and from first person to third person, in other words from spoken autobiography to written biography. There is also a significant shift in the way time is managed since this biographical recount depends on circumstances of exact location in time rather than conjunctions to move events along. This circumstantial scaffolding is strongly associated with initial position (Theme) in each clause, highlighted in bold face in the text below.

[3:2] Nganyintja AM

Nganyintja is an elder of the Pitjantjatjara people of central Australia, renowned internationally as an educator and cultural ambassador.

She was born **in 1930** in the Mann Ranges, South Australia. Her early years were spent travelling through her family's traditional lands, living by hunting and gathering, and **until the age of nine** she had not seen a European.

At that time her family moved to the newly established mission at Ernabella, 300km to the east of the family homeland. They were **soon** followed by most of the Pitjantjatjara people, as they were forced to abandon their Western Desert lands during the drought **of the 1940s**.

At the mission, Nganyintja excelled at school, becoming its first Indigenous teacher. She married Charlie Ilyatjari and began a family that would include four daughters, two sons, eighteen grandchildren and ever more great-grandchildren. **In the early 1960s** the family moved to the new government settlement of Amata, 100km east of their traditional lands, which they visited with camels each summer holiday, renewing their ties to the land and educating their children in their traditions.

Then **in 1979** they were able to buy an old truck and blaze a track through the bush to re-establish a permanent family community at Nganyintja's homeland of Angatja.

In those years the tragedy of teenage petrol sniffing began to engulf the Pitjantjatjara people. Nganyintja and Ilyatjari established a youth cultural and training program at Angatja, and worked for many years to get young people out of the settlements in the region and educate them, both in their cultural traditions and in community development skills. In addition, Nganyintja became a widely respected leader and spokesperson for her people.

During the 1980s Nganyintja and Ilyatjari hosted many visits from students and organisations interested in learning about Indigenous Australian culture. **In 1989** they established a cultural tourism venture known as Desert Tracks, that has brought hundreds of Australian and international visitors to Angatja, and provided income and employment to many Pitjantjatjara people, as well as winning major tourism awards.

In 1993 Nganyintja was awarded the Order of Australia Medal for her services to the community.

In Lavina's spoken recount, cause and effect were signalled explicitly by *so*, but in this written biography causal relations tend to be left implicit, for the reader to infer:

> …the Pitjantjatjara people…were forced to abandon their Western Desert lands **(because of)** the drought of the 1940s.

> …teenage petrol sniffing began to engulf the Pitjantjatjara people. **(so)** Nganyintja and Ilyatjari established a youth cultural and training program

> Nganyintja and Ilyatjari hosted many visits from students and organisations interested in learning about Indigenous Australian culture. **(so)** In 1989 they established a cultural tourism venture

And in writing, cause also comes to be expressed within clauses:

> Nganyintja was awarded the Order of Australia Medal **for** her services to the community

Here the reason for Nganyintja's award is realised as a circumstance, in which her activities in serving her community are nominalised as *services*. In a more spoken paraphrase, this reason might be expressed as a complete clause linked by a conjunction, 'because she served the community well'. Nganyintja's biography also features an ongoing prosody of evaluation focusing on her achievements, which are sometimes set against the deprivations of her people.

[3:2'] ... **renowned internationally as an educator and cultural ambassador.**

... the Pitjantjatjara people, as they were **forced to abandon** their Western Desert lands

... Nganyintja **excelled at school, becoming its first Indigenous teacher.**

... they were **able to buy** an old truck and **blaze a track** through the bush

... **the tragedy of teenage petrol sniffing began to engulf** the Pitjantjatjara people.

... worked for **many years**... hosted **many visits**

... brought **hundreds of Australian and international visitors**

... Nganyintja became **a widely respected leader and spokesperson** for her people.

... **winning major tourism awards.**

... Nganyintja **was awarded the Order of Australia Medal** for her services to the community.

Compared with the story genres presented in Chapter 2, these biographical recounts differ with respect to both time and evaluation. Temporally, they focus on a lifetime of experience rather than a few successive events. This means that we hop through time, from one significant phase to the next, rather than moving successively through the events of one activity sequence or another. Serial time gives way to episodic time, as experience is packaged into phases. A key resource for managing temporal packaging of this kind is circumstances of location in time, realised as Theme in the first clause of each episode – a pattern which is stronger in the written biography than in the spoken autobiography, whose time management through conjunctions is more like that of story genres. These developments in time management, from personal recounts to spoken autobiography to written biography are illustrated in Table 3.1. The personal recount, *Greg's story* from Chapter 2, records a series of events within a single tragic episode of his life, and the events in this sequence are mainly added one to the next with the conjunction *and*. The biographies record a series of episodes, with the spoken text primarily using temporal conjunctions to scaffold the sequence, and the written one primarily using temporal circumstances. These trends are shown in Table 3.1, from spoken to written, from first to third person, from serial to episodic time, and from adding events to dating episodes.

As far as evaluation is concerned, the biographical recounts differ from stories, in that they are less concerned with putting us in touch with the feelings of Lavina Grey and Nganyintja as they experience the events of everyday life, and more concerned with the achievements that made them respected elders in their communities. The focus of the recounts in other words is on Lavina Grey and

Table 3.1: Organising time in stories and biographies

personal recount	autobiographical recount	biographical recount
first person		third person
serial time	episodic time	
...I went off to school in the morning	I grew up in Wellington NSW...	She was born **in 1930** in the Mann Ranges, South Australia...
and I was sitting in the classroom	I went to Wellington High.	**until the age of nine** she had not seen a European.
and there was only one room...	I left school at 14...	**At that time** her family moved to the newly established mission...
and there was a knock at the door,	I **then** came to Sydney...	
which the schoolmaster answered.	I **then** worked in factories wherever I could.	**At the mission**, Nganyintja excelled...
After a conversation he had with somebody at the door, he came to get me.	**Then** I became a defacto at 17...until the birth of my first child.	**In the early 1960s** the family moved to the new government settlement...
He took me by the hand	I **then** went back home to Wellington to my mother...	Then **in 1979** they were able to...re-establish a family community...
and took me to the door.	**My first job** in the education sector was AEA...	
I was physically grabbed...	I **then** stayed at Murrawina after graduation...	**In those years** the tragedy of teenage petrol sniffing began...
I was taken to a motor bike	The College of Advanced Education came to Murrawina...So three of us applied.	**During the 1980s** Nganyintja and Ilyatjari hosted many visits...
and held by the officer		**In 1989** they established a cultural tourism venture...
and driven to the airstrip		
and flown off the Island.		**In 1993** Nganyintja was awarded the Order of Australia Medal...
often added with *and*	often sequenced with *then*	often dated with circumstances

Nganyintja as public figures, not private ones – on why they matter to more than their family and friends. Once again this is more true of the written biography than the spoken autobiography, which shows us that stories and histories are related families of genres. We'll return to this point in our discussion of topology and learner pathways below.

In summary then, as we move from story to history, temporal organisation shifts from sequence in time to setting in time, and evaluation shifts from personal reactions to public significance. This changing texture is further reinforced as we move from biography to the historical recounts in section 2 below.

3.2 Historical recounts – recording public histories

Historical recounts construct public records of people and the agents and agencies that mediate their fate. As with public discourse in general, these are interested accounts, which construct the past in terms that suit the history makers and the communities they want to align (Martin & Wodak 2003). We'll begin with a text written by Frank Brennan, a prominent Australian human rights activist and Jesuit priest, who is writing here about asylum seekers arriving by boat in Australia. This is an extract from Brennan's book *Tampering with Asylum* which he wrote as part of his work to alleviate the plight of asylum seekers kept indefinitely in detention camps by the Howard government. His purpose in this extract is to contrast earlier Australian governments' humanitarian responses to waves of Vietnamese refugees, with the draconian approach of Howard and his chief ministers.

As with the biographical recount [3:2], historical recounts involve episodic rather than serial time, and episodes are scaffolded by circumstances of location in time (highlighted in the text),[3] together with ordinal and comparative modifiers (first *boatload,* another *two boats,* third *Vietnamese boat,* underlined in the text).

Beyond the episodes signalled by these temporal circumstances is another broader layer of time in this chapter of Brennan's book. As the *first* wave at the beginning of [3:3] indicates, there are more waves to come; text [3:3] is in fact Brennan's recount of the first of four waves of boat people around which he organises a chapter titled 'Four waves, Tampa and a firebreak':

> '**The first wave** of 2,077 Indochinese boat people came to Australia in 54 boats between 1976 and 1981 [p 29]... **The second wave** of boat people commenced with the arrival of a Cambodian boat at Pender Bay near Broome on 25 November 1989 [p 32]... **The third wave** of boat people arrived between 1994 and 1998...These Vietnamese and Chinese boat people were the last victims of the Comprehensive Plan of Action which proposed the compulsory repatriation back to Vietnam of those left in the camps around Asia [p 40]... **The fourth and biggest wave** of boat people in modern Australian history could not be so readily categorised as non-refugees or as refugees who had their claims determined elsewhere. In late 1999 boat people started arriving from Afghanistan, Iraq and Iran via Indonesia [p 40].'

These waves are significant for Brennan because they 'heightened the concerns of government and the public that Australian borders are not secure' [2003: 29]. In 2000, at the height of an Australian election campaign, the Norwegian container vessel MV Tampa became involved in the fourth wave when it picked up 433 asylum seekers from a boat in distress on the high seas, and attempted to bring them to the Australian territory of Christmas Island. Brennan refers to the Howard government's vote-catching response to this incident as a 'firebreak', as it legislated to exclude all offshore islands from its

[3:3]

The first wave of 2,077 Indochinese boat people came to Australia in 54 boats **between 1976 and 1981. In that time,** Australia was to resettle another 56,000 Indochinese through regular migration channels. The first boatload of asylum seekers arrived in Darwin harbour **on 28 July 1976.** The five Vietnamese had made the 6,500-kilometre journey in a small boat. **At the end of that year** another two boats arrived carrying 106 people who were screened for health reasons and then flown to Wacol migrant hostel outside Brisbane. **When** the third Vietnamese boat **of the first wave arrived,** there was some media agitation about the threatened invasion by boat people. One Melbourne newspaper reported that 'today's trickle of unannounced visitors to our lonely northern coastline could well become a tide of human flotsam'. The paper asked how the nation would respond to 'the coming invasion of its far north by hundreds, thousands and even tens of thousands of Asian refugees'. The invasion never occurred. **In 1978** the Communist government in Vietnam outlawed private business ventures. Tens of thousands, mainly ethnic Chinese, then fled by boat. The outflow of Vietnamese boat people throughout the region gave rise to great moral dilemmas in the implementation of government policies. Countries such as Malaysia would periodically declare that their camps were full and they could take no more boat people. They would even threaten to shoot new arrivals on sight. Alternatively, they would provide them with food, fuel and repairs so they could set off for another country. Meanwhile Vietnamese officials were profiting by charging the boat people high departure fees.

Camps were filling around Southeast Asia. There was no let-up in the departures from Vietnam. **In the end** there was a negotiated agreement involving Vietnam, the countries of first asylum such as Thailand and Malaysia, and the resettlement countries, chiefly the United States, Canada and Australia. **In 1982** the Australian government announced that the Vietnamese government had agreed to an Orderly Departure Program. Australian immigration ministers Michael MacKellar and Ian MacPhee were able to set up procedures for the reception of Vietnamese from camps in Southeast Asia as well as those coming directly from Vietnam under a special migration program. With careful management, they were able to have the public accept up to 15,000 Vietnamese refugees a year when the annual migration intake was as low as 70,000.

In 1978 the government set up a Determination of Refugee Status (DORS) Committee which would determine onshore refugee claims. A UNHCR representative joined this committee of pubic servants from the key departments. The committee made only recommendations to the minister. If it rejected an application, it could still recommend that the applicant be given temporary or permanent residence 'on humanitarian or strong compassionate grounds'. **In the early 1980s** the committee considered fewer that 200 applications a year, with less than a one third approval rating.

In 1982 the government decided that even offshore cases would be decided on a case by case basis. It would no longer accept the UNHCR's blanket determination that anyone from Indochina was a refugee. **It was now seven years** since the end of the Vietnam War and it was more likely that some of those departing Vietnamese were economic migrants unimpressed by their economic prospects under a communist regime rather than refugees who were fleeing in fear of persecution. **At the same time** the government set up a Special Humanitarian Program to complement the offshore refugee program. **In the first year,** there were 20,216 offshore refugees and 1,701 applicants approved for migration to Australia under the Special Humanitarian Program. **Within eight years** there were only 1,537 under the offshore refugee category and 10,411 under the Special Humanitarian Program. Onshore, it was also possible for persons to gain residence on humanitarian or compassionate grounds. **Initially** it was assumed that there would be only a few hundred of such onshore cases a year. That all changed when the courts got involved.

In 1985 the High Court by the narrowest of margins (3 to 2) decided that ministerial decisions rejecting the grant or extension of an entry permit on the grounds that the applicant was not a refugee were reviewable by the courts. Also the failed applicant would be entitled to a written statement of reasons for the minister's rejection. From now on, refugee status was to be a matter of law rather than unreviewable ministerial or bureaucratic decisions rejecting people's humanitarian claims. Neither parliament nor the government had foreseen such court intervention.

Brennan 2003: 29–31

international obligations to accept refugees, thus creating a legal no-mans-land between the Australian mainland and an imagined 'bushfire' of asylum seekers streaming in from Middle Eastern conflicts. The aim was to stop refugees getting to the jurisdiction of Australian courts, thus circumventing the 1985 High Court decision.

For Brennan, then, what happened is packaged as unauthorised arrivals by boat, leading to the legislative clampdown; the arrivals themselves are divided into four waves; and each wave is itself phased into episodes through paragraphing, temporal circumstances and comparative identification. These layers of time are illustrated in Figure 3.1. The episodes are nested within the four waves, and the waves and episodes follow each other in succession (indicated by arrows).

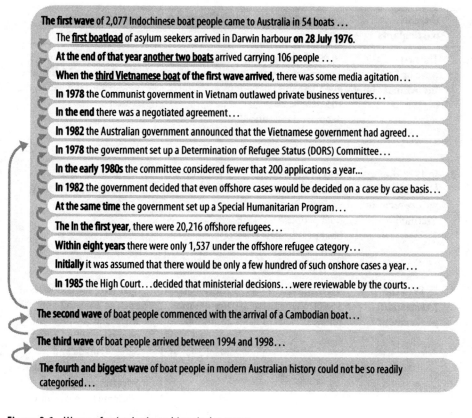

The first wave of 2,077 Indochinese boat people came to Australia in 54 boats . . .

The **first boatload** of asylum seekers arrived in Darwin harbour **on 28 July 1976.**

At the end of that year another two boats arrived carrying 106 people . . .

When the **third Vietnamese boat** of the first wave arrived, there was some media agitation . . .

In 1978 the Communist government in Vietnam outlawed private business ventures . . .

In the end there was a negotiated agreement . . .

In 1982 the Australian government announced that the Vietnamese government had agreed . . .

In 1978 the government set up a Determination of Refugee Status (DORS) Committee . . .

In the early 1980s the committee considered fewer that 200 applications a year . . .

In 1982 the government decided that even offshore cases would be decided on a case by case basis . . .

At the same time the government set up a Special Humanitarian Program . . .

The In the first year, there were 20,216 offshore refugees . . .

Within eight years there were only 1,537 under the offshore refugee category . . .

Initially it was assumed that there would be only a few hundred of such onshore cases a year . . .

In 1985 the High Court . . . decided that ministerial decisions . . . were reviewable by the courts . . .

The second wave of boat people commenced with the arrival of a Cambodian boat . . .

The third wave of boat people arrived between 1994 and 1998 . . .

The fourth and biggest wave of boat people in modern Australian history could not be so readily categorised . . .

Figure 3.1 Waves of episodes in an historical recount

Further analysis would reveal additional layers of temporal phasing within this structure, which readers are invited to pursue. Not that this pursuit would be without its indeterminacies, presumably since Brennan is not definitively concerned with partitioning time at this level of detail. The important point as far as historical recounts are concerned is that time is phased into an indefinite number of layers, and this elasticity can be deployed to develop long chronicles, time upon time.

Alongside this layered phasing of events, historical recounts are also organised by the groups and agencies participating in the events. In Brennan's recount [3:3], the major players include the boat people/refugees, the governments of south-east Asia and Australia, and the High Court. As we saw for stories, switching from one to another participant in the Theme of clauses, alongside new settings in time, can signal new phases of the text, displayed in Table 3.2.

Table 3.2 Participants in three phases of text [3:3]

	thematic participants	groups of people	public agents	public agencies
1	The first wave of **2,077 Indochinese boat people**	56,000 Indochinese; asylum seekers; the five Vietnamese; 106 people; boat people; unannounced visitors; Asian refugees		Australia; migration channels; one Melbourne newspaper; the paper; the nation
2	In 1978 **the Communist government in Vietnam**	tens of thousands; mainly ethnic Chinese; Vietnamese boat people; boat people; new arrivals...them... they; the boat people	Vietnamese officials	countries such as Malaysia... they...they;
3	In 1978 **the [Australian] government**	Vietnamese...those; 15,000 Vietnamese refugees	Australian immigration ministers Michael MacKellar and Ian MacPhee...	Vietnam; the countries... such as Thailand and Malaysia; resettlement countries...the United Sates, Canada and Australia; the Australian government; the Vietnamese government; the public
4	In 1985 **the High Court**	the applicant		parliament nor the government

As Table 3.2 reveals for the four phases of text [3:3], people generally appear in groups (e.g. *56,000 Indochinese, unannounced visitors*). On three occasions lexical metaphors are used to evaluatively quantify their numbers:

the first **wave of** 2,077 Indochinese boat people
today's **trickle of** unannounced visitors
a **tide of** human flotsam

The exception to this pattern is individuals acting in institutionally defined roles (*ministers Michael MacKellar and Ian MacPhee*), and generic individuals (*the applicant*). Alongside people, a range of agencies are noted, including nations (*Australia*), governments (*the Communist government in Vietnam*), public institutions (*the High Court*), and the media (*one Melbourne newspaper*).

While the global function of historical recounts is recording rather than explaining history, there is a growing use of implicit cause to connect events, for example:

…the Communist government in Vietnam outlawed private business ventures. **(so)** Tens of thousands, mainly ethnic Chinese, then fled by boat.

Countries such as Malaysia would periodically declare that their camps were full and **(so)** they could take no more boat people…

Camps were filling around Southeast Asia. There was no let-up in the departures from Vietnam. **(so)** In the end there was a negotiated agreement…

It was now seven years since the end of the Vietnam War and **(so)** it was more likely that some of those departing Vietnamese were economic migrants…

Nominalisation is also used to explain (e.g. *106 people who were screened for* **health reasons**), and to reason within the clause:

The outflow of Vietnamese boat people throughout the region
<u>gave rise to</u>
great moral dilemmas in **the implementation** of government policies

In addition, historical recounts are generally more abstract that biographies. Brennan uses nominalisation to construe several abstract participants, as highlighted below:

regular **migration** channels
some media **agitation** about the **threatened invasion** by boat people
the **coming invasion** of its far north by … of Asian refugees'
The **invasion**
high **departure** fees
no **let-up** in the **departures**
the **resettlement** countries

> **procedures** for the **reception** of Vietnamese
> a special **migration** program
> the annual **migration** intake

Of all the history genres we are considering here, the historical recount is arguably the most important, since it can be episodically expanded as outlined above to scaffold the organisation of sections, chapters, books and multi-volume chronicles – the 'grand narratives' of modernist history (as Lyotard 1984 has referred to them). Where necessary of course, serially unfolding recounts can be included within these. Brennan takes up this option in [3:4] below in order focus precisely on the contested sequence of events in which Captain Rinnan of the *Tampa* found himself embroiled in August 2001. Here one episode of Brennan's fourth wave of boat people is expanded as events sequenced in time, with individuals as actors and speakers (in bold), but without the additive and temporal conjunctions characteristic of spoken recounts.

[3:4]

On 29 August the *Tampa* entered into Australian territorial waters approaching Christmas Island. **The prime minister** told parliament that **the captain** had decided on this course of action because **a spokesman for the asylum seekers** 'had indicated that they would begin jumping overboard if medical assistance was not provided quickly'. **Captain Rinnan** gave a different reason for this decision: 'We weren't seaworthy to sail to Indonesia. There were lifejackets for only 40 people. The sanitary conditions were terrible.' **The SAS** came aboard and took over *Tampa*. **An Australian Defence Force doctor** was given 43 minutes to make a medical assessment of the 433 asylum seekers. **He** reported, 'Four persons required IV (2 urgent including 1 woman 8 months pregnant).' **Captain Rinnan** was surprised at the prompt medical assessment, because **his crew** had already identified ten people who were barely conscious lying in the sun on the deck of the ship. **The prime minister** then made a finely timed ministerial statement to parliament insisting that 'nobody – and I repeat nobody – has presented as being in need of urgent medical assistance as would require their removal to the Australian mainland or to Christmas Island'. **One hundred and thirty-one fortunate asylum seekers** were granted **immediate asylum** by the New Zealand government. **The rest**, having been transported to Nauru, waited processing under the evolving Pacific Solution. [Brennan 2003: 42–43]

Brennan's purpose here is to exemplify an aspect of the spin doctored mendacity and shameless inhumanity which became the hallmark of Prime Minister Howard's neo-con regime, and its effects on hapless refugees (cf. Marr & Wilkinson 2003). So whereas the events involve specific actors and speakers, the episode concludes with its outcomes for groups of asylum seekers. Brennan uses the recount genre to let the events speak for themselves, but within this neutral arena manages appraisal contrasts to guide the reader towards a judgement, from *conditions were **terrible**, **surprised** at the prompt medical assessment, people who were **barely** conscious*, to Howard's ***finely timed** ministerial statement*, and ***fortunate** asylum seekers granted **immediate** asylum*, while *the rest…waited*.

Moving in the opposite direction, elasticity of time can be exploited to condense potentially layered events into a single clause. In [3:5] below, Robert Tickner, Minister for Aboriginal and Torres Strait Islander Affairs in the Labor governments that preceded Howard's, recounts the events surrounding the 'Koowarta case', in which a conservative state government in Queensland attempted to prevent an Aboriginal community from acquiring a pastoral property, motivated purely by racial hatred. Tickner packs the Koowarta case into a series of nominal groups, representing four episodes (in bold), before evaluating the Queensland government's actions.

[3:5]

The Koowarta case was an extraordinary saga involving **attempts to purchase a property** by Aboriginal interests, **the refusal by the Bjelke-Petersen government** to transfer property to Aboriginal people, **the successful challenge** to this refusal in the High Court, and finally **the circumvention of the High Court decision** invalidating the Queensland government action, by gazetting the area as a national park and therefore making it no longer available to purchase by Aboriginal people. The actions of the Queensland government, which was as rabidly anti-environmental as they were anti-Aboriginal, showed that they hated the 'blacks' even more than they hated the 'greens'.

[Tickner 2001: 20]

As we have seen, episodic time reconstrues serial time as phases of activity; and once phased, these packages of time can be named (e.g. *waves of boatpeople, the actions of the Queensland government*). Events become things. And these 'things' can be used to preface or sum up events. This motif of 'looking forward and looking back' is crucial to the presentation and interpretation of history, and is intimately linked with the ways that events and agents are valued. Appraisals tend to be relatively intense in previews, validated by events or arguments, and further intensified in reviews. For example, Tickner's recount begins by appreciating the case as an *extraordinary saga*, and ends by interpreting what it showed about the negative feelings held by Bjelke-Petersen's government for blacks and greens. Both the appreciation and the affect are strongly amplified (*extraordinary, rabidly, hated*). The patterns of episodes and values are illustrated in Figure 3.2. The intense appreciation of the preview, and even more intense judgement of the review scope over the intervening episodes, indicated by shading in the diagram.

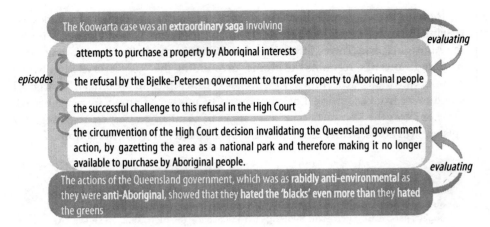

Figure 3.2 Nominalised episodes and scope of values

One further dimension of temporal scaffolding we should mention here is the use of 'time lines' to provide a synoptic overview of key events. Tickner provides a 13 page time line at the beginning of his book, a small part of which is exemplified in Table 3.3 below.

Table 3.3 from Tickner's 'Time line of events' [2001: xx]

...	
March 1993	McArthur River mine issue begins to surface in public debate
21 March 1993	Joint Australian business community statement in support of protection of existing titles
22 March 1993	Lois O'Donoghue, ATSIC Chairperson, writes to Prime Minister in opposition to any suspension of Racial Discrimination Act
24 March 1993	Office of Indigenous Affairs established in Department of Prime Minister and Cabinet
6 April 1993	Mabo Ministerial Committee meets industry representatives and Prime Minister later addresses Evatt Foundation dinner
18 April 1993	WA pastoralist warns of civil war over Mabo
27 April 1993	Mabo Ministerial Committee meets Aboriginal representatives and receives Peace Plan
...	

These time lines have a strong field focus, and support readers in keeping track of significant events in the sequence in which they occurred. But they are not history – not just because they are so cryptic, but more importantly because they do not necessarily match up with interpretations of the past which phase it into evaluated chunks of activity. For this task we have history discourse proper, as

---

[3:6]

On 22 March 1993, Lois O'Donoghue wrote to the Prime Minister, formally alerting him to ATSIC concerns about any attempt to erode the operation of the RDA (Racial Discrimination Act) to validate titles. She enclosed a copy of a pre-election statement of ATSIC's preliminary response to the Commonwealth consultation, which argued for extensive government action and included:

- proposals to support the RDA;
- revival of native title following the expiration of a finite grant of an interest in land; land rights legislation to address the position of dispossessed people;
- the establishment of a specialist tribunal to adjudicate on native title claims;
- the concept of representative bodies for indigenous people that would lodge claims and conduct negotiations;
- royalty payments;
- a public education program to explain the effect and importance of the Mabo decision; and
- a proposal for an international convention on the rights of indigenous people

In hindsight it is quite remarkable that with one or two exceptions this agenda of indigenous aspirations was to be acted on by the Labor government.

On March 29 the new Minister for Resources, Michael Lee, moved to hose down the concerns of the oil industry by emphasising in a speech to the annual conference of the Australian Petroleum Exploration Association that 'advice to the Government suggests that the offshore petroleum legislation and its administration do not contravene the Racial Discrmination Act' and that 'there is no evidence to suggest that the Mabo decision has major implications in terms of management of petroleum exploration activity in Commonwqealth waters'. Tim Fisher, for his part, suggested to the conference that 'Mabo has the potential to threaten the sovereignty of a great deal more land – and sea'.

The next day Patrick Dodson wrote to the Prime Minister raising broader issues that needed to be addressed in any government response and calling for national discussions with indigenous people leading to meetings between COAG (Council of Australian Governments) and representatives of the broader indigenous community. Moves to reform the Canadian Constitution in the early 1980s had led to comparable negotiations between representatives of Canada's indigenous peoples and the leaders of the Canadian national and provincial governments. But Australia, or more specifically its state and territory governments at this time, lacked the maturity and respect for indigenous people displayed by their Canadian counterparts.

[Tickner 2001: 109–110]

---

exemplified in the historical recount developed by Tickner around the intervention by Lois O'Donoghue, then Chairperson of the Aboriginal and Torres Strait Islander

Commission, in proposals to erode Australia's Racial Discrimination Act in order to limit Indigenous claims to pastoral lands.

Note in passing the use of nominalisation in O'Donoghue's bullet point agenda of indigenous aspirations to envision future time – the phases of activity which ATSIC wanted the government to enact and most of which Tickner suggests his government turned into realis history during their term in office.

- **proposals** to support the RDA;
- **revival** of native title following the **expiration** of a finite grant of an interest in land;
- land rights legislation to address the position of **dispossessed** people;
- the **establishment** of a specialist tribunal to adjudicate on native title claims;
- the concept of representative bodies for indigenous people that would lodge claims and conduct **negotiations**;
- royalty payments;
- a public education program to explain the **effect** and **importance** of the Mabo **decision**; and
- a **proposal** for an international convention on the rights of indigenous people.

3.3   Historical accounts and explanations – explaining the past

Alongside packaging the past into phases of activity, historians undertake to explain it – to say why one episode arose from another. We have already seen a few examples of this in biographical recounts, and a few more in the historical recounts, both of which foreground time over cause. We refer to texts that foreground cause over time as historical accounts. Tickner's description of the beginning of the land rights movement in Australia provides a relatively clear example of an historical account. Here reasons and consequences are highlighted, including circumstantial and verbal realisations.

[3:7]

In another part of Australia, Aboriginal people were themselves acting to assert their rights. On 23 August 1966 Vincent Lingiari, a Gurindji elder, led his people off the cattle station operated by the giant Vesteys pastoral organisation **in protest against their wages and conditions**. Their calls **for Commonwealth involvement** also strongly argued the case for land to establish their own cattle station. They subsequently sent a petition to the Governor-General, **with no immediate result**. Their stand against injustice, however, **attracted national publicity** for Aboriginal land rights grievances. The strike developed into a seven-year campaign by the Gurindji **for the return of their traditional lands** and became a *cause célèbre* across Australia. The campaign was strongly supported by the trade union movement and **sparked a campaign** for human rights, including land rights, by many Aboriginal people. It was a cry **for Commonwealth leadership** that would not be acted upon until the election of the Whitlam government.

[Tickner 2001:8]

There is only one explicitly temporal relation, signalled by the conjunction *subsequently*. Otherwise Tickner draws on various clause internal resources to explain what led to what. Causal circumstances are used to explain why Lingiari led his people off (*in protest against their wages and conditions, for the return of their traditional lands*), and what the Gurindji were appealing for (*for Commonwealth involvement…leadership*). These nominalised appeals are verbally connected (*argued, acted*) to further abstractions (*the case, the election*), and processes are also used to causally connect the Gurindji walk-off to a burgeoning land rights movement (*attracted national publicity, sparked a campaign*).

Realising cause inside the clause enables historians to fine tune causality by deploying verbs which elsewhere literally construe material and verbal activity (*argue, act, attract, spark*) but here enact finely differentiated types of cause and effect relations. This indefinitely enhances historians' resources for explaining how one event affects another and is one important sense in which written language elaborates the meaning potential of a language.

Nominal, prepositional and verbal realisations of cause inside the clause are typical of historical accounts (and of explanations as we shall see below). Manne begins text [3:8] in just these terms…

> The Howard government's **unwillingness** to apologise
> <u>determined</u>
> the nature of its **response** to other recommendations contained in *Bringing them home*.

…before unpacking what he means in clauses connected by causal conjunctions (highlighted below):

[3:8]

The Howard government's unwillingness to apologise **determined** the nature of its response to other recommendations contained in *Bringing them home*. **Because** it refused to consider the present generation of Australians legally or morally responsible for the mistakes of the past, it refused altogether *Bringing them home's* recommendation for financial compensation for members of the stolen generations. **Because** it thought the policies of child removal had been lawful and well-intentioned, it treated almost with contempt the arguments in *Bringing them home* which suggested that in removing Aboriginal children from their families by force previous Australian governments had committed serious violations of the human rights treaties they had signed or even acts of genocide. **Because**, nonetheless, it accepted that the Aboriginal children who had been taken from their families has suffered serious harm it was willing to allocate modest sums to assist members of the stolen generations with psychological counselling, family reunion, cultural projects, oral histories and so on.

Manne 2001: 76

[3:9]

The government faced three problems. Or to put it another way, there were **three distinct advantages** that asylum seekers and people smugglers saw in making the perilous journey by boat to Australia.

- **First, if** you made it to Australia, there was a good chance that the Australian authorities would find that you were a refugee. The Immigration Minister, Philip Ruddock, was fond of quoting the statistic that 84 per cent of boat people were being found to be refugees whereas only 14 per cent of the contingent from the same countries of flight and who were presented at the UNHCR office in Indonesia were found to be refugees. Ever since its election in 1996, the Howard government had wanted to reduce the involvement of the courts in reviewing refugee cases, as it thought that the judges were being too soft on applicants and were being too cavalier in their willingness to expand the categories for refugee status under the convention.

- **Second, if** you were found to be a refugee after you have landed in Australia, you were guaranteed residence in Australia. If you had waited in a camp in Pakistan or in a transit city such as Jakarta awaiting a UNHCR determination, you not only had less chance of being found to be a refugee, you also had no guarantee of being resettled in a country where you would feel secure, let alone one in which you could avail yourself of the benefits of life in a first-world, democratic country.

- **Third, if** you were granted permanent residence in Australia, you would over time be able to bring your family to join you and they would be able to travel safely and legally by commercial aircraft. [44–45]

In effect what we have here is an account which moves from a more written nominalised approach to a more active take on reasoning. This move from more written to more spoken textures is a familiar trope in history discourse as historians use less nominalised language to 'substantiate' more abstract interpretations. As readers we experience the shift to 'spoken' texture as evidential.

[3:10]

In retrospect, the removal of Aboriginal people from the pastoral industry was a monumental policy failure. The dilemma facing policy makers at the time the equal wage case was being debated was this: on the one hand, Aboriginal stock workers were being discriminated against in relation to their wages and conditions and this could not continue, but on the other hand, it was clear to everyone that the institution of equal wages would result in the whole-scale removal of Aboriginal people from cattle station work to social security on the settlements – and the latter path was chosen.

Of course, with hindsight this choice has had **tragic consequences**.

First, the cultural impact of the removal of families from their traditional lands in pastoral properties was obviously massive and today inestimable.

Second, there are the social results of the removal of Aboriginal families from work on stations to no work on settlements.

Third, we would not have had the difficulties in relation to the Wik case and the issue of coexistence of native title on pastoral leases had Aboriginal groups remained on those properties.

[Pearson 2000: 167]

As we can see in [3:8] cause is becoming multi-dimensional rather than linear. We don't simply have one thing leading to another but three dimensions of a political position giving rise to different effects. The inevitable monoglossing linearity of grand narratives has at times to be arrested so that different factors can be brought into play. Because of this historians have evolved a pair of complementarity genres which stop time as it were and deal with complex inputs to and outputs from events. Texts which focus on multiple factors leading to some event have been termed factorial explanations; those which focus on multiple outcomes of events are known as consequential explanations.

In [3:9], Brennan uses a factorial explanation to outline three reasons why asylum seekers would travel to Australia by boat. He signals these as *three distinct advantages*, then numbers them as *first, second, third*, and makes explicit that they are conditioning factors with the conjunction *if*.

[3:11]

Some key consequences of the decision need to be emphasised. The Mabo judgment did not challenge any of the legal rights and interests of non-Aboriginal Australians. Its effect was to recognise that native title may continue to exist in those parts of Australia where Aboriginal people still occupied or had sufficient continuing association with their traditional lands, but in no case could the rights of any other landholder be eroded. Furthermore, any hope indigenous people had of challenging the sovereignty or supreme law-making power of the parliaments was unambiguously buried for all time by the court. The court made clear in its judgement that governments acting within their powers could extinguish any native title by granting the land to non-native title holders in a manner that was inconsistent with native title, and that they had done so over much of the continent, for example wherever there had been a grant of freehold interests. The question to be asked in the case of each type of crown grant or crown dealing with the land was whether native title rights could continue to exist over the land after the grant, as it could, for example, in the case of crown land being converted to a national park or following the grant of an exploration licence.

A key question that was left up in the air was whether grant of a leasehold interest, such as pastoral lease, extinguished native title. This was the issue that the High Court was subsequently to consider in the Wik case when it ruled in favour of Aboriginal people. But it was clear from the Mabo decision itself that whatever interest Aboriginal people might continue to have in such land, it would always be subject to and overridden by any valid interest held by non-indigenous Australians. Thus not one square centimetre of land held by non-indigenous Australians was put at risk by the Mabo decision. Viewed in this context, the Mabo decision is by no means radical, but it did bring Australia to a position of basic recognition of the concept of indigenous title to land, and it had huge symbolic value as well as practical consequences.

Another principle flowed from the decision that was crucial to the protection of indigenous rights and to the need for a national response to Mabo. Even after Mabo, Commonwealth, state and territory governments could legislate to take away the native title rights recognised by the High Court, provided they acted within the limits of their law-making power. There is no constitutional constraint that requires a state government to pay fair compensation when acquiring the property of citizens. States and territories are, however, bound by the provisions of the RDA (Racial Discrimination Act), which requires them to treat indigenous people no less favourably than others in the community.

[87–88]

3.4 Expositions, discussions and challenges – debating the past

The recounts, accounts and explanations we have reviewed to this point all deal with unfolding time. In recounts one event follows another, in accounts one event leads to another, and in explanations more than one event causes another or some event leads to more than one other. At this point we turn from genres organised around events as they unfold in the world to genres which unfold upon themselves; we turn in other words from field time to text time – from genres of recounting, accounting and explaining to genres of argumentation.

Perhaps the best known of these is exposition, in which some thesis is expounded and argued for. Argumentation is required since the historian sees what s/he wants to say as in some sense contestable, and requiring motivation if it is to be accepted by a wider readership. The last twenty years has seen liberal Australian historians successfully contest the hitherto dominant construction of European colonisation as a peaceful occupation of a largely empty land. This revision of history has helped Indigenous Australians gain recognition of their native title, as exemplified by Eddie Mabo's famous 1992 High Court Victory. However in the subsequent reactionary

[3:12]

Thesis
The over-reliance on the government's own records grossly distorts Windschuttle's understanding of the realities of frontier life **for two reasons**.

Argument1
First, despite *Fabrication's* claim that 'except for a handful of gaps, there are good records of the activities of almost the entire colonial population from 1803 to the 1840s,' it was not until 1824 that Governor Arthur instituted a comprehensive system of public record-keeping. The preceding two decades of government records have enormous gaps. So few records of Governor Collin's time (1804–10) survive that in 1925 his burial cask was re-opened in a search for long-lost documents. In 1820, Commissioner Bigge heard many excuses about this topic. Governor Davey (1813–17) claimed he had sent most of the many documents missing from his term of office to the Earl of Harrowby. One senior civil servant gave the excuse to the commissioner that 'very considerable difficulties arise from the insufficiency of stationery.' Another claimed that 'about a year ago a case containing all my papers was stolen. 'Government record keeping improves somewhat with the arrival of Sorrell in 1817, except in relation to documents pertaining to Aborigines. Sorell virtually never mentions Aborigines in his dispatches to London and ignores them altogether in his lengthy hand-over report to Arthur in 1824. Even the meticulous Arthur largely followed the same practice of keeping London out of the Aboriginal issue until 1827. Quite simply, like any good administrator, neither Sorell nor Arthur actively sought information in those areas they would rather not know about, let alone apprised a meddling London of the uncomfortable facts. Only when the level of killing became such a prominent public issue from 1827 onwards, with such a dramatic impact on profit, colonisation and the operation of the penal system, did Arthur change tack.

Relying for the most part on the official government record for information on the Aborigines before 1827 is **therefore grossly inadequate**. *Fabrication's* claim that 'Few colonial encounters anywhere in the world are as well documented as those of Van Dieman's Land' is only true for the years 1827 to 1832.

Argument2
And once the violence got out of hand, **almost the opposite problem** faces the historian. Arthur was very aware of the political implications of the violent dispossession and possible extinction of the Aborigines. The wide reporting of the violence had caused concern to grow among the politically powerful missionary societies in Britain, who were well connected to the House of Commons and other seats of power. Arthur – once again like any other competent government administrator – now set out to cover his own and the government's back by sharing the responsibility for actions and policies and documenting every move. The government's very real policy dilemmas, and its genuinely difficult choices, are thus well recorded at this time. Committees were set up wherever possible, and settler input sought, to ensure that 'blame' was widely shared. None of this is to imply that Arthur lacked a genuine humanitarian concern. It is simply to point out that this governor was the finest administrator of the Van Diemonian era, that running a large penal colony doubling as a rapidly growing settlement on another people's land was no easy matter, and that it was not by chance that he was one of the two governors on Van Dieman's Land before 1850 to leave the posting with career prospects enhanced and his official reputation intact. Such hidden considerations do not mean the 17 volumes of official records are not a very important source. Windschuttle, however, is too easily duped when he confuses quantity for completeness. The fact that Arthur covered himself so well does not mean that he revealed – or even knew – every aspect of the conflict.

Reiteration of Thesis
By relying to such a degree on the government record of the time, Windschuttle remains ignorant of the period until 1827 and inherits a distorted and unbalanced perspective on the height of the war years. This is true not only of the direct conflict with the Aborigines but also of the realities of European life outside the main settlements. The narrow selection of sources results in a profound ignorance of the basics of Van Diemanian economy, society and politics, which in turn leads to a series of elementary errors.

[Boyce 2003: 27–29]

climate of the Howard government, neo-conservative writers have been encouraged to challenge what they and Howard refer to as the 'black arm-band' view of Australian history, which they characterise as foisted on the Australian public by unscholarly and ideologically driven liberals (Manne 2001). Prominent among these neo-conservatives is historian Keith Windschuttle, who published his notorious *The Fabrication of Aboriginal History* in December 2002, denying the well-documented 19th century genocide of Aboriginal Tasmanians.

Exposition [3:12] is from one of a number of replies of liberal historians attacked by Windschuttle, that are published in Manne (2003). Here James Boyce motivates his thesis that Windschuttle has relied too much on official government records at the expense of other primary sources. In broad outline, Boyce presents two arguments in favour of his position. The first is that there are enormous gaps in the Tasmanian government's record keeping, and the second is that later on, documentation proliferated as a kind of smoke screen for violent dispossession. He scaffolds his exposition with conjunctions (*first, therefore, and, by*), metadiscourse (*reasons, problem),* and reiterations of his position (all highlighted in the text below). And Boyce reiterates his thesis twice, once after each argument, to drive home his position (underlined below). On the basis of this scaffolding, the stages of his exposition can be labelled as Thesis^ Argument1^Argument2^Reiteration of Thesis (inserted as headings [in 3.12]).

Of course Boyce presents values judiciously, from his Thesis that *over-reliance on government records* **grossly distorts** *Windschuttle's understanding of the realities,* to an intense series of condemnations in the Reiteration stage. In between he continually piles praise on Tasmania's founder hero Governor Arthur, in contrast to his dissembling predecessors, and excuses Arthur's manipulation of record keeping to cover himself. He thus avoids antagonising his readers' loyalties, while concluding each Argument with Windschuttle's foolishness. These patterns are displayed in the extract of the text's appraisals in Figure 3.3. The diagram illustrates how judgements of Windschuttle (in bold) in the Thesis and Reiteration scope forward and backward over the text (indicated by shading), while judgements of him in the conclusion of each Argument scope backward over the Argument.

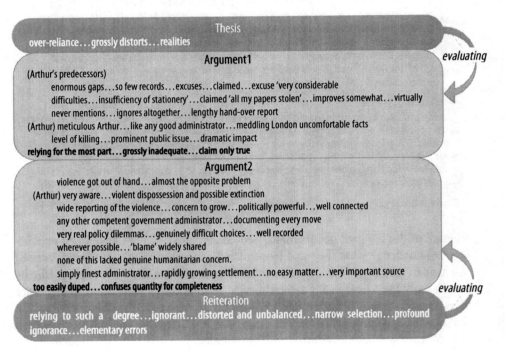

Figure 3.3 Values in stages of an exposition

Expositions in general vary with respect to the number of arguments included to motivate a thesis, although three arguments is a common rhetorical trope. They also vary with respect to reiterations of the thesis, generally favouring a single reiteration following the arguments. In these terms, Boyce has one argument less and one reiteration more than many of the expositions we have encountered (cf. Martin & Rose 2003/2007). But this flexibility is of course built into the telos of the genre, allowing it to be fine tuned to the issue to hand.

Complementing exposition is the discussion genre, in which more than one position on an issue is explicitly tendered. In text [3:13] below Peter Mares relays the views of Philip Ruddock, then Minister for immigration, as he outlines three competing visions for population management in Australia.

[3:13]

At the Knox auditorium Mr Ruddock's performance is polished and professional, if perhaps a little tepid. He begins by… The minister moves on to outline **three competing visions** for Australia's population in the century ahead. **The first scenario** is the high-immigration model favoured by some business groups, which call for Australia's net migration intake to be set at 1 per cent of existing population per year. The red line on the graph trends alarmingly upwards, predicting an 'inevitably rising' population, which would hit 65 million in the year 2007. According to the minister, the business groups' goal of 1 per cent net migration betrays 'a certain lack of realism'. **The second scenario** is net zero migration, the model pushed by sections of the environmental movement and by groups such as One Nation, which say that Australia should take just enough migrants to replace the number of people who permanently depart the country each year. With falling birthrates, this would se Australia's population slump from 20 million to 14 million within the next century. The green line on the graph sags in a depressing downward arc, heading inevitably towards zero. **The minister's final forecast** is reassuring – according to him, if we hold fast to the current government policy, Australia's population will increase gradually for the next forty years before settling comfortably at around 23 million. This favourable outlook is represented on the graph by a blue line, which rises gently and unthreateningly before charting a stable course between the extremes of green and red.

[Mares, P 2001 *Borderline: Australia's treatment of refugees and asylum seekers*. Sydney: UNSW Press (Reportage Series) 141–142]

So where expositions are organised around arguments for a single position, discussions are scaffolded around competing positions. Typically, one of these will be promoted and the others undermined, so that the discussion resolves in the direction of a single position; the genre is thus not as even handed as its multi-voicing might imply. This is clear from the appraisal choices in [3:13]. As Ruddock's graphs reveal, Goldilocks tries the business position, which is too fast, then the green position, which is too slow, and then the government position, which is just right:

> The first scenario …
>> The red line on the graph trends **alarmingly** upwards
>> …**betrays 'a certain lack of realism'**.

> The second scenario …
>> The green line on the graph **sags** in a **depressing** downward arc…

> The minister's final forecast
>> is **reassuring** … This **favourable** outlook is represented
>> on the graph by a blue line, which rises **gently** and **unthreateningly**…

It's democracy in action – we're told what to think!

Complementing these promotional genres is the challenge, which sets out to demolish an established position. Challenges are in effect anti-expositions – their mission is to rebut arguments which might be offered in support of a position and proffer counter-arguments. In [3:14] Father Brennan returns to attack the Howard government over the rationality of its mandatory detention policy for asylum seeking boat people. He uses metadiscourse (*rationale, objection, case*) to position arguments for and against mandatory detention (in bold below), and uses negation to deny potential counterarguments (underlined).

[3:14]

During the firebreak period, the government made an example of the Afghans, the Iraqis and the Iranians in detention. If they had been released into the community while their cases were being determined, they could have commenced their orientation to life in the community, given that most of them would be staying at least three years on a temporary protection visa. The modest number whose claims were rejected could have been treated in the same way as all other onshore asylum seekers. Their numbers would <u>not contribute significantly</u> to the 60,000 overstayers in the community.

There can be **no objection** to detention while a person is awaiting removal from the country once a decision on refugee status is made. There is **no case** for detaining one particular group before a decision is made when that group is known historically to contain a much higher percentage of refugees than all other groups. There is **no case** for detaining them further while their appeals are processed, especially when it is known that they are at least six times more likely than other asylum seekers to succeed on appeal. The injustice of this discriminatory detention would be heightened if, as is likely, the detention in remote places were contributing to more regular bad decision making at the primary stage. If the government's chief concern was to limit the number of unlawful overstayers in the community, the savings from <u>not holding unlawful</u> arrivals in protracted detention during the processing stage could be devoted to increased surveillance of all overstayers in the community. This would facilitate the orderly departure from Australia of overstayers, regardless of their racial, national or religious identity. Though there are 60,000 overstayers a year, our government locates only about 15,000 of them a year. The Australian public's fixation with boat people is highlighted when you consider that only 308 unauthorised boat arrivals were removed from Australia in 2001–2002, while another 10,894 persons who had no authority to be in Australia were removed. Where were the other 49,000? Would it really have mattered if those 308 boat people had been in the community rather than in detention at taxpayers expense? There is **no coherent rationale** for keeping all unauthorised asylum seekers in detention during the second stage of their processing. After ten years of such detention, there is **no proof** that it operates as a deterrent. With the fourth wave of boat people, mandatory detention was imposed on a group of whom 90 per cent were proved to be refugees.

Brennan 2003: 112–113

Overall Brennan's challenge is organised around implicit concession – the government might think so, but in fact they are wrong. After three rounds of this repartee, the challenge concludes that its opposition is wrong (i.e. there is no coherent rationale for mandatory detention). This concessional rhetoric is outlined below:

During the firebreak period, the government made an example of the Afghans, the Iraqis and the Iranians in detention.
(but in fact)
If they had been released into the community…they could have commenced their orientation to life in the community…

There can be no objection to detention while a person is awaiting removal from the country…
(but in fact)
There is no case for detaining one particular group before a decision is made…

(If) the government's chief concern was to limit the number of unlawful overstayers in the community,
(but in fact)
the savings from not holding unlawful arrivals…could be devoted to increased surveillance of all overstayers…
(so)
There is no coherent rationale for keeping all unauthorised asylum seekers in detention…

Like historical accounts and explanations, expositions, discussion and challenges rely heavily on nominalisation to construe events as things and explain how one thing leads on to another. Examples from [3:12] and [3:14] above illustrate the use of explicitly causal verbs connecting events inside the clause:

The wide reporting of the violence
   had caused
concern to grow among the politically powerful missionary societies in Britain

The narrow selection of sources
   results in
a profound ignorance of the basics of Van Diemanian economy, society and politics,

which in turn
   leads
to a series of elementary errors.

The wide reporting of the violence
   had caused
concern to grow among the politically powerful missionary societies in Britain

Boyce pushes this one step further, nominalising the causal connection as *impact* in *Only when the level of killing became such a prominent public issue from 1827 onwards, with such a dramatic* <u>impact</u> *on profit, colonisation and the operation of the penal system, did Arthur change tack* (cf. *the level of killing* <u>impacted</u> *on profit etc.*):

the level of killing …from 1827 onwards
with such a dramatic impact on
profit, colonisation and the operation of the penal system

And both Boyce and Brennan 'borrow' action verbs into the same agentive structure to increase their causal repertoire:

> The over-reliance on the government's own records
>   grossly distorts
> Windschuttle's understanding of the realities of frontier life for two reasons.

> 'very considerable difficulties
>   arise from
> the insufficiency of stationery'.

> Government record keeping
>   improves somewhat
> with the arrival of Sorrell in 1817

> the detention in remote places
>   were contributing to
> more regular bad decision making at the primary stage

> the savings from not holding unlawful arrivals in protracted detention…
>   could be devoted to
> increased surveillance of all overstayers in the community

> This (= increased surveillance of all overstayers in the community)
>   would facilitate
> the orderly departure from Australia of overstayers

Nominalisation of this order also facilitates evaluation, as we shall see in the next section.

3.5 Packaging value – what history means

Alongside explaining, history involves interpretation – giving value to the past. It's not just about what happened and why, but in addition what it means. So to understand how history genres are organised, we need to look more carefully at how they evaluate what's gone on.

As outlined in Chapter 1, appraisal theory provides us with a useful tool for mapping evaluation. We'll concentrate on attitude (types of evaluation) and graduation (strength of feeling) here. Tickner's condensed recount of the Koowarta case (text 3.5 above) illustrates the way in which appraisal can be used to bracket events with evaluation; he begins by appreciating the case as an *extraordinary saga*, and ends by interpreting what it showed about the negative feelings held by Bjelke-Petersen's government for blacks and greens. Both the appreciation and the affect are strongly amplified (*extraordinary, rabidly*).

> **[3:5]**
>
> The Koowarta case was an **extraordinary saga** involving attempts to purchase a property by Aboriginal interests, the refusal by the Bjelke-Petersen government to transfer property to Aboriginal people, the successful challenge to this refusal in the High Court, and finally the circumvention of the High Court decision invalidating the Queensland government action, by gazetting the area as a national park and therefore making it no longer available to purchase by Aboriginal people. The actions of the Queensland government, which was **as rabidly anti-environmental as they were anti-Aboriginal**, showed that they **hated the 'blacks' even more than they hated the 'greens'**.
>
> [Tickner 2001: 20]

Similarly, Pearson introduces his consequential explanation with intense negative appreciation of the outcomes of the equal wages decision:

> **[3:10]**
>
> In retrospect, the removal of Aboriginal people from the pastoral industry was a **monumental policy failure**. … Of course, with hindsight this choice has had **tragic consequences**.

And Boyce's Thesis and its two Reiterations involve negative appreciation of Windschuttle's perspective alongside negative judgement of his capacity as an historian.

> The over-reliance on the government's own records **grossly distorts** Windschuttle's understanding of the realities of frontier life for two reasons.
>
> …
>
> Relying for the most part on the official government record for information on the Aborigines before 1827 is therefore **grossly inadequate**.
>
> …
>
> By relying to such a degree on the government record of the time, Windschuttle remains **ignorant** of the period until 1827 and inherits a **distorted and unbalanced** perspective on the height of the war years. … The narrow selection of sources results in a **profound ignorance** of the basics of Van Diemanian economy, society and politics, which in turn leads to a series of **elementary errors**.

Across genres then we can see that historians are disposed to both preview and review events, factors/consequences and arguments with intensified evaluations by way of interpreting them. Nominalisation of events obviously plays an important role in this since resources for construing and grading attitude are richest in English nominal group structures:

> a monumental policy failure
> tragic consequences
> (Relying…on the…government record) is … grossly inadequate[1]
> a distorted and unbalanced perspective
> a profound ignorance

To see how this works in longer texts, we'll consider [3:15] below, which comes earlier in the Brennan chapter from which we took [3:14] above. In this text Brennan deploys a range of recounts to exemplify the federal government's failure to protect children in mandatory detention. This time, instead of analysis we'll deploy synthesis, and build the text up gradually from its phases. We begin with an autobiographical recount from the mother of a 7-year-old child injured by a detention centre guard in March 2002.

[3:15']

My son was with me in Oscar compound during the disturbance in the early hours of Saturday 30 March 2002. He and I were both hit by tear gas even though we were not trying to escape. I was blinded for about a minute and I took my son to my chest and embraced him to protect him. I started to move away from the scene with my son. Then an ACM guard came and bowled over me and struck my son with a baton.

On Tuesday 2 April, I told my story to Father Brennan and the lawyers at Woomera. I then went to the doctor on Wednesday 3 April 2002. The doctor made a report which I attach to this letter. I asked the lawyers to make a complaint. One and a half months later two policemen came to see me. I told them what happened to my son. They said they would return with an interpreter from Adelaide and with Federal Police and someone from Children's Services and with a camera for an interview with my son. Then about one week later, and before the United Nations came to visit Woomera, I was interviewed by Geoff Cardwell of the South Australian Police about the incident. He said he was the boss of the other police who had come. He said it was not the responsibility of Federal Police because they would come only for damage to property. He said Child Service would not come because their responsibility was child abuse and relationships between children and parents. He gave me a card with the reference PIR/02/966813. He recorded our conversation. He was interested only in the events which occurred on the evening of Friday 29 March 2002. He told me that the doctor and ACM had not made any report of my son's injury to Children's Services. I asked him about my rights. He told me, 'You can't do anything because you are captive in here and when you get out and get your visa, you can continue your protest and maybe you can get your rights.' He asked whether I saw who hit my son. I said I did not see because the guard was wearing a mask. He said, 'We can't catch him because you didn't see him.' I said, 'It's not important who hit my son, just it is important that ACM action that they hit children, because it is their habit in our compound.'

I trusted the government to protect my son. I hope my complaint can help other mothers and children. I am only a single mother in detention who wants the government to care for us.

Compared with texts [3:1] and [3:2] above, this recount has much less ongoing evaluation. It is only towards the end of the text that we find some projected evaluation, as the mother quotes herself: *'It's not **important** who hit my son, just it is **important** that ACM action that they hit children, because it is their habit in our compound.'* Our reading of this is that the text to this point is in fact a piece of testimony, probably transcribed by lawyers as part of a report to the Australian Human Rights and Equal Opportunity Commission. As such it presents itself as factual evidence, reporting what people said but not what the mother feels – until the last paragraph that is, where her affectual disposition in making her complaint is finally made explicit:

I **trusted** the government to protect my son. I **hope** my complaint can help other mothers and children. I am only a single mother in detention who **wants** the government to care for us.

The voice of the text appears to us to shift here – from documentation to emotional appeal; from an audience of judicial commissioners in fact to a range of interested observers, including perhaps the media and their readership at large. By the same token, in spite of the inhumanity of the events to hand, the text expresses affect, not judgement; there is no explicit moral indictment by the mother of what has been done to her son.

Brennan's voice on the other hand becomes explicitly judgemental. He introduces the mother's recount in factual terms, as part of his historical recount of government behaviour; but he follows up her story with as series of pointed rhetorical questions, in effect accusing the government of irresponsible buck-passing as far as the investigation was concerned.

[3:15″]

Mr Ruddock's own chief of staff had referred the matter to the South Australian Family and Youth Services on 29 April 2002 once a new search of medical records revealed there was a problem. On 10 July 2002 the mother reported to the Human Rights and Equal Opportunity Commission:

> **[3:15′ here]**

On 22 August 2002 Mr Ruddock advised, 'I understand that South Australian police investigations are continuing. Meanwhile, the Department is examining an ACM report into the matter, received on 5 August 2002 to determine what action, if any, is required.' The mother of the boy never received a report on her complaint. On 3 February 2003 the Minister wrote again, advising that 'the matter was referred to the AFP' who 'determined that there was insufficient evidence relating to the identity of the alleged offender.' Who does investigate assaults in detention centres? The Australian Federal Police (AFP) or the state police? Or nobody?

Expanding further, this historical recount (3.15") is prefaced by an autobiographical recount by Brennan, in which he documents his own dealings with authorities over this matter.

[3:15‴]

I communicated information about injuries to children at Woomera to the Minister and to the Department of Immigration and Multicultural and Indigenous Affairs (DIMIA) on 4 April 2002. Some of this information, including the claim that a seven-year-old boy was hit with a baton and exposed to tear gas, was then published in the *Canberra Times* on 18 April 2002. Within six hours DIMIA had publicly refuted the claim on its website, saying, 'This department has no record of injuries to a 7-year-old sustained during the disturbance at Woomera detention facility on Good Friday… If Father Brennan has information or evidence of mistreatment of detainees he should report it to the appropriate authorities for investigation.' I had seen the bruises with my own eyes. I had heard reports of tear gas hitting children even from the ACM (Australian Correctional Management Pty Ltd) manager at Woomera. I lodged a complaint about the department's spin doctoring. It took the secretary of the department more than three months to conduct the inquiry. The department could strenuously deny allegations within six hours, then take more than three months to acknowledge their error. The acting secretary of the department explained that their public misinformation occurred because 'a number of communication problems in the Department allowed the matter to escalate to the stage where Mr Foster [Director, Public Affairs, DIMIA] posted inaccurate information.' According to the departmental inquiry, this escalation took place over four days. The public rebuttal was issued within six hours of the publication of my remarks – hardly any time at all for communication problems or escalation to impede the single-minded objective of denying that there had been injury to children.

Like the mother's story, this recount is relatively devoid of evaluation; overall it is designed to set the record straight, in the face of a Howard government and politicised bureaucracy whose operational dictum became 'Lie first; cover up later.' It does of course explicitly charge DIMIA with spin-doctoring, a negative judgement which the rest of the recount corroborates.

Let's now place these recounts in context, as part of an argument by Brennan about the government's failure to provide basic protection and services for persons, especially children, in detention. In this section of his challenge to detention policy he is discussing the hazy line of authority for detainees, between state and federal governments and their various institutions. At issue here is the incapacity of the government to deal with child abuse:

> **[3:15]**
>
> Let me give one example of the incapacity of the Canberra bureaucracy to deal credibly with reports of child abuse and neglect in detention because of their need to pursue a hot political agenda.
>
> [3:15''' = Brennan's autobiographical recount]
>
> [3:15'' = Brennan's historical recount]
>
>   [3:15' = mother's autobiographical recount]
>
> The cursory and dilatory nature of DIMIA's inquiry invokes no public confidence that there will not be a recurrence of cover-ups or neglect of credible claims of injury to children in detention, where they are being used as a means to an end. In this instance, the Commonwealth department was guilty of a negligent or wilful cover-up regarding the investigation of child abuse in detention centres. If children are to be held in detention with their parents, they should be held in facilities where there is ready access to state Children's Services departments. The policy parameters of their detention should be sufficiently humane to win the support of both the federal government and the state governments, regardless of which party is in power. It is obscene that defenceless children are used as political footballs by political spin-doctors.
>
> [Brennan 2003: 101–104]

Brennan's actual text then begins with an explicit judgement of Canberra's incapacity, which he exemplifies with his own autobiographical recount, follows up with his historical recount (which includes the mother's autobiographical recount), and concludes with a damning judgement of a negligent or wilful cover-up amounting in his terms to an obscenity. The ways in which these genres are stitched together is indicative of the way in which genres participate in macro-genres, a topic we'll return to in Chapter 4 below.

The patterns of both text staging and values are diagrammed in Figure 3.4. Intensity of appraisals and their scope over text stages are indicated by shading. These include the judgements that open and conclude Brennan's recount, the affect that concludes the mother's recount, while the intense judgements in Brennan's recount and conclusion scope over the whole text.

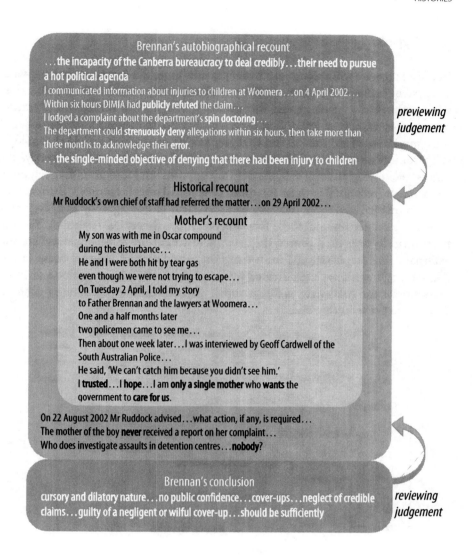

Figure 3.4 Pattern of recounts within recounts within history texts

Discussion to this point puts us in position to note some important correlations in history discourse, recurring across genres. On the one hand we have an association of previews and reviews with explicit evaluation and nominalisation; and on the other we have an association of the body of text with more factual, less nominalised textures. Rhetorically speaking, this constructs the factual, concrete bodies of texts as evidence for their more value laden, more abstract, prospective and retrospective conclusions. What we experience as serial time, we read as historical waves – of interpretation, grounded in memories, interpreted again, and grounded, and so on – the past breaking upon the present, time upon time.

3.6   Typology – classifying difference

In this section we will arrange our history genres as we did for stories in Chapter 2, as a system network in Figure 3.5. This is fundamentally a taxonomic exercise, classifying genres as a typology, and this means privileging one dimension of texture over another as more or less critical for categorisation. In Figure 3.5 we've privileged the opposition of field time to text time, separating texts which unfold chronologically from those which unfold rhetorically (basically recounts and accounts vs the others). Following on from this, the network opposes texts foregrounding temporal connections (recounts) to those foregrounding causal ones (accounts). The recounts are then divided into those focusing on individuals (autobiography and biography depending on person) and those focusing on groups (historical recounts). Turning to rhetorically organised genres, the network distinguishes those organised around external cause (explanations) from those organised around internal cause (arguments). Arguments are then divided into organised around one position or more (expositions and challenges vs discussions), with expositions promoting a position and challenges rebutting one.

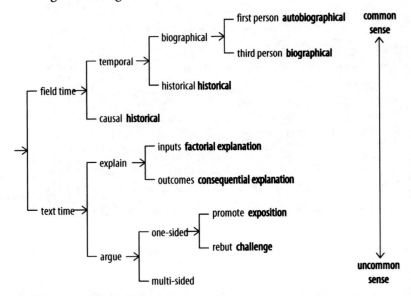

Figure 3.5   A typological perspective on relations between history genres

Typology creates categorical distinctions, where thinking about things as ranged along a cline might be more productive. For example it forces us to distinguish between recounts and accounts as distinct categories, when from another perspective what we have is texts unfolding through time, some of which create more causal connections than others. In our experience, historical accounts are the least 'categorical' of the genres reviewed above, emerging now and again from historical recounts; but they are in some sense less 'institutionalised' than recounts, explanations and the arguing genres. One implication of this is that we would expect to find many more texts straddling the border of recount and account than across the boundaries of other genres.

Another set of oppositions that might be better treated as a cline is the exposition, challenge and discussion group. From the perspective of appraisal theory what distinguishes these genres is the degree of heteroglossia as far as alternative positions is concerned. Expositions efface alternatives, challenges deface them and discussions include but deprecate them.

As an alternative to Figure 3.5 we might have promoted temporality vs causality as our first cut, thereby opposing recounts to accounts, explanations and arguments at primary delicacy. The important point is that because the network is a hierarchy, privileging has consequences for the categorisation as a whole. In choosing to organise our system as we have, we have brought out one cline that is significant for the learner pathway discussed in the following section. This is a cline of abstraction, from the discourse patterns of autobiographical recounts that most closely resemble those of everyday commonsense, to those of written argument genres that are most remote from the unfolding event time of everyday experience.

3.7 Topology – proximating likeness

The alternative to taxonomising of the kind displayed in Figure 3.5 is topology, which allows us to relate genres as more or less like one another, from as many angles as we wish. We'll illustrate topological analysis of history genres here from the perspective of pedagogic discourse (Bernstein 2000), drawing on work by Coffin 1997, Coffin 2006. The basic question we are asking here is how best to apprentice students into the discourses of history reviewed above. In Bernstein's terms we want to build a stairway of recontextualisation, from everyday discourse to academic history.

3.7.1 Recount genres

We start with the assumption that the closest relevant 'domestic' genre for secondary school students is the personal recount introduced in Chapter 2 – because this genre reconstructs what happened as events unfolding through time. The first move which students have to make in moving from personal recounts to history is to learn to manage episodic time alongside serial time. And this means organising texts around phases of activity scaffolded by clause initial circumstances of location in time – the move from 'and then' to 'later on in another period of time' (from 'sequence in time' to 'setting in time' in Gleason's terms).[5]

Of course as we have seen above in [3:4], and this is where topology is important, history genres do deploy serial time where required – to focus step by step on a sequence of events. In our experience this happens more often in autobiography than biography, and less often in historical recounts than in either of these genres. This has partly to do with access to detail, and partly to do with the focus of historical recounts – which is to package time into phases, which might in turn be nominalised (and possibly named; e.g. the Depression, the Cold War).

Alongside this move from serial to episodic time, students need to shift from 1st person reference to 3rd person, and from specific participants to generic ones. Once again these are not categorical distinctions. Personal and autobiographical recounts do feature 1st person reference, especially as Theme; but the narrator interacts with other participants as the texts unfold. Similarly, personal, autobiographical and biographical recounts feature individuals, although reference is made to groups of people as well; historical recounts on the other hand foreground groups of people over individuals, although the 'grand narratives' of modernist history include specific reference to great men (sic) by way of enacting their patriarchal reading of the past. A summary of these time management and participant identification variables is presented in Table 3.4.

Table 3.4 Key features of four recount genres

GENRE [staging]	INFORMAL DESCRIPTION	KEY LINGUISTIC FEATURES (Halliday 1994, Martin 1992)
personal recount [Orientation^Record]	agnate to story genres; what happened to me	serial time; 1st person (& 3rd); specific participants
autobiographical recount [Orientation^Record]	the story of my life [oral history]	episodic time; 1st person (& 3rd); specific participants
biographical recount [Orientation^Record]	the story of someone else's life	episodic time; 3rd person (specific); other specific & generic participants
historical recount; [Background^Record]	establishing the time line of the grand narrative	episodic time; 3rd person; mainly generic participants (but specific 'great men')

Because we are dealing with clines rather than categorical distinctions, and because more than one variable is relevant, topological analysis is a useful tool for modelling relations among the recount genres. Although topology is theoretically multidimensional, it is difficult to clearly diagram more than two dimensions at a time – so we'll set aside person and restrict ourselves to individual vs generic reference and serial vs episodic time here.[6] Figure 3.6 below plays these vectors off against one another to create a space in which recounts can be mapped as more or less focused on individuals or groups and as unfolding more or less through serialised events or phases. In these terms, personal recounts are relatively serial and individual, compared with historical recounts which are relatively generic and episodic. Autobiography and biography come somewhere in between, with autobiography leaning towards personal recount, and biography towards historical recount.

The precise positioning of these genres in the landscape is not at issue here, and would have to be pursued on the basis of quantitative analysis of a corpus of the relevant genres in any case. Our purpose at this point is simply to signal the complementarity of typological and topological perspectives on genre relations. Topology is of course a useful tool for exploring the fit between specific texts and the genre they realise. For example, a personal recount which includes several phases of sequenced events would move down the time variable in Figure 3.6 towards autobiography (more setting in time); by the same token, an autobiography which expands detailed sequences of events within phases would move up towards personal recount (more sequence in time). The elasticity of discourse and the attendant facility with which texts adapt to their context means that now and again we'll come across texts which are difficult to categorise as one genre or another (i.e. texts that 'blend' genres). At the same time, the metastability of culture as a predictable system of genres means that we regularly recognise and participate in texts as enacting one genre or another.[7]

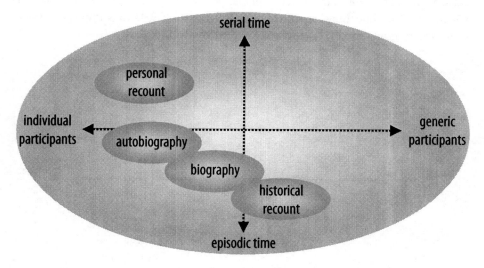

Figure 3.6 A topological perspective on recount genres

3.7.2 Historical accounts and explanations

The next move students need to make is from recounts to accounts, and this involves moving from temporal to causal connections between events. Cause can of course be realised between clauses through conjunctions (e.g. the factorial explanation [3:8] above), but as we have indicated, in accounts it tends to be realised inside the clause through nouns, verbs and prepositions. For this to happen one or both of the events being connected have to be nominalised in order to have them functioning inside the clause as participants or circumstances. Accordingly, historical accounts draw on grammatical metaphor much more heavily than recounts (although for time packaging reasons historical recounts are already moving in this direction). Since grammatical metaphor is a resource for reading and writing that develops after puberty in secondary school, the move from recounts to accounts is a very significant one in the development of apprentice historians.

Factorial and consequential explanations share this predilection for realising cause inside the clause. They differ from recounts and accounts in that chronology is not used to organise texts. Rather, explanations are organised rhetorically, beginning with the event being explained and then unfolding through a set of relevant factors or consequences. Since these factors and consequences are not ordered in time with respect to one another, students have to learn to put them into a sequence appropriate to the explanation. In other words they have to organise text time independently of field time, since texture is no longer determined by chronology.

Although sequence becomes a matter of texture, causality remains a matter of what caused what in the world. In a sense, explanations are simply complicated accounts in which more than one thing leads on to or on from another. Relations among recounts, historical accounts and explanations are approximated in Figure 3.7.

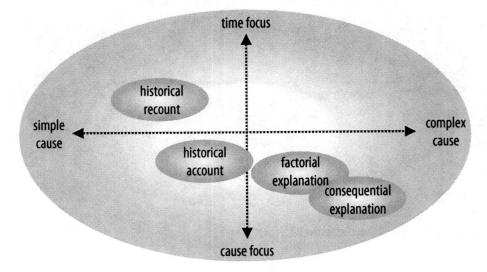

Figure 3.7   A topological perspective on explanatory genres

Because learning to manage cause inside the clause and sequence texts rhetorically is fundamental to the apprenticeship of young historians, accounts and explanations are highly favoured examination genres in Australian secondary schools. Students who cannot deploy the key features of these genres, outlined in Table 3.5, will fare poorly in test situations – however well they know what happened. What happened is not history; it's story. For history, understanding why things happened is critical. And for understanding students need accounts and explanations and control of the linguistic resources which realise them.

Table 3.5 Key features of historical accounts and explanations

GENRE [staging]	INFORMAL DESCRIPTION	KEY LINGUISTIC FEATURES (Halliday 1994, Martin 1992)
historical account; [Background^Account]	naturalising linearisation rendering the grand narrative inevitable	text unfolding through cause and effect; cause within clause; 3rd person; mainly generic & nominalised participants
factorial explanation [Outcome ^ Factors]	complexifying notion of what leads on to what	text internal organisation of factors; factors externally linked to outcome; cause within clause; 3rd person; mainly generic & nominalised participants
consequential explanation [Input ^ Consequences]	complexifying notion of what leads on from what	text internal organisation of consequences; consequences externally linked to input; cause within clause; 3rd person; mainly generic & nominalised participants

3.7.3 Exposition, challenge and discussion

Beyond chronicling and explanation we move to history at risk – the task of motivating interpretations. As with explanations, these genres unfold rhetorically rather than chronologically; unlike explanations, their notion of cause is also rhetorical. They are concerned with why a contestable reading of the past is motivated, not simply with what caused what. In Halliday and Hasan's 1976 terms this means that consequential links are internal rather than external – why I'm arguing that 'x', as opposed to why 'x' happened.

Thus Pearson, in [3:10] above, treats it as uncontroversial that the equal pay decision was a monumental policy failure with tragic consequences; he treats this as given, and presents the decision's outcomes. Boyce on the other hand, in [3:12], above treats Windschuttle's over-reliance on government sources as controversial. He's not explaining why Windschuttle did what he did or what it's effects were; rather he moves on to prove his point, arguing that relevant government records were scarce early on and later on plentiful but misleading. Although there is a tendency for contestable positions in explanations to be less heavily evaluative than contestable ones in arguments, what is more critical is how historians position us with respect to appraised events: are they explaining what happened, or convincing us they're right?

Topologically speaking we will encounter texts which blur this distinction, as in the following factorial explanation cum exposition by Evans (1997), with which he concludes his biography of Deng Xiaoping. The text [3:16] starts out as if it is listing factors which will impede the growth of political and cultural freedom in China; but it concludes by taking these as the basis for arguing that freedom is a long way away. This kind of slippage between how a text begins and how it ends is an important aspect of the dynamism of texture, taking advantage here of the topological affinity of explanations and expositions just reviewed.

> **[3:16]**
>
> The experience of other developing countries, not least the countries which underwent the profoundest changes in the nineteenth century, suggests very strongly that rising levels of prosperity and education lead to pressure for wider political and cultural freedom. There is plenty of evidence, not least the democracy movements of 1986 and 1989, that this is also true in Chine. In China, however, there are **factors** which could both modify the degree of pressure and increase resistance to it. One such factor is that the state has been an ideological state throughout China's history as a unified country. The state has been the custodian and propagator of a complete ideology and of an associated morality and not just an apparatus for control by an individual, a class or an interest. This tradition is still strong. Another factor is that Chinese society's experience of open competition for political power has been wholly unfavourable, from the days of corrupt parliamentary democracy in the early years of the Republic to the Cultural Revolution. It is not difficult for those who are dedicated to party leadership to obtain an echo when they argue that renewed competition would lead to social and political chaos. A third factor which could retard the development of political freedom is that the degree of economic and cultural freedom enjoyed by most Chinese had increased greatly during the past twenty years, and is still increasing. The law is still harsh – and arbitrary; political dissent outside very narrow limits is still not tolerated; and large numbers of political and other prisoners still live and work in worse than spartan conditions. But for all the Chinese who keep out of political and other trouble, life is no longer rigidly controlled, or even narrowly circumscribed. This is clear from the behaviour of Chinese to one another – in markets, on trains and buses, and in parks and other public places – and also from their reaction to foreigners. They no longer try to avoid public contact with foreigners and are often ready to be seen answering foreigners' questions. It is also clear from the nightlife of the cities, the way in which the urban young dress, and the extent to which they know about developments in the youth culture of the rest of the world.
>
> It may **therefore** be quite a long time before political freedom breaks out in China. Meanwhile, the world will continue to wonder that a country boy with a sketchy education could have left his stamp so strongly, and on the whole to their taste, on the people of the world's most populous country. [Evans 1997: 331–2]

Challenges may have a similar organisation to expositions, with an introductory 'anti'-thesis subsequently undermined by the arguments why it is wrong (e.g. Tutu's challenge discussed in Martin 2003). Alternatively, specific aspects of the general position being attacked may be introduced and rebutted piece by piece, as with Brennan's challenge (3:14 above). Discussions involve additional organisational decisions about the number of positions around an issue to be canvassed and how certain positions will be negatively evaluated and another positively viewed. Space precludes consideration of the finer points of internal conjunction, appraisal and hierarchy of periodicity in arguing genres here. A few key parameters are outlined in Table 3.6, and diagrammed in Figure 3.8.

Table 3.6 Key features of exposition, challenge and discussion

GENRE [staging]	INFORMAL DESCRIPTION	KEY LINGUISTIC FEATURES (Halliday 1994, Martin 1992)
exposition – one sided; promote [Thesis^Arguments]	problematic interpretation that needs justifying	internal conjunction keying on thesis
challenge˙ – one sided; rebut [Position^Rebuttal]	someone else's problematic interpretation that needs demolishing	internal conjunction keying on thesis
discussion – multi-sided; adjudicate [Issue^Sides^Resolution]	more than one interpretation considered	internal conjunction keying on thesis; & internal organisation of points of view

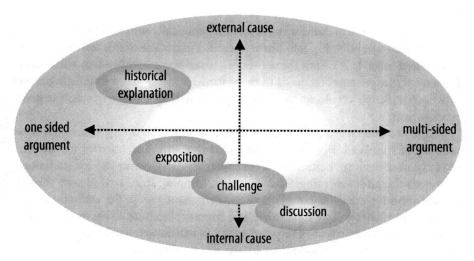

Figure 3.8 A topological perspective on argument genres

3.7.4 Learner pathways through history genres

From the textures outlined in Tables 3.3 through 3.5, a spiral curriculum can be developed that leads learners through the genres of history, and the linguistic hurdles each one presents, illustrated in Figure 3.9 (based on Coffin 1997).

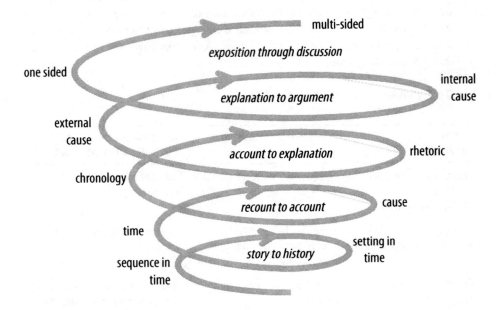

Figure 3.9 A spiral curriculum for history genres

The basic idea here is to come up with an ontogenetically sensitive topology which can facilitate apprenticeship into history genres. An outline of this learner pathway is presented in Table 3.7, with the genres discussed above arranged on a cline from those most like personal recounts to those furthest away. Major linguistic hurdles have been included in column three, by way of signalling significant stages in genre development.

We're not of course arguing here that stages cannot be skipped along a learner pathway of this kind. But we would predict that jumping hurdles will require extra cycles of deconstruction and joint construction of exemplars for students to latch onto the additional linguistic demands. Jumping from oral history directly to exposition for example would entail involving students in the shifts from time to cause, from chronology to rhetoric and from explanation to motivation noted above – in short a leap from everyday orality to institutionalised literacy. This is a lot of language learning for students to handle in a single go.[8]

Table 3.7 Learner pathway and linguistic hurdles for history genres[9]

GENRE [staging]	INFORMAL DESCRIPTION	HURDLES
personal recount **[Orientation^Record]**	**agnate to story genres; what** **happened to me**	*sequence in time...*
autobiographical recount [Orientation^Record]	the story of my life [oral history]	*...to setting in time*
biographical recount [Orientation^Record]	the story of someone else's life	
historical recount; [Background^Record]	establishing the time line of 'grand narrative'	*temporal connections &* *concrete participants...*
historical account; [Background^Account]	naturalising linearisation of 'grand narrative '	*...to causal connections &* *abstract participants...*
factorial explanation [Outcome ^ Factors]	complexifying notion of what leads on to what	*...to complex causal* *relations...*
consequential explanation [Input ^ Consequences]	complexifying notion of what follows on from what	
exposition – one sided; promote [Thesis^Arguments]	problematic interpretation that needs justifying	*...to complex rhetorical* *relations*
challenge – one sided; rebut [Position^Rebuttal]	problematic interpretation that needs demolishing	*one side-ed argument....*
discussion – multi-sided; adjudicate [Issue^Sides^Resolution]	more than one interpretation considered	*...to multi-sided adjudication*

4 Reports and explanations

4.0 Classifying and explaining

Whereas history functions as capital for negotiating control of the social world, the broad social function of science is to facilitate control of the natural world. In this respect, science works hand in glove with industry: industry providing the material resources science needs for investigating nature; science providing the discursive resources industry needs for exploiting nature. Science in this view is a set of semiotic practices; it is concerned with manipulating material activities, but these activities are informed by what science has to say about the world; industrial practices and products make sense within the technical discourses that science has accumulated over the five centuries since Galileo described the movement of the earth around the sun. The historical development of scientific discourse from this moment has been mapped by Halliday 1993, 1998, 2004. Genres in the sciences have been described by Halliday & Martin 1993, Lemke 1990a&b, 1998, Martin 1986, 1989, 1990, 1998, Martin & Painter 1986, Rose 1997, 1998, Rose et al 1992, Unsworth 1997a,b&c, 1999, 2001a&b, 2004, Veel 1997, 1998, Wignell 1997, Wignell, Martin & Eggins 1993.

From this body of research we are able to make a broad generalisation that science semioticises the natural world by generalising about things and processes in four regular ways: by classifying and describing phenomena, by explaining how processes happen, by instructing how to observe phenomena (e.g. in experiments), and by recounting and interpreting what was observed. So four families of genres that characterise science are **reports** that classify and describe, **explanations** of causes and effects, **procedures** for observing and experimenting, and **procedural recounts** for reporting on observations and experiments (cf Veel 1997). In this chapter we will analyse a range of reports and explanations. Procedures and procedural recounts will be addressed in Chapter 5, as they function to direct activities in industry.

Reports and explanations draw on two complementary sets of resources that language provides for construing relations between phenomena, focusing on one hand on **entities** – their description, classification and composition, and on the other hand on **activities** – in sequences of cause and effect (Martin 2007 a, b). In the history of scientific fields description and classification tends to precede explanation of causes. In astronomy and physics for example, telescopes enabled classification of parts of the solar system centuries before Newton explained why they moved as they do, and the relation between the most general physical classes of matter and energy was not explained until Einstein's theory of general relativity in the last century. Today physicists have decomposed matter into some 40 subatomic particles, but they are not yet able to explain how they function to compose protons, neutrons and electrons, the building blocks of atoms. Likewise the major activity of biology was for centuries the description and classification of species, until Darwin explained how they came to be so through natural selection. And until very recently the major activity of linguistics remained the description and classification of elemental particles – phonemes, morphemes and syntactic rules – at least until Halliday among others began to explain how they function to realise social contexts.[1] In this chapter we will follow a similar course, beginning with classification and composition in reports, followed by causal relations in explanations. In the final section we will use the principles developed here to describe multimodal texts, including the structures of visual images and their relations to verbal texts.

4.1   Reports: classifying and describing things

Science classifies and describes phenomena in three types of reports. **Descriptive** reports classify a phenomenon and then describe its features. **Classifying** reports subclassify a number of phenomena with respect to a given set of criteria. **Compositional** reports describe the components of an entity.

4.1.1 Descriptive reports

The purpose of a descriptive report is to classify and describe a phenomenon, so its stages are most generally Classification followed by Description. Classification and description of species in biology is a common site for descriptive reports, illustrated in text [4:1] about the canonical group of reptiles in Australia known as *goannas*.

[4:1] Goannas

Australia is home to 25 of the world's 30 monitor lizard species. In Australia, monitor lizards are called goannas.

Goannas have flattish bodies, long tails and strong jaws. They are the only lizards with forked tongues, like a snake. Their necks are long and may have loose folds of skin beneath them. Their legs are long and strong, with sharp claws on their feet. Many goannas have stripes, spots and other markings that help to camouflage them. The largest species can grow to more than two metres in length.

All goannas are daytime hunters. They run, climb and swim well.

Goannas hunt small mammals, birds and other reptiles. They also eat dead animals. Smaller goannas eat insects, spiders and worms.

Male goannas fight with each other in the breeding season. Females lay between two and twelve eggs.

Silkstone 1994

This report from a school textbook first classifies the phenomenon as a group of species known as monitor lizards or goannas, and then describes them in terms of four sets of characteristics – their appearance, behaviour, feeding and breeding habits. Each characteristic constitutes a phase of the Description, and this phasal structure is made explicit with paragraphing. The generic structure is set out as follows, with stages and phases labelled, and key elements in bold.

[4:1'] Goannas	
Classification	
	Australia is home to 25 of the world's 30 **monitor lizard species**.
	In Australia, monitor lizards are called **goannas**.
Description	
appearance	Goannas have flattish **bodies**, long **tails** and **strong** jaws.
	They are the only lizards with forked **tongues**, like a snake.
	Their **necks** are long and may have loose folds of skin beneath them.
	Their **legs** are long and strong, with sharp **claws** on their feet. Many goannas have stripes, spots and other **markings** that help to camouflage them.
	The largest species can grow to more than two metres in **length**.
behaviour	All goannas are **daytime hunters**.
	They **run, climb and swim** well.
feeding	Goannas hunt **small mammals, birds and other reptiles**.
	They also eat **dead animals**.
	Smaller goannas eat **insects, spiders and worms**.
breeding	**Male goannas fight** with each other in the breeding season.
	Females lay between two and twelve eggs.

The appearance phase of [4:1] describes parts of goannas, illustrated in Figure 4.1 with the central Australian species *Varanus gigantus*, the one that can grow to more than two metres in length.

adapted from Scott & Robinson 1993:44

Figure 4.1 Goanna species described in text [4:1]

The descriptive phases in [4:1] are common in reports about animal species in biology, but descriptive reports are common across many fields. An example from a very different field is the following text [4:2], from a senior secondary textbook in the field of technology design.

[4:2] Ergonomics

Ergonomics can be defined as the design of work so that the best is made of human capabilities without exceeding human limitations.

Standards Association of Australia, *Australian Standard*

1837–1976: Ergonomics in Factory and Office Work,

Standards Australia, North Sydney, 1976.

The evolution of a product or design based on ergonomics relates the product or design to the physical needs of the user. These physical needs include not only size and position but other aspects such as floor surfaces, illumination levels, hand grips, switch standards and vision. Understanding the physical needs of the user allows the designer to cater for individual differences and to create products that cater for the needs of the majority of consumers. Ergonomics is to do with the human body as a whole but it also involves the function of parts of the body and the ease with which humans perform simple tasks.

Warner et al 1995

This report uses a quoted definition for its Classification stage. The phenomenon it describes is not a physical entity as in the zoology report above, but a field of activity – an abstract entity. The Description stage then includes two phases: the first describes the physical needs of users in terms of aspects of a designed product – *size, position* and so on; the second in terms of aspects of the user – *individual differences, the human body as a whole, parts of the body.*

As we saw for stories and history, common stages of a genre may be found across different fields, but phases within each stage are more likely to vary from field to field and text to text.

4.1.2 Classifying reports

While descriptive reports describe characteristics of one class of phenomenon, classifying reports subclassify members of a general class. Crucial to this genre are criteria for classification, and the same phenomena may be classified differently according to various criteria. The following text [4:3] subclassifies groups of organisms according to whether they produce chemical energy, or consume those that do, and this generic organisation is explicitly signalled in the first stage.

[4:3] Producers and consumers

We have seen that organisms in an ecosystem are first classified as producers or as consumers of chemical energy.

Producers in ecosystems are typically photosynthetic organisms, such as plants, algae and cyanobacteria. These organisms build organic matter (food from simple inorganic substances by photosynthesis).

Consumers in an ecosystem obtain their energy in the form of chemical energy present in their 'food'. All consumers depend directly or indirectly on producers for their supply of chemical energy. Organisms that eat the organic matter of producers or their products (seeds, fruits) are called primary consumers, for example, leaf-eating koalas (Phascolarctos cinereus), and nectar-eating honey possums (Tarsipes rostratus).

Organisms that eat primary consumers are known as secondary consumers. Wedge-tailed eagles that prey on wallabies are secondary consumers.

Some organisms consume the organic matter of secondary consumers and are labeled tertiary consumers. Ghost bats (Macroderma gigas) capture a variety of prey, including small mammals.

Kinnear & Martin 2004: 38

The system for classifying phenomena can vary even within a single field. Here organisms are classified as producers or consumers, but they are also classified within biology on various other criteria, such as genetic relations. So classifying reports begin by stating the Classification system, followed by the Types. Within the Types stage, text [4:3] has two layers of classification, including subtypes of *consumers*. Each type and subtype is defined and exemplified as a distinct text phase with its own paragraph, set out below, with types and subtypes in bold and classification criteria marked.

[4:3'] Producers and consumers

Classification system

We have seen that organisms in an ecosystem are first classified as producers or as consumers of chemical energy.

Types

type 1 **Producers** in ecosystems are typically photosynthetic organisms, such as plants, algae and cyanobacteria. These organisms (**criteria**) build organic matter (food from simple inorganic substances by photosynthesis).

type 2 **Consumers** in an ecosystem (**criteria**) obtain their energy in the form of chemical energy present in their 'food'. All consumers depend directly or indirectly on producers for their supply of chemical energy.

subtype 2.1 Organisms that (**criteria**) eat the organic matter of producers or their products (seeds, fruits) are called **primary consumers**, for example, leaf-eating koalas (Phascolarctos cinereus), and nectar-eating honey possums (Tarsipes rostratus).

subtype 2.2 Organisms that (**criteria**) eat primary consumers are known as **secondary consumers**. Wedge-tailed eagles that prey on wallabies are secondary consumers.

subtype 2.3 Some organisms (**criteria**) consume the organic matter of secondary consumers and are labeled **tertiary consumers**. Ghost bats (Macroderma gigas) capture a variety of prey, including small mammals.

The taxonomy of classification realised in text [4:3] is represented in Figure 4.2. Classification taxonomy diagrams are organised as left-right 'system networks'. Although biologists often use top-down tree diagrams to illustrate such classifying taxonomies, in SFL these are reserved these for compositional taxonomies, to illustrate the relations of whole to their parts, see below.

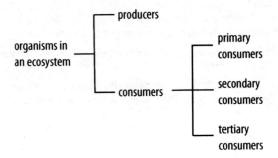

Figure 4.2 Classification taxonomy in a classifying report

In academic fields that take the form of a 'coherent, explicit, and systematically principled structure, hierarchically organised, as in the sciences' (Bernstein 1999), the global structure of textbooks is typically that of classifying reports, of types and their sub-types. That is, the field as a whole is organised in textbooks as a taxonomy of types, and the description of each type gives the criteria for its classification within the taxonomy. Bernstein refers to knowledge structure of this kind as hierarchical. *Genre Relations* is an example of this pattern, which is discussed further below in terms of 'macrogenres'. In fact all fields involve some degree of taxonomic organisation, but this organisation may be more and less elaborate and criteria may not be explicitly stated, as in many fields of everyday activity, or they may be contested by competing interest groups, as in humanities or political fields. The taxonomic organisation of 'vertical' technical fields is the result of research and negotiation over decades or centuries.

4.1.3 Compositional reports

Whereas classifying reports are concerned with membership in classes of phenomena, compositional reports are concerned with another dimension of organisation – parts of wholes. The following report [4:4] about a mangrove forest lists the organisms that compose the forest community. The forest is the whole (illustrated in Figure 4.3), the organisms are its components.

Figure 4.3   Mangrove forest

[4:4] Mangroves: part of a community

When you walk into a mangrove forest, you may at first think that grey mangroves are the only living organisms there. However, look and listen and you will find evidence of other living occupants of the forest.

Many different kinds of organisms share the living space with the grey mangroves. Fish and shrimp are found in the brackish waters. At low tide, you may notice small crabs scurrying into burrows in the mud. Even if you miss the crabs you will see evidence of their presence from holes in the mud leading to their burrows. At low-tide periods, various molluscs, such as snails and whelks, graze on algae that form a green film on parts of the muddy forest floor. Spiders spin their webs between branches of the grey mangroves to catch passing insects. Lichens grow on the trunks of mature mangrove trees. Many bird species feed on the nectar and pollen of the mangrove flowers and on the insects that live in the mangrove trees. At low tide, mudflats on the deepwater side of the mangrove forests are feeding sites for other bird species, such as the striated heron, *Ardeola striatus*, that feeds on snails and crabs. All these different kinds of organisms are part of the living **community** of the mangrove forest.

Kinnear & Martin 2004: 5

Here the first stage classifies the entity to be de-composed, and the compositional organisation is explicitly signalled as *evidence of other living occupants*. The next stage then sets out the Components of the entity, numbered as follows, with each organism in bold.

[4:4'] Mangroves: part of a community

Classification of entity

When you walk into **a mangrove forest**, you may at first think that grey mangroves are the only living organisms there. However, look and listen and you will find evidence of other living occupants of the forest.

Components

Many different kinds of organisms share the living space with the **grey mangroves**.

Fish and shrimp are found in the brackish waters. At low tide, you may notice small **crabs** scurrying into burrows in the mud. Even if you miss the crabs you will se evidence of their presence from holes in the mud leading to their burrows.

At low-tide periods, various **molluscs**, such as snails and whelks, graze on algae that form a green film on parts of the muddy forest floor.

Spiders spin their webs between branches of the grey mangroves to catch passing insects.

Lichens grow on the trunks of mature mangrove trees.

Many bird species feed on the nectar and pollen of the mangrove flowers and on the insects that live in the mangrove trees.

At low tide, mudflats on the deepwater side of the mangrove forests are feeding sites for **other bird species**, such as the striated heron, *Ardeola striatus*, that feeds on snails and crabs.

Definition

All these different kinds of organisms are part of the living **community** of the mangrove forest.

Note that each organism is named and their location and/or activities are then given. This is a common pattern in compositional reports, giving entities/parts alongside their activities/functions within the whole. In science textbooks, reports and explanations may finish with a technical definition, as in [4:4] above. The definition distills the detailed information presented, becomes part of the taxonomic organisation of the technical field.

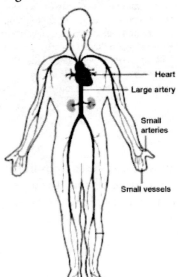

Another common site for compositional reports is in anatomy and physiology. In this field such reports first classify a body system and explain its function. Then the components of the system and their functions are given, then the subcomponents and their functions. Text [4:5] illustrates this pattern for human circulatory system. Figure 4:4 illustrates some components of the system.

Figure 4.4 Human circulatory system

> **[4:5] Transport in the body**
>
> Transport systems are need inside the body of all living things. In humans the blood or circulatory system carries digested food and other materials around the body. The blood contains 20 billion tiny cells floating in a liquid called *plasma*. The cells are of two different kinds *red cells* which carry oxygen and *white cells* which attack germs. Platelets which are microscopic discs, help in blood clotting.
>
> Red blood cells are made in bone marrow. They live for about 100 days and then they are destroyed by the liver. The bone marrow makes new cells to replace the destroyed cells. White blood cells protect the body against toxins and infections. The chemicals into which food has been broken-down are carried to all the body's cells in the blood. Blood also carries waste away from the cells.
>
> The blood moves through a series of tubes called *blood vessels*. The tubes could be compared with the road network of a country. However there are no head-on crashes as the tubes are strictly one-way.
>
> Blood is pumped around the body by the heart. Tubes called *arteries* carry blood away from the heart. Except for the artery to the lungs they carry bright red blood, rich in oxygen. Tubes called *veins* bring blood back to the heart. Except for the vein from the lungs they carry dark red blood, short of oxygen. The smallest arteries and veins are linked by tiny tubes called *capillaries*. Through their fine walls, oxygen and the chemicals from food are delivered to the cells all over the body, and waste products are collected.
>
> Watson 1999:94

The entity here is the circulatory system, and its function is *carries digested food and other materials around the body*. Its parts are given in italics: *plasma, red cells, white cells, platelets, blood vessels, heart, arteries, veins* and *capillaries*, and the function of each is given. The components of this anatomy report are thus structure-&-function, reflecting the component-&-activity pattern seen in the ecology compositional report [4:4] above. But here the composition is organised in a hierarchy at three levels, a compositional taxonomy. Compositional taxonomies are represented as top-down 'tree diagrams', as in Figure 4.5.

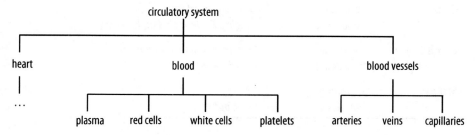

Figure 4.5 Compositional taxonomy in text [4:5]

4.2 Explanations: how processes happen

Explanations are concerned with explaining how processes happen. To this end they imply sequences of causes and effects: process x occurs, so process y results, which in turns causes process z, and so on. This kind of logical pattern has been termed an **implication sequence** (Wignell, Martin & Eggins 1993). The typical structure of explanations is to start by specifying the Phenomenon to be explained, followed by the implication sequence that explains it, the Explanation stage. Explanation genres are of four general types: they may consist of a simple sequence of causes and effects; a **sequential** explanation; they may involve multiple causes, a **factorial** explanation, or multiple effects, a **consequential** explanation; or the effects may vary depending on variable conditions, a **conditional** explanation.

In the sequence of an explanation, logical relations between events are temporal – either succeeding each other in time or happening at the same time. But an effect may be more or less obliged to follow its cause, and a causal event may be more or less likely to occur. In other words, **consequence** modulates a temporal sequence with obligation, there is some reason why an effect <u>must</u> follow its cause. This is the meaning of 'because, so, therefore' and so on. On the other hand **condition** modalises a causal event with probability: a condition <u>may</u> be present, and if it is the effect is obliged to follow. This is the meaning of 'if…then'. Thirdly if an effect should follow another, and for some reason it doesn't, this must be conceded. This is the meaning of 'however, but, nevertheless' and so on. These and related consequential meanings are set out in Table 4.1.

In written explanations, causal relations need not be made explicit. That is the causality may not be explicitly realised as causal conjunctions like 'because, so, therefore', but can be implicit in the explanation genre. The genre is typically announced in the Phenomenon stage, so the reader can infer causal relations where they are not stated.

Table 4.1 Some consequential relations and common conjunctions

Cause	expectant	because, so, therefore
	concessive	although, even though, but, however
Condition	expectant	if, then, provided that, as long as
	concessive	even if, even then
Means	expectant	by, thus
	concessive	even by, but

4.2.1 Sequential explanations

Sequential explanations are typically constructed as a series of events, in which an obligatory causal relation is implied between each event. The following example [4:6] explains how wetlands are formed along the coastline of northern Australia, by water flowing during the tropical wet season. The explanation genre is signalled in the first sentence *Many of the wetlands of the north have been **formed**...* The Explanation stage answers the question 'how are they formed?'.

[4:6] A lowland freshwater wetland – Lower Mary River

Many of the wetlands of the north have been formed by the large rivers that flow from the rugged escarpments that fringe the Top End coastline. In the wet season huge volumes of water flow from the escarpments. When this water hits the flood plains it slows down and spreads out forming the wetlands. The wetlands border the sea, however a series of sand ridges stopped sea water flowing into the wetlands. This kept the wetland water fresh.

Scott & Robinson 1993: 92

The Explanation here consists of two phases, the first explaining how the wetlands are formed in lowlands and the second explaining how the water is kept fresh. The implication sequence is explicated in Figure 4.6, in which the stages of Phenomenon and Explanation are labelled, relations between events are diagrammed with arrows, and these are glossed with explicit conjunctions.

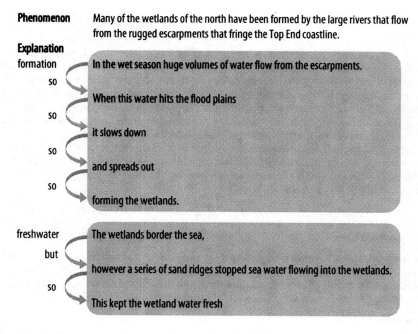

Figure 4.6 Implication sequence in sequential explanation [4:6]

In text [4:6] the technical term for this type of wetland was given in the title. However, explanations can either begin or conclude with a technical definition of the explained phenomenon.

Recognising the implied causal relations in [4:6] depends on imagining the geographic field of the Top End topography and climate, and expectancy implicit in each step. Wet season rainfall exceeds 1200mm. The escarpments are high plateaux. So the water is expected to flow rapidly from the escarpments to the flood plains, where it is expected to slow down and spread out on the flat ground. In the last phase, an expectant relation between bordering the sea and sea water flowing in is countered by concessive *however*, so the sand ridges are expected to keep the water fresh. In other words the series of consequential relations glossed here as 'so' are implicit in the genre and the field, and must be explicitly countered where required.

Sequential explanations vary widely according to the particular phenomenon being explained. Text [4:7] below explains the role of fire in the growth cycles of the Mallee ecosystem. This cycle is defined partway through as a **succession**. The implication sequence is also followed by an Extension stage that contrasts Aboriginal and European influences on the fire regime.

The implication sequences of [4:7] are diagrammed in Figure 4.7. There are four phases in the succession cycle, and two in the Extension stage, contrasting Aboriginal and European influences.

[4:7] Fire – a natural process which is now significantly influenced by humans

Since the advent of the present vegetation pattern around 10,000 years ago, fire has been crucial in modifying the Mallee environment. Regeneration of the Mallee depends on periodic fires. Old mallee produces a build-up of very dry litter and the branches themselves are often festooned with streamers of bark inviting a flame up to the canopy of leaves loaded with volatile eucalyptus oil. A dry electrical storm in summer is all that is needed to start a blaze, which, with a very hot northerly wind behind it will race unchecked through the bush. The next rain will bring an explosion of ground flora; the summer grasses and **forbs** not able to compete under a mallee canopy, will break out in a riot of colour. New shoots of mallee will spring from the lignotuber and another cycle of **succession** will begin. The dead branches become hollows for Major Mitchell cockatoos and other birds on whose eggs the goanna feeds. The more open bush provides green 'pick' for kangaroos and emus. The low shrubs give a home for zebra finches, but the abundant litter need by the mallee fowl to build a nest is no longer available.

Traditionally, Aborigines would periodically have lit small areas to flush out game and provide some fresh grass for later in spring. The result of this over generations would have been a patchwork of small moderate burns.

The European settlers, however, brought with them a very different attitude to fire. Fire was seen as danger to crops and livestock and should be extinguished if possible. The result of this is that litter builds up until it all goes up in one fierce blaze, usually in the middle of summer when conditions are very hot.

Corrigan 1991:100

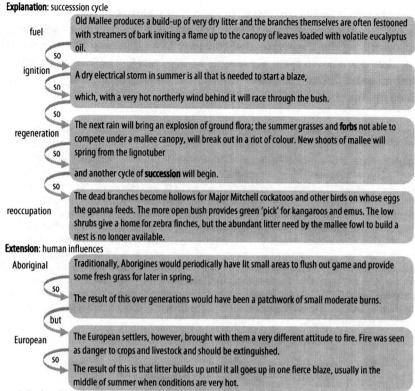

Figure 4.7 Implication sequence of mallee succession [4:7]

This pattern in an implication sequence, of a series of phases succeeding each other, is a common explanation pattern, diagrammed in Figure 4.8. Unsworth 1997, 2001 describes a comparable pattern for explanations of coal formation, for which he terms each phase a 'transformation' and the explanation type 'transformational'. Here we will group these as a variety of sequential explanations. The Extension giving human influences is a feature of the field of geography, and related school sciences. This syndrome is discussed by Veel 1998.

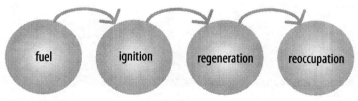

Figure 4.8 Series of phases in sequential explanation [4:7]

From the macro scale of ecosystems, to the micro scale of cell structures, text [4:8] below explains the formation of DNA in cell nuclei. It begins with a compositional report describing the *nucleotides* that compose DNA, followed by an explanation of how they combine to form the double helix of DNA. The technical density of the text makes it difficult to follow without the accompanying diagram, which is included as Figure 4.9.

[4:8] Deoxyribose nucleic acid

The genetic material deoxyribose nucleic acid (DNA) is a polymer of nucleotides. Each nucleotide unit has a sugar (deoxyribose) part, a phosphate part and an N-containing base. There are four different kinds of nucleotides be cause four different kinds of N-containing bases are involved. The four different N-containing bases are **adenine, thymine, cytosine** and **guanine** and the four different nucleotides are denoted by the letters A, T, C and G because of the kind of base each contains. Examine figure [4.9]. The nucleotide sub-units (a) are assembled to form a chain (b) in which the sugar of one nucleotide is bonded with the phosphate of the next nucleotide in the chain. Each DNA molecule contains two chains (c) that bond with each other because the bases in one chain pair with the bases in another. The base pairs between the two strands, namely A with T, and C with G, are said to be complementary base pairs. The two chains form a double-helical molecule of DNA (d) that combines with certain proteins to form a chromosome (e). These chromosomes reside in the nucleus of a cell (f) and the DNA they contain carries the genetic instructions that control all functions of the cell.

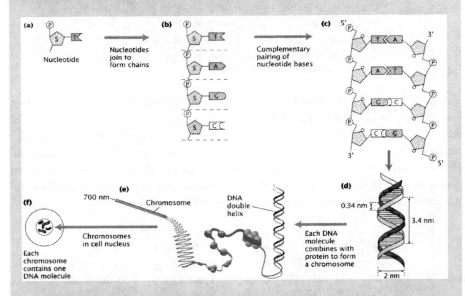

Figure 4.9   Deoxyribose nucleic acid (Kinnear & Martin 2004: 99)

The compositional report defines DNA compositionally as a *polymer*, i.e. made up of smaller molecules, and then sets out the components. The explanation then explains how the components combine to form the polymer. This implication sequence is diagrammed in Figure 4.10 below, with processes of combining in italics: *assemble, bond, pair, combine.* There are two phases in the Explanation stage, explaining the formation of chains from nucleotides, and the formation of chromosomes from chains, and an Extension giving the location and function of DNA in the cell.

As well as causal links leading from one step to another, glossed with 'so', there are also reasons that follow some steps, glossed with 'because'. However understanding the sequence depends not only logical relations, but on lexical relations. The key lexical item here is **chains**, highlighted in bold.

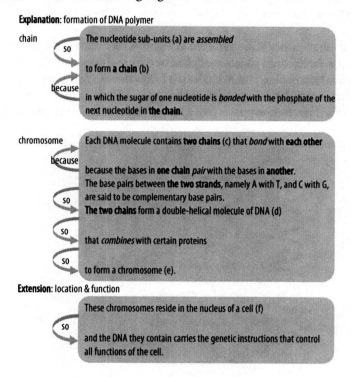

Figure 4.10 Implication sequence of DNA formation in explanation [4:7]

Here the Extension reflects a syndrome of the physiology field, to give functions for physiological structures, as we saw in the anatomical report [4:5]. It is also noteworthy in this text how a technical term is arrived at in steps, beginning with a process: *the bases in one chain **pair** with the bases in another*, which becomes a nominal group: *the **base pairs***, and is finally defined as a technical term: *said to be* ***complementary base pairs***.

Another pattern in sequential explanations is described by Unsworth 2001, for explanations of sound waves, exemplified in text [4:9]. Here the implication sequence consists of three phases, compression of air, followed by 'stretching' of air, followed by *a series of compressions and stretchings*.

[4:9] What causes and transmits sounds?

Figure 15.1 shows a vibrating object [producing sound waves]. As the object moves to the right it pushes or compresses the air particles next to it. The compressed air particles then push on the particles to their right and compress them. As each air particle pushes on the next one to its right the compression travels through the air. When the vibrating object moves back to its left the air particles next to it are no longer being pushed. They spread out or are stretched apart. As a compression travels through the air it is followed by the stretching apart of air particles. Because the vibrating object continually moves back and forth a series of compressions and stretchings of air particles is sent out from the object. Chapman et al. 1989: 280–281

This implication sequence is diagrammed in Figure 4.11. Events in the compression and 'stretching' (i.e. rarefaction) phases are linked by time and cause, but the last phase combines these two into a series. That is, it does not follow them in field time; rather it is linked to them by reasoning that is internal to the text, glossed here as 'thus'. As it combines the compression and rarefaction phases into a series, Unsworth calls this phase 'seriation'.

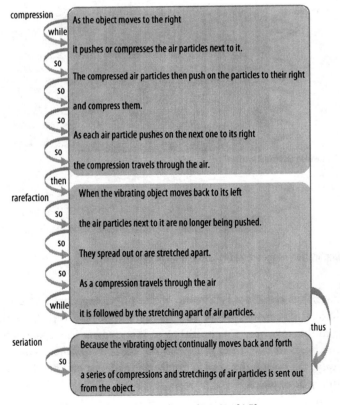

Figure 4.11 Implication sequence of sound waves in explanation [4:7]

This kind of structure is not simply serial, as in the preceding explanations. The compression and rarefaction phases are a series, but the seriation phase is linked to both in an orbital structure, diagrammed in Figure 4.12.

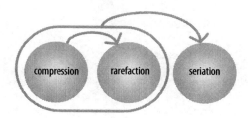

Figure 4.12 Orbital structure of sound explanation

4.2.2 Factorial explanations

We saw in Chapter 3 that historical events may be explained by two or more contributing factors. The same broad pattern is also commonly seen in scientific factorial explanations. The following example [4:10] explains how the Acacia tree species *mulga* survives long droughts by reference to three factors, its shape, its colour, and the food supplied by its own leaves.

[4:10] The mulga tree

How can plant life grow so well in such dry, hot and infertile places?

Surviving the long drought

The mulga tree likes long droughts – if it is too wet mulga trees will not grow.

The shape of the mulga tree is the key to it surviving dry times. The branches of the mulga fan out from the bottom – like a huge half moon. The branching leaves and stem catch the rain and it trickles down to the soil. This traps more rainfall than if the tree grew straight up. The mulga catches more water than a gum tree. The water is stored in the soil to be used by the tree during the next drought. Even the mulga's leaves help it to survive the drought. They are a silvery grey colour. The sun's rays bounce off the leaves helping the plant to stay cool. Also the mulga tree makes its own food by dropping thousands of leaves.

Scott & Robinson 1993: 22

Here the genre is announced in the form of a 'how' question interrogating the Phenomenon. The three factors constitute three phases: since the shape is the 'key' factor it is given a whole paragraph; then colour takes two sentences, and food takes one. The explanation is diagrammed in Figure 4.13, and the three factors are labelled.

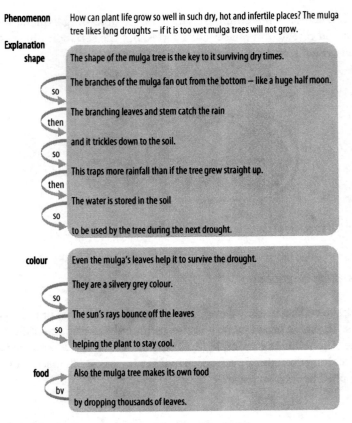

Phenomenon   How can plant life grow so well in such dry, hot and infertile places? The mulga tree likes long droughts – if it is too wet mulga trees will not grow.

Explanation shape

The shape of the mulga tree is the key to it surviving dry times.

so → The branches of the mulga fan out from the bottom – like a huge half moon.

then → The branching leaves and stem catch the rain

and it trickles down to the soil.

so → This traps more rainfall than if the tree grew straight up.

then → The water is stored in the soil

so → to be used by the tree during the next drought.

colour

Even the mulga's leaves help it to survive the drought.

They are a silvery grey colour.

so → The sun's rays bounce off the leaves

so → helping the plant to stay cool.

food → Also the mulga tree makes its own food

bv → by dropping thousands of leaves.

Figure 4.13 Implication sequence in factorial explanation [4:10]

Each factor is announced and then explained. In the first phase, relations between events are either causal or simply temporal succession. Firstly <u>because</u> of the shape, the leaves and stem catch the rain, which <u>then</u> trickles down, and so on. In the second phase, specialised field knowledge is required to recognise the implicit causal relation between the leaves' colour and sun's rays bouncing off. The third phase also requires specialised field knowledge to recognise the causal relation between dropping leaves and making food. Here the causal relation is expressed as means 'by', in order to thematise the factor in a single complex sentence. As each factor contributes independently to the effect, factorial explanations have an orbital structure, with the effect as nucleus, diagrammed in Figure 4.14.

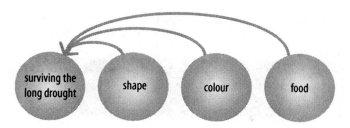

Figure 4.14 Orbital structure of factorial explanation [4:10]

4.2.3 Consequential explanations

As with history's consequences for society, a single event may have two or more consequences in the natural world. Text [4:11] explains three consequences of clearing the woodlands of southern Australia: death of remaining trees, erosion of land, and destruction of habitat.

[4:11] Woodlands of the south

In southern Australia the woodlands have been cleared to plant crops like wheat and other cereals. Sheep and cattle are grazed on introduced pastures. When the land was first cleared small clumps of trees or single trees were left for shade. Today these trees are reaching the end of their lives and dying.

The clearing of the trees has caused problems in using the land for farming. Without trees the land has been eroded by wind and rain. Today farmers are replanting the trees to try to stop this erosion.

Animals like the common dunnart rely on the fallen logs for shelter. The logs of old trees have hollows in them and the small animals of the woodlands hide in these. If these logs are cleared and removed the animals no longer have places to shelter.

Scott & Robinson 1993: 114

Each consequence is a phase here. The first is announced by time *When the land was first cleared….* The second and third are given their own paragraphs. The phasal structure and causal relations are diagrammed in Figure 4.15.

Here the Phenomenon is not an effect, as we have seen in other explanations, but the cause of three effects. In the first and second phases of the explanation, consequential relations are implicit in the field, i.e. that clearing occurred many decades ago, and that stopping erosion is in farmers' interest. The causal relation between clearing and erosion is realised within one sentence as a phrase *without trees*. In the third phase, the field is made very explicit, and the consequential relation is modalised as conditional 'if'. As each consequence follows independently from the cause, consequential explanations have an orbital structure, with the cause as nucleus, diagrammed in Figure 4.16.

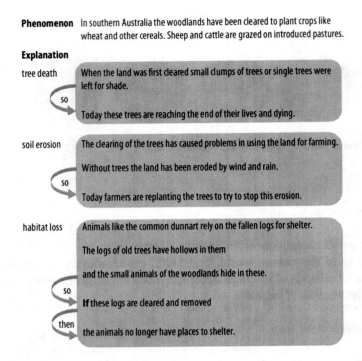

Figure 4.15 Implication sequence in consequential explanation [4:11]

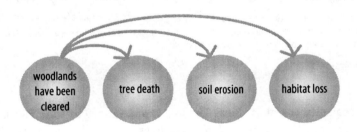

Figure 4.16 Orbital structure of consequential explanation [4:11]

4.2.4 Conditional explanations

Like other types of explanations, conditional explanations imply obligatory relations between events, but they construe effects as contingent on variable factors. Text [4:12] explains what happens to animal populations under three conditions:

if predators are absent, if prey are too few, and if numbers of both predator or prey fall and build up again.

[4:12] Predator and prey population numbers

Population size of one species can be affected by the size of the population of another species. This is true in the case of a predator species and the prey species on which it feeds. Over time, several outcomes are possible:

- If the predators are absent, the prey population will increase exponentially but will eventually 'crash' when its numbers become too high to be supported by the food resources in the habitat.
- If the prey population is too small, the predator population will starve and die. In some cases, cycles of 'boom-and-bust' can be seen in both populations, with the peak in the predator population occurring after the peak in the prey population. Why?

Kinnear & Martin 2004: 15

In conditional explanations the Phenomenon typically generalises the variability of causation, as in *can be affected*, and the contingency of effects is often explicit, as in *several outcomes are possible*. Here the first two conditional phases are demarcated as dot points, while the third asks student readers to hypothesise the condition for the *'boom-and-bust'* effect. Phases and relations are set out in Figure 4.17.

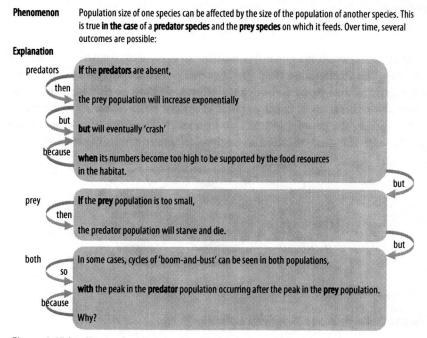

Figure 4.17 Implication sequence in consequential explanation [4:11]

Here we have interpreted the relation between each condition as internal contrast, glossed with 'but'. The relation between these and the generalisation is lexical: *in the case of a predator species and the prey species* is repeated as *If the predators* and *If the prey*. In the first Explanation phase, the chain of reasoning involves three causal steps following the condition, the obligatory 'then', concessive 'but' and consequential 'because'. Likewise the second phase involves obligatory 'then' following the condition. The third phase presents a possible effect *In some cases...*, and asks the student reader to imagine a condition.

Conditional explanations are found across all technical fields in varying forms. Another illustration, text [4:13] is from secondary school physics, explaining why objects sink or float in fluids.

[4:13] Buoyancy and Density

If the object is completely submerged it displaces its own volume of fluid. The weight of displaced fluid, and therefore the upthrust, will depend on the density of the fluid.

If the density of the fluid is less than the average density of the object, the weight of the displaced fluid will be less than the weight of the object and the object will sink.

If, on the other hand, the density of the fluid is greater than the average density of the object, the weight of the displace fluid will therefore exceed the weight of the object. The net upward force will then cause the object to rise to the surface where it will float.

Heading 1967

Here the Phenomenon is a general condition for buoyancy, *upthrust will depend on the density*. The Explanation then specifies two possible conditions, less or greater density, causing two possible buoyancy effects, sinking or floating. The contrast between the conditions is made explicit as *on the other hand*. As the conditions together specify the generalisation, conditional explanations also have an orbital structure, with the generalisation as nucleus, diagrammed in Figure 4.18.

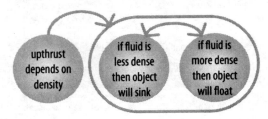

Figure 4.18 Orbital structure of conditional explanation [4:13]

A comparable generic structure is described by Unsworth 1997 for explanations of the seasons. One such implication sequence is extracted as text [4:14].

[4:14] Seasons of the Earth

As a result of the tilt of the Earth's axis the southern hemisphere is inclined towards the sun in December and away from the sun in June. When the southern hemisphere tilts towards the sun, it receives more of the sun's rays at an angle closer to 900 and it experiences summer. During this time the northern hemisphere points away from the sun and is experiencing winter. When the southern hemisphere tilts away from the sun, most of the sun's rays strike the Earth obliquely and their heating effect is less. During this time the southern hemisphere has its winter. The northern hemisphere at the same time points toward the sun and has its summer.

This implication sequence is diagrammed in Figure 4.19. The two conditions are the southern hemisphere tilting towards or away from the sun, and the effects are summer or winter. Each is also expanded with the effect on the northern hemisphere. Again we have interpreted the relation between the two as contrast with 'but', and again their relation to the generalisation is lexical.

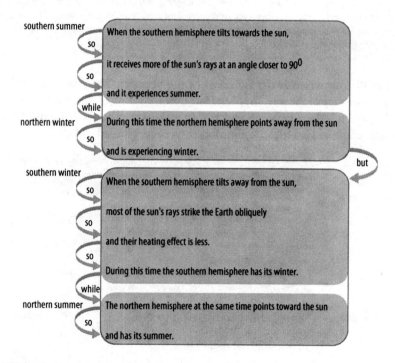

Figure 4.19 Implication sequence of seasons explanation [4:14]

4.2.5 Technological explanations

Explanations are not only used in science for explaining natural process; they are also common in industry for explaining technological processes, and follow very similar discourse patterns. The following [4:15] is a technological explanation from a manual for operating part of a blast furnace in a steel mill. Steel is produced by burning massive quantities of coal, and hot combustible gas is discharged in this process. A large chamber called a brassert is used to cool and clean the gas so it can be used in other activities of the steel mill.

> **[4:15] Brassert**
>
> The main function of the brassert is to cool down the blast furnace gas discharged from the furnace and to also partially remove dust and grit from the gas. To achieve this increased gas cleanliness, the gas must pass through the brassert at a reasonably slow velocity. Thus, the semi clean gas enters the bottom section of the brassert via a main from the dustcatcher.
>
> Inside the brassert two ring mains (top and bottom sprays) supply salt water to the brassert sprays. There are 24 sprays on each ring main, each spray projecting into the brassert. The primary salt water is supplied to the top ring main by one of two (2) pumps, located in the recirculating fresh water (RFW) pumphouse, located under the emergency head tank. Secondary salt water is supplied to the lower ring main from the power house. The water sprays in the brassert cools the gas stream and also combines with the gas, dust, etc, and precipitates (by gravity) at the base of the brassert. The mud precipitated is periodically removed by the brassert dump valves located at the base of the brassert. (Abeysingha 1991)

Here the Phenomenon is the function of the brassert. The Explanation involves four phases, entry of the gas, supply of salt water, cooling of the gas, and removal of mud. Logical relations between and within phases are shown in Figure 4.20. Here temporal relations also include simultaneous time, glossed as 'while'.

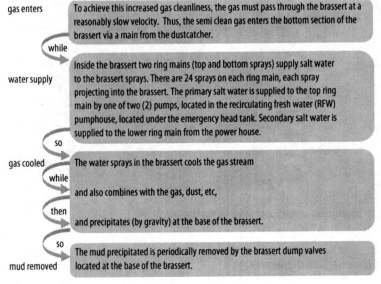

Figure 4.20 Implication sequence in technological explanation [4:15]

This technological explanation displays similar discourse patterns to the geography explanation of wetland formation [4:6]. It is sequential, and causal and temporal relations are often implicit. Furthermore in both the geography and technology explanations, substances move through a series of locations. In [4:6] water was associated with the escarpments, flood plains, sand ridges and wetlands. Here gas, water and mud pass through various locations within and outside the brassert. As the explanation of lowland freshwater wetlands was embedded in the Top End topography, here the explanation of gas cooling in the brassert is embedded in the topography of the blast furnace. Alongside explaining it realises a composition taxonomy of its components, shown in Figure 4.21

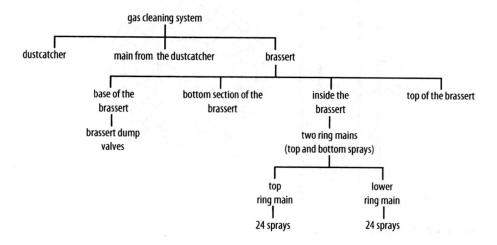

Figure 4.21 Composition taxonomy realised in technological explanation

The composition of the gas cleaning system realised in the explanation is re-expressed as a series of diagrams in the operating manual, one of which is shown in Figure 4.22. On the left the tall brassert structure is shown in a cut-away elevation view, with the *gas outlet* labelled at the top, then the *2 ring mains*, labelled as *top sprays* and *bottom sprays*, then the gas inlet (*from the dustcatcher*) in the *bottom section*, with the *dump valve* at the *base of the brassert*. On the right is a plan view of the *brassert spray arrangement*, showing the *24 sprays* of the *top ring main* and *lower ring main*.

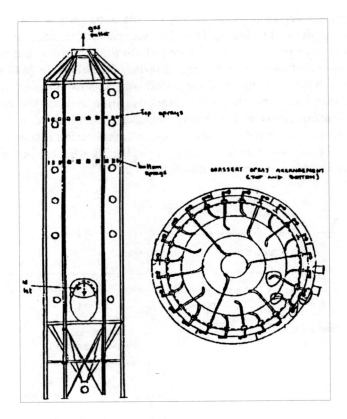

Figure 4.22 Brassert spray arrangement

4.3   Genres in science

Although the focus of this chapter has been on reports and explanations, we have been particularly interested in their roles in science, and have also introduced some other genres used in science. As we did for history, we can construct a typology of these genres, but this time based on criteria most relevant to the field of science. A key difference between reports and explanations is the role of time in their structuring: explanations construe sequences of activities, while reports are focused on entities, organised by classification and composition, rather than unfolding time. This structuring principle can also be extended to other genres used in science: time structured genres also include procedures, and procedural recounts (Chapter 5) and historical recounts (Chapter 3); non-time structured genres also include expositions and discussions (Chapter 3). This typology of genres in science is set out in Figure 4.23.

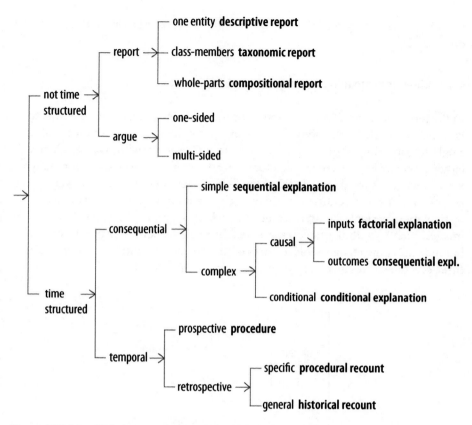

Figure 4.23 A typological perspective on relations between genres in science

4.4   Multimodal reports and explanations

Written reports and explanations in science and technology fields are rarely found without accompanying illustrations in the form of diagrams, charts, photographs, line drawings and maps, that support the reader to interpret the verbal text. Conversely, such visual supports can rarely stand alone without verbal text to explain them. In any textbook there is a complex set of relations between verbal and visual components of such multimodal texts, that may be left implicit for the reader to infer. In this section we will describe multimodal reports and explanations from three perspectives: firstly types of ideational meanings construed by visual images (following Kress & van Leeuwen 1996, O'Toole 1994, Unsworth 2001a); secondly types of textual organisation characteristic of visual images (following Kress & van Leeuwen 2006), and thirdly types of relations between visual and verbal genres in multimodal texts, using Halliday's 2004 logicosemantic categories. As reports and explanations are focused on technical fields, we have set aside interpersonal meanings enacted by technical images at this point (cf Martin 2001c, 2004c for discussion).

4.4.1 Ideational meanings construed by visual images

In the terms developed in this chapter, the focus of visual images in scientific texts is either on entities – classifying or de/composing them, or on activities – either a single activity (simple) or a sequence (complex). Categories within an image may be either explicitly labelled, or implicit for the reader to infer – from the accompanying verbal text or assumed knowledge of the field. Images may also be relatively iconic representations of an entity or activity, such as a photograph or realistic drawing, or they may be symbolic representations such as diagrams. In between, indexical images, such as outline drawings, are neither realistic icons, nor purely symbolic, but indicate some recognisable features of the represented entity or activity.[2] These three sets of features give the options in Figure 4.24.

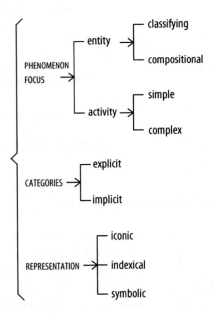

Figure 4.24 General options in technical images for ideational meanings

A classifying image that is explicit and iconic is Figure 4.25, which classifies types of environment in Australia's Western Desert, with realistic drawings. Each landscape type is labelled with its Pitjantjatjara name: *puli* (rocky ranges), *kurku* (mulga plains), *pana* (grass plains), *tali* (sand ridges), *karu* (creeks and rivers) and *pantu* (salt lakes).

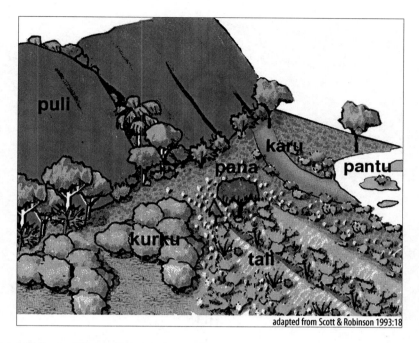

adapted from Scott & Robinson 1993:18

Figure 4.25 Types of Western Desert environment

This iconic classifying image can be contrasted with <u>symbolic</u> classifying images such as the system networks in Figure 4.23, and those used throughout *Genre Relations* to classify genres. In these diagrams, a single left entry condition with multiple right exit features symbolises the relation of class to members, as shown in Figure 2.26.

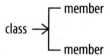

Figure 4.26 System network: an explicit symbolic classifying image

A compositional image which is explicit and indexical is Figure 4.4, reproduced here, that indicates parts of the human circulatory system in outline form, with labels for the heart and blood vessels. Another is Figure 4.22 above, that indicates the parts of the brassert spray arrangement as a cutaway diagram, with labels for the various sprays.

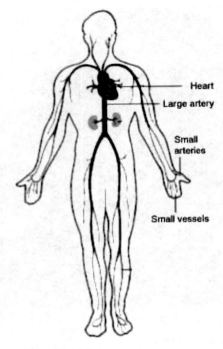

Figure 4.4' Explicit, abstract compositional image

A compositional image which is explicit and symbolic is the compositional taxonomy of parts of the circulatory system in Figure 4.5, reproduced here. In this tree diagram, a single top entry point with multiple lower features symbolises the relation of whole to parts.

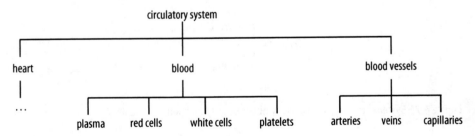

Figure 4.5' Compositional taxonomy in text [4:5]

An implicit iconic compositional image is Figure 4.1, reproduced here, which displays the parts of a goanna in pictorial form without labels; rather each part is assumed from the associated verbal descriptive report [4:1]. Another implicit iconic compositional image is

Figure 4.3 above, that displays components of the mangrove forest without labels, specifically the grey mangrove trees that are identified in the associated verbal report.

adapted from Scott & Robinson 1993:44

Figure 4.1' Goanna species described in text [4:1]

Activities are construed in technical images by means of vectors. These are made explicit in technical diagrams with lines and arrows with labels. A complex activity image that is explicit and symbolic is the explanation of DNA formation in Figure 4.9, reproduced here, in which four labelled vectors indicate chemical activities that produce each structure in the sequence. In addition all of the diagrams we used to illustrate the structures of explanations, in section 4.2 above, are explicit symbolic complex activity images. Vectors in these diagrams include logical relations between activities, as well as serial and orbital relations between genre stages.

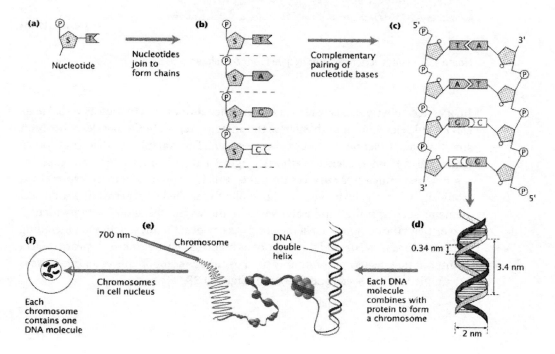

Figure 4.9' Deoxyribose nucleic acid

Vectors may be implied by the direction of a body or gaze. For example, in Figure 4.27 from a geography textbook, a researcher's gaze is directed towards the spinifex grass plain lying before her. The accompanying verbal text explicates this gaze as the activity of field work. As it construes a single activity this photograph is a simple activity image that is implicit and iconic.

The mulgara at Uluru National Park

Fig 3.5
Lynn Baker doing field work in the spinifex plains which overlie a buried river system.

Scott & Robinson 1993:54

Figure 4.27 Implicit vector indicated by gaze (Scott & Robinson 1993:54)

Images need not be exclusively focused on either entities or activities, as verbal texts can include elements of both, such as the anatomy report [4:5], that describes both structures and functions of the circulatory system. For example, the following double page spread from a science textbook (Figure 4.28) includes a diagram explaining how the mulga tree survives droughts; this is a complex activity, represented iconically as a realistic drawing, and is explicitly labelled (it also includes indexical elements such as sunray and water vectors). But within this global activity focus it also displays the components of the mulga tree relevant to these activities, including its leaves, flowers, seeds, and the shape of its branches. Furthermore Unsworth 2001a points out that insets are commonly used to enlarge components of an image, as is exemplified for the seeds and flowers in Figure 4.28.

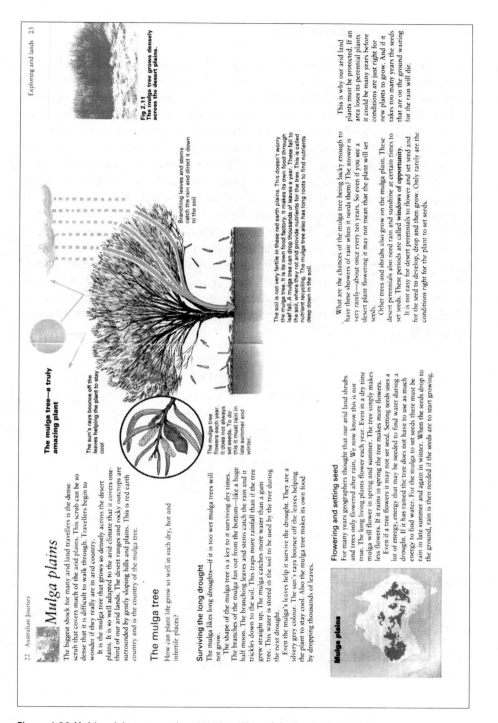

Figure 4.28 Multimodal reports and explanations (Scott & Robinson 1993: 21–2)

4.4.2 Textual organisation of images

Kress & van Leeuwen 2006 identify five types of structures that can contribute to the textual organisation of images, and form the basis of our framework here (with some fine-tuning of interpretation and terms).[3] Firstly the centre-margin axis may indicate the relative relevance of elements; the more central the image, the more relevant it may be to the text as a whole. Secondly, the left-right axis of an image may indicate whether the information it presents is given or new, where given means that some aspect of the image is presumed from the preceding text or the context (e.g. reader's field knowledge), and new means the information may be unknown to the reader. Thirdly the top-bottom axis may indicate whether the substance of an image is more ideal or more real, where the ideal can mean a generalised 'essence', while real is more specific, down-to-earth or practical. Fourthly, the strength of boundaries between image and text may indicate stronger or weaker classification of meanings. And fifthly, the relative salience of images on a page, that draws readers' attention to one image before another, may be indicated by a number of factors, including size, colour intensity, the strength of vectors, as well as centre-margin, left-right, top-down positions. These options in textual organisation are set out in Figure 4.29.

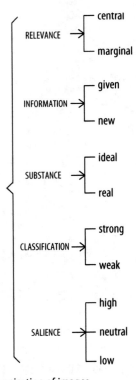

Figure 4.29 Options for textual organisation of images

These options are summarised in Table 4.2.

Table 4.2 Options for textual organisation of images

RELEVANCE	central	more relevant to text as a whole
	marginal	relevant to few elements of text
INFORMATION	given	presumed from preceding pages or context
	new	unknown to the reader
SUBSTANCE	ideal	generalised essence of information
	real	specific, down-to-earth or practical information
CLASSIFICATION	strong	visual text strongly bounded from verbal text
	weak	elements of visual text intrude into verbal text
SALIENCE	high	attracting attention before other elements
	neutral	equal prominence with other elements
	low	other elements attract attention first

We can illustrate each of these axes with respect to the double page spread in Figure 4.28 above. Firstly the relation between the large central and small marginal images is clearly one of relative salience. The reader's attention is drawn first to the central diagram, which is given maximal salience by its large size and central positioning, as well as colour intensity and vector strength, while the map and photograph are small, marginal, low key, and so less salient. In terms of relevance, the central diagram has by far the greatest relevance, as it restates four factors of the verbal explanations (sun rays, catching rain, falling leaves, flowers and seeds), whereas the marginal map and photograph are only relevant to one element each of the verbal report (further discussion below).

In terms of information, the map at lower left is a repeated motif in each section of this textbook on Australian landscapes, so in this respect it is given information. In contrast the photograph on the top right is probably the first image that many students have seen of mulga trees in arid lands, so is presented as new information. Perhaps because the map is given, it has a title but no caption, so that its relation to the verbal text must be inferred, whereas the photograph has a caption that explicitly reiterates the verbal text.

In terms of substance, the central diagram is also positioned at the top of the page. It is an ideal set of meanings, in that it construes a relatively abstract set of relationships not accessible to commonsense observation. However the top-bottom positioning of the smaller images appears to be dictated more by marginality than a real-ideal contrast, since if anything the photograph may be considered more 'real' than the map. And finally in terms of classification, boundaries between visual and verbal texts are generally strong, except for the inset showing flower and seeds, which intrudes into the text, drawing attention to its relation to the relevant explanation below. The values in these axes are summarised in Figure 4.30.

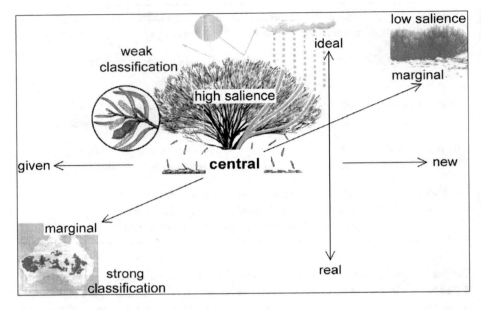

Figure 4.30 Textual organisation of double page (Figure 4.28)

4.4.3 Logical relations between visual and verbal texts

Multimodal texts such as Figure 4.28 consist of a set of smaller verbal and visual texts, of varying genres. There are three visual components: a map, a diagram and a photograph, with accompanying verbal captions. The map is an explicit indexical compositional image, showing mulga plains as a component of the Australian continent. The photograph is an implicit iconic classifying image showing the species of mulga trees. The diagram, as we have discussed above, is an explicit complex activity image explaining how the mulga survives droughts.

And there are three verbal texts. The first is a descriptive report headed *Mulga plains that* describes the salient features of this landscape type; the second headed *The mulga tree* is a factorial explanation (analysed as text [4:10] above); and the third

Flowering and setting seed is a conditional explanation that explains the conditions under which the mulga will reproduce. Each of these verbal and visual texts are related to each other by logicosemantic relations of expansion or projection (see section 1.5.3 in Chapter 1). To begin with relations between the verbal texts: the report *Mulga plains* is enhanced by the explanation *The mulga tree* by explaining how mulga survives; and *Flowering and setting seed* adds a further explanation. (It could have been explicitly added with the conjunction 'furthermore'.)

On the other hand, the visual texts elaborate the verbal texts, restating (in another form) summarising (in less detail), specifying (in more detail) or repeating certain meanings. The quality 'mulga tree grows so densely' in the verbal report *Mulga plains* is specified by the photograph, showing exactly what it looks like, which is in turn summarised by its caption 'The mulga tree grows densely across the desert plains'. The lexical repetition between verbal report and image caption also contributes to the cohesion of the multimodal text as a whole. Secondly, the spatial extent 'covers one third of our arid lands' in the descriptive report *Mulga plains* is specified by the map, that shows exactly which third it covers, and this is summarised by the map's title *Mulga plains*.

Thirdly several factors in the explanation *The mulga tree* are elaborated in the central diagram. At the top, vectors between the sun and tree restate the activity 'sun's rays bounce off the leaves', and these words are repeated in the caption to left of the diagram. At the right, the vectors from schematised clouds to branches to ground restate the activity 'branching leaves and stem catch the rain and it trickles down to the soil'. Again these words are repeated in the caption to the right of the diagram. At the bottom, the implicit vector of falling leaves restates the activity 'dropping thousands of leaves'. This factor is then explained in greater detail in the caption at bottom.

And fourthly, the activities of 'flowering and setting seed' in the next verbal explanation are specified by the inset image, and summarised in the associated label. So logical relations between verbal and visual texts are elaborating (restating, summarising, specifying or repeating). The captions attached to images further elaborate the image in these ways, or enhance it by explaining, and captions may also repeat elements of the associated verbal texts. These relationships are summarised in Table 4.3, and diagrammed in Figure 4.31 (*overleaf*).

This has not been an exhaustive survey of possible logicosemantic relations between visual and verbal texts. For example, relations may also include extension (and/or), as well as other kinds of enhancement (time/manner/place). Rather the aim here has been to illustrate the potential for analysis using the criteria we have developed in this section.

Table 4.3 Logical relations between verbal and visual texts in Figure 4.27

verbal text		visual text	caption
Descriptive report Mulga plains			
dense scrub	= specify	photograph implicit iconic	= summarise
covers one third of our arid lands	= specify	map implicit indexical	= summarise
x (explaining causes)			
Factorial explanation The mulga tree		diagram	
sun's rays bounce off the leaves	= restate	vectors explicit symbolic	= restate
branching leaves and stem catch the rain and it trickles down to the soil	= restate	vectors explicit symbolic	= restate
dropping thousands of leaves	= restate	vectors implicit iconic	x explain
+ (adding another factor)			
Conditional explanation Flowering and setting seed			
flowers and seeds	= specify	inset drawing implicit iconic	= summarise

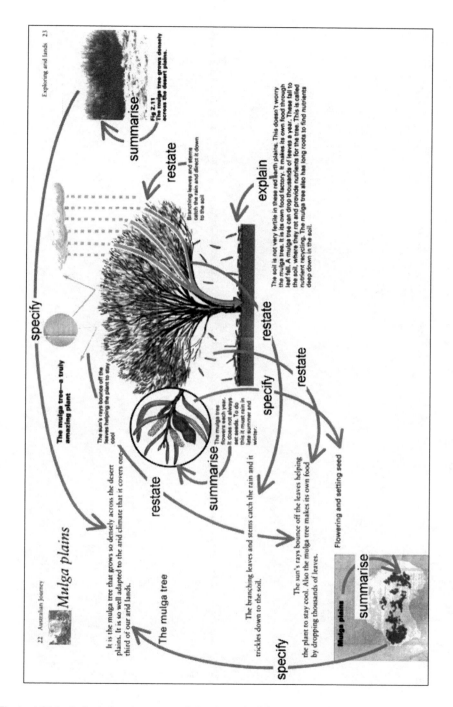

Figure 4.31 Logical relations between verbal and visual texts (in Figure 4.28)

5 Procedures and procedural recounts

While Chapter 4 was concerned with genres that describe and explain the world, here we are concerned with genres that direct us how to act in it. Procedures are a central feature of many contexts: domestic, recreational, educational, scientific and industrial. We will illustrate a few of these variations here, but our particular concern is with procedures and procedural recounts used in the workplace, and their relationships to education. This focus emerges from a major research project on literacy in science and science based industries, which mapped relations between writing at each level of industry, from the factory floor to research laboratories, with writing at each stage of the science educational sequence, from primary school to doctoral research (Rose 1997, 1998, Rose et al 1992, Veel 1997, 1998). After grounding the discussion in some procedures of the household, recreation and school, including Indigenous Australian contexts, we will trace this industrial hierarchy, from simple to increasingly more complex operating procedures in industry, and then to the procedural recounts that technicians and scientists use to effect changes in scientific knowledge and its applications.

The texts we use to illustrate this journey are from the steel mills of Australia's biggest company, BHP. At the time of the research in the early 1990s, BHP steel manufacturing was engaged in a huge program of restructuring and retraining of its workers. Thousands of jobs that had hitherto been learnt through demonstration and practice were now being codified in manuals, and workers who had immigrated over preceding decades, from poor agricultural backgrounds with minimal education, now had to learn to read these manuals to keep their jobs. This was part of larger national and global process of industry restructuring, which is having far-reaching effects on education, from vocational strands in secondary schools, to an upwards shift in qualifications at all levels of vocational and professional training (e.g. Bernstein 1996, 2000, Harvey 1989, Gee et al. 1996, Golding et al 1996, Lankshear et al. 1997, Muller 2000, National Training Board 1991, Taylor et al 2000). After spending millions of its own and taxpayers money on retraining its workers, BHP has now retrenched most of them and moved their work overseas where manual labour is cheaper and the profits larger. But the pedagogising of work, the shift from hands-on to formal training, continues around the world, and with it grows the need to read the genres illustrated here.

5.1 Procedures: directing specialised activities

Procedures are pedagogic texts in that they teach the reader how to perform a specialised sequence of activities in relation to certain objects and locations. This activity sequence has a specialised function in the culture, instrumental or ritual, and requires esoteric knowledge to be performed – expert mentoring is required. Some procedures can in principle be demonstrated without a verbal text, simply by performing each step while the learner watches. But in practice, demonstrations are almost always accompanied by verbal instruction. If we think of any activity we have shown to others, or been shown ourselves, we will be hard pressed to think of one without verbal accompaniment (see Muller 2000: 75-93, Painter 1984, 1998) Written procedures go a step further than this to mediate the author's expertise, directing the learner what to do at each step, in relation to explicitly named objects and locations. Oral procedures accompanying an activity need not be so explicit, as processes, objects, locations and the sequence itself can be indicated with reference items, 'now do this here'.

5.1.1 Everyday procedures

Procedures accompanying an activity are the principal way in which learners are instructed by experts to perform specialised activities across cultures. The pedagogic relation is direct, personal, here and now (see Gamble 2004 on craft pedagogies). The following example, text [5:1], is from the Indigenous hunting-gathering culture of Australia's Western Desert. The language is Pitjantjatjara and the speaker is instructing a learner how to dig out the nests of *tjala* honey ants,

Figure 5.1 *tjala* honey ant

shown in Figure 5.1. This species stores honey in the distended abdomens of certain individuals in chambers a metre or more underground. To find the chamber the digger must recognise and follow a tiny tunnel that twists and turns, and dig and place the earth very carefully, and it is these activities that require expertise. In [5:1] the speaker directs the learner where to dig and place earth, and how to recognise the ants' tunnel. Objects and locations are not named but indicated with reference items, in bold in both the Pitjantjatjara and English translations.

[5:1] Digging for *tjala*

*piruku   wati-wani   **nyangatja***
more   across-throw-!   here
Again throw (the earth) **over here!**

***palatja**   kura-ring*
that   bad-become
That's no good.

*nya-wa   **nyangatja**   wirunya*
look-!   this   good
Look, **this** is good.

nyaratja-lta**   nyina-nyi   **paluru
yonder-at.that   sit-PRES   it
There **it** is, **over there.**

***munkarra**   ma-tjawa*
other side   away-dig-!
On the **other side**, dig **over there**.

***nyangatja**   katja*
here   son
Here, son.

*tjinguru   **nyarangka**   nyina-nyi   urilta*
maybe   yonder   sit-PRES   outside
Maybe it's **over there**, on the **outside**.

*uwa   ala palatja   **pala palu-la**   arka-la*
yes   'as I said'   there that-at   try-!
Yes, you see, try **that there!**

from Rose 2001a

In this sequence, activities are directed with imperative commands (marked with -!), and evaluations are given (*that's bad, this is good*) and attention directed (*there it is, maybe it's over there*) with statements. An advantage of oral instruction accompanying activity like [5:1] is that the procedure can be continually adjusted to match the particular condition of each step of the activity, and the learner's actions can be directed, monitored and corrected as required. A disadvantage with such instructions is that they can only be given as the activity is performed. There is no way we could interpret the activity simply from the transcription here. Written procedures overcome this limitation, but the cost is that at each step, the process, objects, and locations must be explicitly named, and the activity must follow a specific sequence.

Perhaps the most widely experienced written procedures are cooking recipes, which import the specialised context of culinary arts into the domestic kitchen. These consist of two stages, typically titled Ingredients and Method or Instructions. The following example [5:2] instructs the kitchen gourmet in how to cook kangaroo meat.

[5:2] Kangaroo Fillet With Redcurrant Reduction Sauce

Ingredients

100 – 130g (3 – 4 oz) kangaroo fillet (or strip loin) per person
1 tsp (1/6oz) olive oil
2 cups (16oz) low-salt (gluten-free) beef stock
1 cup (8oz) red wine
3–4 tsp (1/2oz) redcurrant jelly

Instructions

1   Brush kangaroo with olive oil and pan-fry over high heat to seal until brown on all sides.
2   Place on a baking tray and roast at 200 C (375 F) for 5 minutes.
3   Meanwhile pour remaining ingredients into frying pan and boil over high heat until reduced to a thick and syrupy sauce.
4   Remove kangaroo from oven, cover with foil and rest for 10 minutes.
To serve: Slice kangaroo and spoon over sauce.
          Serve with sliced potatoes cooked in the oven until crunchy and a steamed green vegetable such as asparagus.

Milan 1999

Like the instructions for finding *tjala*, this recipe entails a sequence of imperative commands for acting on various objects in a series of locations. All these elements must be made explicit for the novice kangaroo cook. In Indigenous Australian cultures preparation of kangaroo meat is equally prescribed, by religious tradition rather than culinary authority (cf Levi-Strauss 1978); but it is learnt like the *tjala* activity, by repeated modelling and instruction in context, as the child is learning in Figure 5.2.[1]

Figure 5.2   Step 1 in kangaroo cooking: burn off the fur (photograph J.P. Reser in Horton 1994:532)

Another common context for procedures is tourist guides and promotions, that lead the reader through a series of locations. This group of procedures has been termed **topographic procedures**. The following example [5:3] from a tourist promotion uses the procedure patterns of activities, things and places to tell us what to expect on a tour at Uluru (Ayers Rock). The series of locations is in bold.

[5:3] Uluru Sunrise Climb and Base Tour

Rise early this morning to travel **to the Uluru sunrise viewing area.**

Watch the first rays of dawn set the Red Centre alight whilst enjoying a warming cup of tea or coffee.

After the sun has risen you will be transferred **to the base of the Uluru climb**…After the climb, join your AAT Kings Driver/Guide for a tour **around the base of Uluru.**

Travel by coach to the Mutitjulu Walk where you will be escorted **into the beautiful Mutitjulu Waterhole.**

View Aboriginal rock art and learn about the area as your Driver/Guide points out some native flora…

Travel **around the base of Uluru** in the comfort of the coach…

Visit **the Uluru-Kata Tjuta Cultural Centre**, where you can learn about Aboriginal culture…,

before returning **to Ayers Rock Resort.**

traveloneline.com 2004

This is of course a somewhat different experience of central Australia than that of the learner down a hole digging for *tjala*!

Closely related to the recipe genre are procedures for conducting science experiments and observations in schools. These typically include the stages **Equipment & materials** and **Method**. The following example [5:4] initially seems very close the recipe genre, as the first phase involves cooking.

[5:4] Chicken neck

For this exercise you will need the neck of a cooked chicken. Place the neck in a saucepan. Cover it with water. Add 3 tablespoons of vinegar or a teaspoon of detergent to the water. This should help you to loosen the meat on the neck.

When the water is cool remove the neck. Carefully take away as much of the meat as you can. You may need tweezers to help you. Wash the neck bones. Then gently dry them with tissue paper.

Now you can observe the chicken neck vertebrae. In your notebook write down what a vertebra looks like. Draw a picture of a vertebra.

Grossbard & 1978:36

Here the **Equipment & materials** stage is realised by the first line, followed by a series of steps in the **Method**. However the Method includes three phases distinguished by paragraphing, as follows:

[5:4']

Equipment & materials

For this exercise you will need the neck of a cooked chicken.

Method

cook	Place the neck in a saucepan.
	Cover it with water.
	Add 3 tablespoons of vinegar or a teaspoon of detergent to the water. This should help you to loosen the meat on the neck.
prepare	When the water is cool remove the neck.
	Carefully take away as much of the meat as you can. You may need tweezers to help you.
	Wash the neck bones.
	Then gently dry them with tissue paper.
observe	Now you can observe the chicken neck vertebrae.
	In your notebook write down what a vertebra looks like.
	Draw a picture of a vertebra.

In the cooking phase, [5:4] resembles a domestic recipe, but then the bones are prepared rather than the meat, using tweezers and tissues, and the last phase is clearly scientific experiment, both in the processes *observe, write, draw* and in the technical term *vertebrae*. In this it converges with the following procedure [5:5] from a geography textbook.

[5:5] **Observing desert ranges**

...

Step 1	Carefully observe Fig 2.8. Identify its main features. Write these down.
Step 2	Select a full page in your notebook...
Step 3	Look at Fig 2.8 again...Look carefully at the features...
Step 4	Use a pencil to sketch the important features you can observe in the background...
Step 5	Now sketch the important features you can observe in the middle ground...
Step 6	Now sketch the important features you can observe in the foreground...
Step 7	Line drawings are a summary of the observations you make. It is also important to make a summary of the major features in note form. This can be done by making notes around the line drawing...The headings which should appear on your page are Landforms, Vegetation, Soil and Refuge Islands.

Scott & Robinson 1993:21

Clearly 'observing, drawing and writing' are key processes in scientific activity, and scientific procedures function to direct learners to do them. As much as in the oral procedure [5:1], domestic recipes and so on, they are directed through a series of imperative commands, together with statements that classify and evaluate. But in Step 7 of [5:5] the imperative pattern shifts to a declarative pattern *It is also important to make a summary…, This can be done…, The headings which should appear…* Why? Because there is more than one possible course to follow, like the conditional explanations we saw in Chapter 4; so commands must be modulated to allow for these other possibilities. This problem and strategies for its solution recur throughout the following sections.

As we move up the educational and occupational hierarchy, from the factory floor to the research laboratory, workers' choices for actions diversify and more information is required to make decisions. All procedures dictate a sequence of activities, in relation to objects and locations, but sequences complexify, demanding action gives way to presenting information, and specialised tools give way to technical abstractions. These changing patterns are tracked in the following sections.

5.1.2 Operating procedures – steps in a specialised activity

Each of the texts we have show so far are varieties of simple procedures. Like recounts or sequential explanations they consist of a sequence of steps following each other in time. Likewise, at the lowest levels of the workplace hierarchy, simple procedures direct workers to operate technology. Minimal information is given about the technology; either workers do not need to know this information, or it is assumed that they already know it. These types of procedures are very common at the basic operator level of manufacturing, in the 'Standard Operating Procedures' (SOPs) written for process workers. In common with more complex procedures, simple procedures typically begin with a Statement of Purpose. This may be simply a title for the activity sequence, which embodies the purpose of the procedure as follows in [5:6].

[5:6] TO ISOLATE PRECIPITATOR ELECTRICALLY

Move the main isolator switch (CFS) in the precipitator switch room to the OFF position

and tag, 'OUT OF SERVICE'.

Lock the main isolator switch switching arm using 'Castell Key 2'

Remove the 'Castell Key 2'

and attach an 'OUT OF SERVICE' tag to the key identifying No 12 Tar Precipitator. Place the 'Castell Key 2' in the shift supervisor's office.

Coke Ovens By Products Department 1991

This simple procedure involves six steps. It is written for workers in a blast furnace of a steel mill. The workplace hierarchy is explicit in two ways: in the explicit detail for each step of the safety procedure, allowing no options for decision making, and in the last command to place the key *in the shift supervisor's office*. It differs from domestic procedures in the density of specialised terms associated with the technology. Such specialised terms can become quite complex, but the principles of their construction are regular. Each component of the technology is a member of a class of items, and is subclassified to the left of the item, such as *main isolator switch*. And each item can also include subcomponents, and these parts are de-composed to the right of the item, such as the *arm* of the *switch*. These patterns of classifying to the left and composing to the right are shown in Figure 5.3.

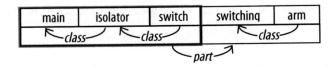

Figure 5.3   How specialised terms are constructed

Operating procedures are also very comon in domestic contexts for using domestic technology, including the ubiqitous VCR instruction manual as in [5:7].

[5:7] Basic Connections

It's essential that your video recorder be properly connected. Follow these steps carefully. THESE STEPS MUST BE COMPLETED BEFORE ANY VIDEO OPERATION CAN BE PERFORMED.

1   CHECK CONTENTS
    Make sure the package contains all of the accessories listed in 'Specifications' (pg. 47).
2   SITUATE RECORDER
    Place the recorder on a stable, horizontal surface.
3   CONNECT RECORDER TO TV
    The connection method you use depends on the type of TV you have.
    RF CONNECTION
    • To Connect To A TV With NO AV Input Terminals . . .
        a Disconnect the TV aerial cable from the TV.
        b Connect the TV aerial cable to the ANT. IN jack on the rear panel of the recorder.
        c Connect the provided RF cable between the RF OUT jack on the rear panel of the recorder and the TV's aerial terminal.

JVC 2000

Like the workplace procedure, the VCR instruction manual begins with a Purpose (*your video recorder be properly connected*), here also with a warning, and its Method includes a multitude of specialised terms within series of procedural steps (*RF connection, AV Input Terminals, TV aerial cable, ANT. IN jack, RF cable, RF OUT jack, aerial terminal*). Some of these specialised terms are defined visually by the accompanying diagram, Figure 5.4, and steps in the connection procedure are reiterated as vectors in the diagram. The complementarity here between the verbal and visual texts illustrates the point made in 4.4 above, that each may be required to successfully read the other. For the average reader, procedure [5:7] is not comprehensible without the accompanying diagram. Insofar as it explains the connection procedure by means of labelled vectors, the image is an explicit indexical complex activity. But it also includes compositional images of the technology, which are presented as iconic drawings, in order to be recognisable for laypeople.

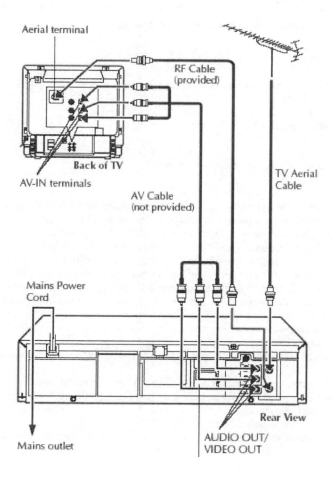

Figure 5.4 Connection diagram for VCR (JVC 2000)

5.1.3 Cooperative procedures: assigning responsibility in teamwork

Cooperative procedures differ from simple procedures in that the tasks prescribed require more than one operator to carry out, and each operator must be identified, as well as what is being acted on. In order to do this, cooperative procedures use a range of strategies to make various people and things explicit at the start of each command. Text [5:8] follows the technological explanation we saw in Chapter 4, about how gas is cooled and washed in the 'brassert washer' of a steel mill blast furnace [4:11]. That text finished with the statement *The mud precipitated is periodically removed by the brassert dump valves located at the base of the brassert.* Procedure [5:8] now directs workers to manually dump the brassert. As in the simple operational procedure [5:6], the first stage is also Purpose, explicitly labelled here, together with the 'scope' and 'definition' of the activity. The Method stage (labelled here as *5.0 Procedure*) is concerned with the technology and its operators, and these are identified at the beginning of each sentence, shown here in bold.

[5:8] Dumping Brassert Washer

1.0	Purpose
	The purpose of this procedure is to establish or outline the steps required in dumping the brassert washer under normal conditions.
2.0	Scope
	This procedure will apply to No 4 Blast Furnace
	[omitted]
4.0	Definitions
	Dump – remove some of the water seal from the brassert.
5.0	Procedure
5.1	Philosophy
	The brassert washer is the second mechanism in the gas cleaning plant at No 4 BF. **The water sprays** used in the gas cleaning process cause dust particles to precipitate out of the gas and form a sludge at the base of the brassert. **Some of this sludge** is not removed by the normal flushing process. **Dumping of the brassert** flushes this sludge out of the base, therefore preventing build up.
5.2	Two trained people are required to safely dump the brassert (one operator and one gas watcher).
5.3	**Operators** should liaise with the general supervisor to ensure the furnace is casting, in case difficulties arise in shutting the slide valves at the base of the brassert, resulting in an unscheduled furnace stop.
5.4	Control room attendant should be notified about intentions (for possible alarm).
5.5	One of the operators should equip himself with a co monitor.
5.6	Ensure no personnel are in the immediate area, such as staves platform and ground level around brassert sump (possibility of gas below).
5.7	Bottom slide valve on brassert cone to be opened fully and then closed (reason, to depressurise area between valves).
5.8	Top slide valve on brassert cone should be opened fully and then closed immediately.
5.9	Bottom slide valve on brassert cone should be opened fully until a turbulence is noted in the brassert sump and then closed immediately.
5.10	Ensure both valves are completely closed.
5.11	Notify general supervisor and control room attendant that dumping has been completed.

Abeysingha 1991

The Method stage (*5.0 Procedure*) includes three phases: *5.1 Philosophy* is a brief implication sequence that recaps and extends the explanation of how the mud accumulates; then 5.2–5.6 is a series of safety procedures; and finally 5.7–5.11 is the step-by-step procedure for dumping the brassert.

Unlike simple procedures, which tend to start each step with the activity to be performed, the starting point for most of the sentences here is with the technology or its operators. In the explanation phase it is the technology that produces the mud. In the safety procedure phase it is the workers: *Two trained people (one operator and one gas watcher), Operators, Control room attendant, One of the operators, no personnel, the general Supervisor.* This is the primary meaning of a cooperative procedure – it is a procedure which involves a team of workers at various levels. In the final phase it is the technology that is operated on: *Bottom slide valve, Top slide valve, both valves.* The cooperative procedure represents part of the communication network of a workplace, specifically those communications involved in performing a particular task. The diagram in Figure 5.5 models the communication network in text [5:8].

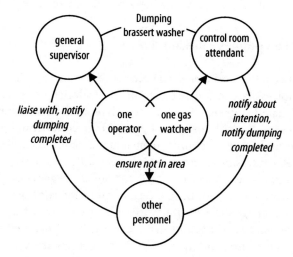

Figure 5.5 Communication network for dumping brassert

Another feature of cooperative procedures [5:8] is that many or most of the commands are followed by reasons for carrying out the commands. At this level of the workplace hierarchy, operators need to know these reasons in order to make independent decisions while carrying out the procedure, shown here in bold:

5.3 Operators should liaise with the general supervisor to ensure the furnace is casting, **in case difficulties arise in shutting the slide valves at the base of the brassert, resulting in an unscheduled furnace stop**.

5.4 Control room attendant should be notified about intentions (for possible alarm).

5.6 Ensure no personnel are in the immediate area, such as staves platform and ground level around brassert sump (possibility of gas below).

5.7 Bottom slide valve on brassert cone to be opened fully and then closed (reason, to depressurise area between valves).

In each of these clause complexes, the command comes first and the explanations follow. For reasons of space these explanations are very compressed. This textual pattern is maintained by the use of ideational metaphors. That is activities are re-expressed as nouns or phrases, and causal relations as verbs. For example 5.3 compresses a complex logical sequence into one sentence, in which 'difficulties arise' and 'unscheduled furnace stops result'. In order to unpack it to a more spoken form, the sequence must be reversed as follows (logical linkers in **bold face**):

Operators should liaise with the general supervisor **to** *ensure the furnace is casting,* **in case** *difficulties arise in shutting the slide valves* **resulting** *in an unscheduled furnace stop.*	'**If** it is difficult to shut the slide valves the furnace might stop unexpectedly **so** operators should liaise with the general supervisor **to** ensure the furnace is casting'

In order to understand and act on this cooperative procedure, operators must be able to unpack this kind of complexity, a literacy skill of a relatively high order.

5.1.4 Conditional procedures – making choices

Written procedures in the workplace can become very complex when the operator needs to make choices about a course of action. These decisions depend on what is happening in the manufacturing process, so at each point there are a number of possible decisions to take. We call this type of procedure a **conditional procedure.**

Text [5:9] is from another operating manual in the same steel mill blast furnace. The title gives its Purpose: *stop gas flow through precipitator.* As gas is produced from burning coal it contains tar, which is precipitated out as the gas cools. The pressure of the gas in the precipitator must be in a certain range for safe operation, and this pressure varies. To manage the pressure, workers have to operate three gas valves: a *bypass gas valve*, an *inlet gas valve*, and an *outlet gas valve.* What they do with them depends on the gas pressure, and the number of tar precipitators in operation.

While the title is the Purpose, the Method stage of [5:9] includes two phases: 1–3 are actions depending on the **number of tar precipitators**; 4–7 are actions depending on the **back pressure** that the exhauster driver has to monitor. The complex relations between the possible conditions in each phase and the alternative actions to take are managed by numbering.

In the simple operating procedure [5:6], numbering referred to temporal succession – each step was numbered and followed each other one after another. In the conditional procedure however, numbers do not refer steps in a sequence but rather to choices for action. The numbered steps *2–3 and 5–7* refer to commands that are not steps in a sequence but are **alternative** actions depending on the conditions. By referring to each of these alternative actions as a number, the commands within the

[5:9] STOP GAS FLOW THROUGH PRECIPITATOR

1 Check the number of the tar precipitators on line to assure an uninterrupted gas flow. Currently four (4) tar precipitators are the minimum number.that have to be on line to maintain an acceptable back pressure range of 8–14 kPa.
If after this precipitator is isolated:
i. There will be fewer than four (4) tar precipitators in operation, go to step 2.
ii. There are four (4) or more tar precipitators in operation, go to step 3.

2 Open tar precipitators bypass gas valve (5 or 6 turns).3 Close the inlet gas valve slowly, and tag, 'OUT OF SERVICE' in two positions:
- Rotork isolator with the lugs tied together,
- Manual valve handle.

4 Exhauster driver to monitor back pressure which must be in the acceptable range if enough precipitators are on line (Range 8–14 kPa).
If when the precipitator by pass gas valve is open:
i. Pressure range is OK, go to step 7
ii. Pressure range is too high, go to step 5
iii. Pressure range is too low, go to step 6.

5 Open the precipitator by pass gas valve until exhauster back pressure is in range.

6 Close tar precipitator by pass gas valve until exhauster back pressure is in range.

7 Close the outlet gas valve slowly, and tag, 'OUT OF SERVICE' in two positions:
- Rotork isolator with the lugs tied together,
- Manual valve handle.

Abeysingha 1991

preceding **conditional** sentences can be kept simple and regular – *(either) go to step 5... (or) go to step 7.* By this means, the conditional sentences focus on the decision to be made, while the following action sentences focus on each of the alternative tasks. These patterns are illustrated in Figure 5.6.

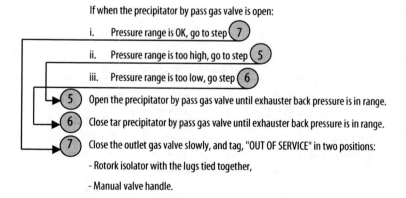

Figure 5.6 Relations between conditions and actions managed by numbering

Restating a procedure with a flowchart

The problem of complex procedures is addressed in many enterprises by the use of flowcharts. Flowchart diagrams translate the complex logical relations in a procedure into a conventional set of visual symbols. In the terms developed in section 4.4, they are explicit symbolic complex activity images. The visual symbols do not operate by themselves however – they link units of written text together, and ultimately any flowchart is dependent on an accompanying verbal text, as we saw for multimodal texts in science textbooks in Chapter 4.

The following flowchart Figure 5.7 restates the conditional procedure [5:9] to assist the learner. It translates the conditional and temporal conjunctions into labelled vectors. The key to reading the flowchart is as follows:

> each step in the procedure is enclosed in a box, with the title of the stage written on top,
> within each step, sub-steps are written and enclosed in smaller boxes,
> temporal succession between each step and sub-step is expressed as lines with arrows,
> decision points are written as questions, enclosed in diamonds with choices expressed as yes (Y) or no (N).

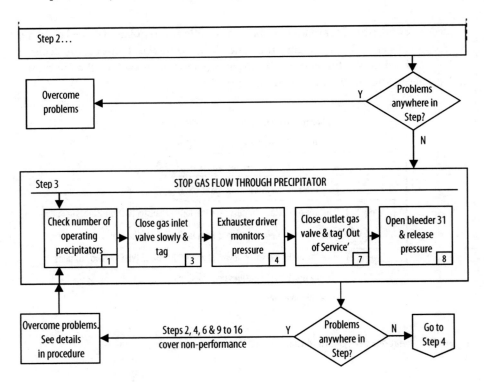

Figure 5.7 Tar Precipitator flowchart (from Abeysingha 1991)

The flowchart 5.7 is a combination of verbal and visual expressions of meaning. But the visual expression is ultimately dependent on the verbal text. The complexity of choices in the conditional procedure cannot be adequately handled in the visual text. So after the decision point *Problems anywhere in step?*, the reader is directed to the verbal procedure:

> *Steps 2, 5, 6 and 9 to 16 cover non-performance->Overcome problems see details in procedure*

Conditional procedures are also common within instruction manuals for domestic technology, as in [5:10].

[5:10] SET VIDEO CHANNEL

Set your TV to UHF channel 40.

- If the two vertical white bars appear clearly on the screen as shown in the illustration (Z "TEST SIGNAL" on page 4), press **OK** and then go to step **4**.

- If the two vertical white bars do not appear clearly, press **OK** and then **PR +** or **–** to set the video recorder to a vacant channel between 28 and 60 which is not occupied by any local station in your area.

    (Ex.)   If channel 50 is available in your area

    Then set your TV to UHF channel 50 and check if the two vertical white bars appear clearly on the screen;

- If so, go to step **4**.

- If not, re-set the video recorder to another vacant channel and try again.

Notes

- If you set the video recorder to a channel which is occupied by a local station or has neighbouring channels that are occupied by local stations, the picture reception quality will be affected and some interference noise will appear on the TV screen. Be sure to select a vacant channel which has no broadcast on neighbouring channels.

- If you cannot obtain the two vertical white bars clearly with any channel between 28 and 60, consult your JVC dealer.

JVC 2000

The patterns of conditions, dependent actions and numbering are uncannily similar between industrial and domestic operating procedures. The complex logical patterns of conditional procedures are also closely related to the conditional explanations we saw in Chapter 4. In both cases the reader is asked to imagine alternative possible eventualities. In the science explanations, these imagined events are intended to lead to students' understanding of abstract physical relationships. The way this understanding is achieved is through conditional relations between events. In the conditional procedure, the imagined events are possible outcomes of actions the operator might take, and the same strategy is used. Again this illustrates a strong functional relationship between literacy learning in middle secondary science, and the literacy demands of technical operations in manufacturing industry.

5.1.5 Technical procedures – applying technicality to technology

Technical procedures are typically used in scientific testing laboratories within manufacturing enterprises. Their function is to enable a technically trained worker to perform a testing procedure on manufacturing materials, using laboratory technology. Reading and acting on these procedures depends on an extensive apprenticeship into the language and field of science involved. The results of the testing are typically recorded by the technical assistant as figures on a pro-forma. These figures will be interpreted by a supervising technician who may write the results up as a technical note (described in the next section). The goal of a technical procedure is to obtain these figures. To do this the technical assistant must 1) prepare a material sample in the manner required by the testing technology, 2) operate the testing technology and record the numerical results, 3) follow a mathematical procedure to convert these numbers to useful figures. There are therefore three typical phases to the Method stage of a technical procedure:

> Sample preparation
> Testing procedure
> Calculation of results

[5:11] Crack examination

Objective

The objective of the test is to determine the extent of HAZ cracking.

Sample preparation

The test section shall be sectioned transverse to the weld joint, ground to a 1200 grit and etched with 2% nital. To assist metallographic examination, the test piece should be cut down to the approximate dimension shown in Fig. 2.

Testing

Crack examination is done by one of two methods, either using an optical microscope or a shadowgraph with a stage that has a digital readout. Firstly using the optical microscope, the microscope is set at 100x. First the vertical leg length of the weld is measured and expressed as a number of fields (fig 3). This leg length is measured from the top of the groove. Similarly the vertical crack length is measured and expressed as a number of fields (fig 3). Secondly using the shadowgraph a similar measure is used. Magnification is set at 100x. The vertical leg length and vertical crack length are measured using the digital readout. This gives the actual measurements in mm instead of in the field.

Results

The vertical crack length is expressed as a percentage of the vertical leg length (I/L) x 100. The four results obtained are averaged to give a result to the nearest 10%. This number is then taken to be the amount of cracking in the weld.

Metallurgical Technology 1991

These are illustrated as follows in the technical procedure [5:11].

The ***Sample preparation*** phase consists of four steps – *sectioned, ground, etched* and *cut down*. The ***Testing*** phase then consists of three subphases, first giving two options, and then the steps for each option in turn. The sequence of steps in this and the ***Results*** phase are shown in Figure 5.8 below.

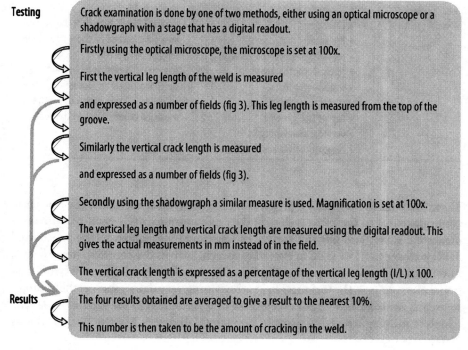

Testing

Crack examination is done by one of two methods, either using an optical microscope or a shadowgraph with a stage that has a digital readout.

Firstly using the optical microscope, the microscope is set at 100x.

First the vertical leg length of the weld is measured

and expressed as a number of fields (fig 3). This leg length is measured from the top of the groove.

Similarly the vertical crack length is measured

and expressed as a number of fields (fig 3).

Secondly using the shadowgraph a similar measure is used. Magnification is set at 100x.

The vertical leg length and vertical crack length are measured using the digital readout. This gives the actual measurements in mm instead of in the field.

The vertical crack length is expressed as a percentage of the vertical leg length (l/L) x 100.

Results

The four results obtained are averaged to give a result to the nearest 10%.

This number is then taken to be the amount of cracking in the weld.

Figure 5.8 Steps in a technical procedure [5:11]

The technical procedure thus has some commonalities with conditional procedures in that multiple options are possible. But it differs from the specialised procedures because the measurements taken are part of a technical field involving mathematics.

Specialised and technical fields

The technical procedure realises the interaction of a two specialised fields – 1) steel fabrication and 2) testing technology, with a technical field – scientific measurement. Extensive knowledge of these fields is assumed on the part of the reader, and additional information is provided to enable the task to be carried out. Terms and clauses that are part of each of these fields are listed in Table 5.1.

Table 5.1 Specialised and technical fields in [5:11]

specialised field 1: metal fabrication	specialised field 2: testing technology	technical field: scientific measurement
• HAZ cracking • test section • sectioned • weld joint	• crack examination • sample preparation • transverse • 1200 grit • 2% nital • metallographic examination • optical microscope • shadowgraph • vertical leg length • top of the groove • vertical crack length • magnification set at 100x	• expressed as a number of fields • measurements in mm instead of in the field • vertical crack length is expressed as a percentage of the vertical leg length (I/L) x100. • four results obtained are averaged • to give a result to the nearest 10%. • number is then taken to be the amount of cracking in the weld.

These three fields exemplify a progression from the most accessible (i.e., closer to commonsense) to the most technical (i.e., uncommonsense). Each field involves ideational metaphor, but the variety of ideational metaphors in the specialised fields is closer to those used in everyday speech, such as the common items *length, examination, preparation, magnification*. On the other hand the variety of ideational metaphors in the technical field is becoming very dense, such as the complex sequence *vertical crack length is expressed as a percentage of the vertical leg length*, which is moving towards scientific English (Halliday & Martin 1993, Halliday 2004).

5.2   Procedural recounts

Above the level of laboratory technicians, step-by-step procedures are relatively uncommon. These are the levels of 'professional' training, qualifications are diplomas to degrees, and workers no longer require detailed procedures to do their jobs. Instead they investigate technical problems, using their knowledge of the technical field and appropriate activities, and report on their investigations in the form of technical notes and research articles. Since both technical notes and research articles recount an investigative procedure, these are forms of procedural recount – a genre we looked at briefly in Chapter 4, in the context of school science. The relationship between procedure and recount is made explicit in the geography textbook *Australian Journey*: first the procedure [5:12].

[5:12] Investigating an arid lands mystery

Geographers are interested in land management issues that affect arid lands... To do this the geographer follows a number of steps:

Step 1 Identify the issue to be studied.
Step 2 Research the background to the issue.
Step 3 Go on the field trip. While on the field trip it is important to:
 • observe and
 • collect information.
Step 4 Use the observations to identify what is happening.
Step 5 Develop a plan to manage the environment.

This procedure is followed by a recount of field research by biologist Lynn Baker, written in terms accessible and appealing to junior secondary students. This is summarised as [5:13].

[5:13] The mulgara at Uluru National Park

Step 1 Identify the issue to be studied.

Before leaving on the field trip to Uluru National Park, Lynn identified the issue she wished to study and spent time researching it. 'I want to find out why mulgara appear to be in some areas and not in others. If I find that the mulgara are rare I want to be able to suggest ways to conserve their habitat.'

Step 2 Research the background to the issue

Lynn didn't just pack her bags and leave for Uluru. She spent time in the library reading what others have found out about arid zone animals....

Step 3 The field trip

...

The work involved in step 3 can be divided into two parts:
1 Making observations
2 Collecting and recording information

Observing the mulgara and its environment

During her first field trips to Uluru, Lynn spent time observing mulgara and the environments where it lives.

...

Collecting and recording information

Now Lynn needed to collect information that would help her find out why the mulgara seemed to be found in different habitats during times of high rainfall and during times of drought. Her first task was to collect data that showed where mulgara were living and where they were not living.

...

Using computer mapping to locate relict drainage environments

Earlier you learnt that old river systems can't be seen when walking over the ground. However, photographs taken by satellites, circling thousands of kilometres above the earth, do reveal these old rivers.

...

[5:13] (Contd)

Step 4 Use the observations to identify what is happening

Lynn's next step was to carefully study her observations to see what they told her... She started to develop a theory:

'The theory is that in the relict drainage area the vegetation remains in better condition than in areas outside its influence. This area is better able to support animals during drought. It becomes an important refuge area for animals like the mulgara during times of drought. The mulgara in this area are better able to survive than those living elsewhere. This is because the plants are able to collect the water from the underground drainage system. When it rains the habitat in the rest of the country improves. The mulgara are able to spread out over the country and I will find mulgara living away from this area again.'

...

Step 5 Develop a plan to manage the environment

Geographers conduct field work to help them decide on ways to manage the environment. When Lynn Baker's work is complete she wants to be able to suggest things that can be done to protect and save the mulgara. This means protecting the environments where it lives.

At this stage Lynn believes the refuge areas that are found in our arid lands must be protected, as the research so far suggests that small animals like the mulgara do rely on them in droughts. ...

Scott & Robinson 1993:54–58

These stages of the procedural recount follow the staging of the principal genres written by technical officers and research scientists – technical notes and research articles respectively. The stages of these genres are correlated with the steps of text [5:13] in Table 5.2. In addition the staging of **experiment reports** written by school science students is included. This type mirrors the experiment procedure patterns, but with a Results stage, as in the research article, sometimes followed by a Conclusion.

Table 5.2 Staging of procedural recounts

Technical Note	Introduction	(Method)	Investigation	Conclusion & Recommendation
Research Article	Introduction	Method	Results	Discussion
Experiment report	Purpose, Equipment & materials	Method	Results	(Conclusion)
Text [5:13]	1 Issue & 2 Background	3 Field trip: observation information	4 Identify what is happening	5 Develop a plan

The common goal of these genres is to improve understanding of a phenomenon and thereby resolve or avert a problem. To achieve this they begin by stating the issue/problem and contextualising this in current knowledge in the **Introduction**. The process of research is then recounted in the **Method** stage, observations are reported as **Results/Investigation** and interpreted in the **Discussion/Conclusion**. In technical notes which directly address application issues, this interpretation is then followed by a **Recommendation**. Clearly text [5:13] recontextualises a research report for secondary students. School science is sometimes criticised for alleged artificiality of experiments and procedural recounts, but the comparison here displays clear consistency between science, science industry and school. This is an important observation, as these fields have co-evolved and are interdependent in material production and production and reproduction of knowledge. In particular, science in school recontextualises not only the scientific fields, but the genres with which they are associated.

In the following three sections we describe these stages for technical notes in the specialised field of welding technology, in the technical field of metallurgy, and for research articles in the scientific field of industrial chemistry. All three are from the same industrial field as our procedures, that of steel manufacturing in Australia.

5.2.1 Specialised technical note – solving problems with technology

In materials and product testing areas of manufacturing enterprises it is necessary to produce written reports on testing to customers. These extended texts are typically known as technical notes. Technical notes are written by technicians and applied scientists, often with data recorded on pro-formas as the Results of technical procedures by technical assistants. The goal of the technical note is produce a set of Recommendations to the client on how to solve a specific production problem, or improve production processes.

Specialised technical notes are concerned with technological problems. Text [5:14] addresses problems with welding certain types of steel, and uses specialised knowledge of welding techniques to solve these problems. The steel mill produces coils of thin steel plate, and the ends of the coils need to be welded together. The particular steel plate produced for the electrical industry has a high content of silicon, and this makes welding very difficult.

[5:14] GTA Welds on hi-silicon coil plates without filler rod addition

Introduction

S&CP roll high silicon steel for applications in the electrical industry.

It is desirable to join coils for processing purposes, but the normal joining processes used by S&CP of flash butt welding has not proved capable of welding these high Si steels. The Welding Development Section of BHP SPPD was asked to evaluate alternative means of joining these coils. This report details results found during gas tungsten arc autogenous welding on four different grades of hi-silicon steel. The steels tested were LS07 (0.7%Si), LS13 (1.3%Si), LS22 (2.2%Si) and LS27 (2.7%Si).

Welder settings

The standard parameters used for the tests are tabulated below:

Gas type	Argon
Flow rate	30cu.ft/hr
Voltage	23–24v
Tungsten tip size	3.2mm ground to a 550 point
Nozzle size	ø 15mm gas cupped
Stand off	2.5mm

Investigation

Problems were encountered during this welding process with weld discontinuities occurring in most of the test pieces. Consistency of weld shape and form was difficult to achieve with burn through occurring both in welds showing good penetration as well as welds made at lower current levels which showed lack of penetration. We found that only a slight increase in amperage of say 5 amps, after a previous weld giving a good clean weld without full fusion, would cause the next weld to burn through with good weld penetration observed on intermittent sections. Tables 1 and 2 show results of weld trials while Rockwell B results are shown in Table 3.

Table 2 – GTA weld results

Conclusion & recommendation

From our weld trials we have proven that these steel grades are capable of being welded by the GTA process. However all process variables have to be 'spot on' to achieve consistent full penetration. We suggest further trial welding using an automatic filler wire feeder to produce more consistent welds. Unfortunately we do not have this equipment at present.

Drmota & Draper 1991

The Investigation stage recounts the procedure that was followed, but unlike the school text [5:13] or the recounts we looked at in Chapters 2 and 3, it does not consist of a series of clauses that follow each other in succession. Instead activity sequences are compressed into single sentences, as we saw for the cooperative procedure [5:8]. These can be unpacked as shown in Figure 5.9.

This activity sequence is packed into a single sentence by reconstruing processes as nouns (*a slight increase, a previous weld, full fusion, weld penetration*) and logical relations between processes as verbs (*giving, would cause*) or prepositions (*after, without, with*). These ideational metaphors allow a series of activities to be packed into nominal groups by means of post-modifying, shown as arrows in Figure 5.10.

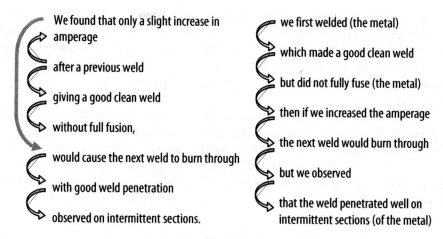

Figure 5.9 Activity sequence compressed in a sentence

nominal group					nominal group		
only a slight increase in amperage	after a previous weld	giving a good clean weld	without full fusion	would cause the next weld to burn through	with good weld penetration	observed on intermittent sections

Figure 5.10 Post-modifying in nominal groups

In scientific writing strings of post-modifiers can get very dense, and we find the beginning of this density in the technical note [5:14], such as the following:

welds showing good penetration

as well as welds made at lower current levels which showed lack of penetration.

Here two nominal groups are linked by *as well as* to form a complex that classifies two types of welds. These two classes of weld are expressed as a taxonomic diagram in Figure 5.11.

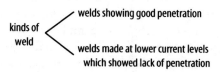

kinds of weld
welds showing good penetration
welds made at lower current levels which showed lack of penetration

Figure 5.11 Classifying in nominal groups

In both nominal groups the characteristics of the weld are the <u>criteria</u> for their classification and these criteria post-modify 'welds'. At this level of the industrial hierarchy we find a mixture of congruent and metaphorical resources used to represent the unfolding of time, and classification of entities. These two semantic domains are starting to coalesce into the same grammatical pattern of nominalisation and post-modification.

Following the recount of the Investigation, results are presented in a table, with numerical values for variations in welding, and verbal comments on the results. In the Conclusion stage, the writers take subjective responsibility for their investigation *We found, From our weld trials we have proven, We suggest further*. They also express feelings *difficult to achieve, a good clean weld, Unfortunately we do not have*. Above this level of industry such explicit personal intrusions become rare.

5.2.2 Scientific technical note – solving technical problems

Scientific technical notes are concerned with technical problems, and are written by applied scientists. Text [5:15] reports the results of chemical testing of a maintenance problem. Metal particles had been found in the oil of gearboxes that drive massive cranes in the steel mill, so the oil was not lubricating the gears properly. The job was find out what was wrong with the oil. It was found that the oil was contaminated with a cleaning compound that thinned it out, reducing its viscosity,and so its effectiveness as a lubricant.

The chemical testing itself would have been done by technical assistants or technicians who may record their results as figures in printed pro-formas, following technical procedures such as [5:8] above. The tertiary trained scientist then interprets these in a technical note with a Discussion and Recommendations for the client.

Like the specialised technical note, the goal of [5:15] is to solve an industrial production problem, and make recommendations for changes in manufacturing or maintenance processes. But a major difference between this and the specialised technical note is that it draws on a scientific field, industrial chemistry. The testing involves the use of technology for measuring 'viscosity' and 'chemical composition' (i.e. phenomena of the scientific field), and the results of these measurements are reasoned about scientifically to arrive at a conclusion and recommendations.

Again activity sequences tend to be compressed into single sentences, such as the implication sequence of observation and reasoning unpacked in Figure 5.12. However the implication sequence in [5:15] is more implicit than in the specialised technical note, in which temporal sequence is explicitly signalled by *after, previous, next*, and the verbs *caused to* and *observed* explicitly express causeand observation. Interpersonally, text [5:15] also effaces the people doing the investigation, shifting responsibility for judgements of cause and proof, from people *We observed* to the observation technique *Infrared examination of the oil suggested*. At this level

[5:15] SUBJECT: OPTIMUL BM460 OIL EX BOS No 1 CHARGER CRANE MAIN HOIST WORM DRIVE GEARBOXES

Samples of Optimul BM460 oil from the main hoist east and west worm drive gearboxes, sampled 15/1/91, were received at the Coke Ovens Laboratory for analysis 18/1/91...

The analyses of the two samples, together with that for new oil, were available 23/1/91 as follows:

Visual examination of the solids indicated the presence of 'bronze' particles 10–20um in both samples plus particles up to 200um in the solids from the west gearbox. The viscosity of the oil in the gearbox after flushing and changing was extremely low, 44.0 cSt @400C. Infrared examination of the oil suggested contamination with perchloroethylene (tetrachloroethylene). Confirmation of this finding was the fact that the gearbox had been flushed out with perchloroethylene. Using the viscosity data it was estimated that the low viscosity gearbox oil contained approximately 21% perchloroethylene.

After the oil was changed again a viscosity determination was carried out. The viscosity of the oil (380 cST @ 400) indicated 1% perchloroethylene or 6% of the 44.0 cST had been left in the gearbox after the last oil change.

With the fact that the viscosity of the later samples had been reduced by perchloroethylene contamination the original samples were checked for perchloroethylene contamination. Based upon the infrared spectrum and the viscosity it is estimated that the west worm gear drive contained approximately 9% perchloroethylene and the east gearbox 1%.

Recommendations
Due to the critical nature of these gearboxes it is recommended that:

(1) A regular checking programme be instituted to monitor the oil quality for physical properties and wear metals.

(2) Whenever flushing and oil changes are carried out viscosity checks should be carried out to determine the possible presence of residual flushing fluid.

The same recommendation should be applied to other similar critical units.

Coke Ovens Laboratory 1991

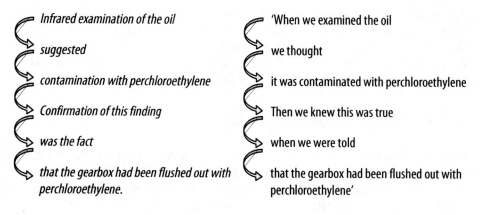

Infrared examination of the oil	'When we examined the oil
suggested	we thought
contamination with perchloroethylene	it was contaminated with perchloroethylene
Confirmation of this finding	Then we knew this was true
was the fact	when we were told
that the gearbox had been flushed out with perchloroethylene.	that the gearbox had been flushed out with perchloroethylene'

Figure 5.12 Implication sequence of observation and reasoning

interpersonal judgements become part of an edifice of abstract entities, grading relations between them as more or less necessary and evident. The world of people and power has been reconstrued as a structure of things and truths. These truths are accumulated as evidence supporting the final Recommendations stage.

Secondly we can note the increasing complexity of specialised terms, such as the title, in Figure 5.13. As we found in the simpler specialised terms, while pre-modifiers classify, specifying members of classes, post-modifiers de-compose, specifying smaller parts of wholes. Although such specialised terms can be very complex, they are made up of components of technology. They differ from scientific technical terms that are defined in scientific texts, and denote abstract taxonomies or explanation sequences (see White 1998 for a fuller discussion of this distinction).

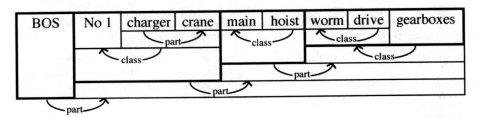

Figure 5.13 Increasing complexity of specialised terms

Although scientific technical note [5:15] does not have headings to signal the stages, it follows the same staging as the specialised technical note [5:14]. The Introduction and Investigation stages are collapsed into the opening paragraph. There is no need to describe the testing procedure in detail, since the reader presumably either knows, or does not need to know, what the tests involve. Instead they are merely named *the normal tests, wear metal analysis*. The Results are expressed as tabulated figures (these are the figures supplied by the technical assistants), and these tables are followed by the Discussion stage – the figures form the topic of the discussion. Only the Recommendations stage has a heading. Here the writers' demands become depersonalised *it is recommended that, programme be instituted, checks should be carried out, same recommendation should be applied.*

5.2.3 Research articles – producing science

Research articles have been a special focus of genre research in the ESP tradition referenced above in Chapter 1 (section 1.3.4). Swales 1990 and 2004 and Paltridge 1997 are key resources; and there has been considerable work on specific stages – introductions (Swales 1990, Hood 2004), abstracts (Salager-Meyer 1990, Hyland 2000), literature reviews (Swales and Lindemann 2002) results sections (Hopkins and Dudley-Evans 1988), discussion section (Dudley-Evans 1994) and the transition from results to conclusions in research articles (Yang and Allison 2003). We won't explore this rich tradition of analysis in detail here since our focus is on genre relations across workplace and educational sectors. Instead we'll pursue the pattern of increasing technicality, vis a vis the other procedural genres, through each stage of the genre.

Whereas technical notes are concerned with issues related to specific contexts – workplaces, plants or enterprises, research articles are concerned with more generally applicable scientific knowledge – adding to and modifying the knowledge base of the scientific field. Stages of a research article are as follows:

Abstract	A brief summary of the experimental method and the results and discussion.
Introduction	Locates the text in the development of the field by reference to previous research. Establishes a problem that previous research has not dealt with. States intention of current research.
Experimental Details (i.e. Method)	Lists experimental methods used, including equipment and procedures.
Results and Discussion	Presents experiment results in graphic and mathematical form. Interprets these results verbally. Reasons about the probable cause of the problem.
Conclusions	Summary of reasoning
References	Previous research

Research articles also typically include acknowledgements, as well as numerical tables, graphs and other graphic illustrations of data.

The following research article [5:16] is in a similar field to that of the technical notes we have seen – steel manufacturing. The theoretical base of this applied field of science is in industrial chemistry. The overall goal of this research article is to find out how different kinds of steel resist wearing. Different kinds of steel are produced by different manufacturing methods, and have different 'micro-structures' that are visible to the scientist through high tech microscopes. The writer therefore needs to draw complex interlocking causal relations between manufacturing methods, structure and wear. Like most problems in the physical sciences, mathematics is used to describe these complex relationships.

At 10 content words per clause, the Abstract of the research article [5:16] has 4 times the lexical density of everyday spoken discourse. Moreover most of these content words are technical terms in the scientific field of metallurgy, making it very difficult to read for outsiders. A synopsis here will help to make it more accessible. It discusses types of steel, which vary in both their carbon content and their micro-structures, set out in Figure 5.14. Steels are made with various carbon contents. Their micro-structure and hardness can be varied by different kinds of heat treatment.

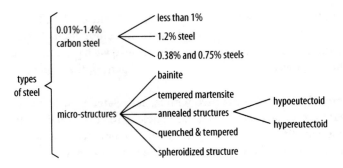

Figure 5.14 Types of steel in text [5:13]

The Abstract summarises relationships between the hardness of these steels, and their resistance to abrasive wear. A direct linear relationship between hardness and wear resistance was found for some steels, but for not for others. The study showed that resistance to wear varied with both carbon content and micro-structure. And the type of wear also varied with both carbon content and micro-structure.

[5:16] A study of the abrasive wear of carbon steels

Abstract

The abrasive wear behaviour of 0.01%-1.4% carbon steels heat treated to various micro-structures and hardnesses was studied using a pin-on-drum machine. For constant hardness and carbon content less than 1.0%, the results show that bainite had the hardest wear resistance, followed by tempered martensite and annealed structures. For 1.2% steel, the annealed structure had wear resistance superior to the quenched and tempered structure and spheroidized structure. Additionally the relationship between relative wear resistance and hardness was linear for annealed steels, but the slope for hypoeutectoid steels was lower than for hypereutectoid steels. A non-linear relationship between wear resistance and hardness of tempered martensite was confirmed for both 0.38% and 0.75% steels. This behaviour indicates that abrasive wear resistance is not simply related to the hardness of materials, but is determined also by the microstructure and fracture properties. Microscopical studies showed the dominant wear mechanism to be microcutting with significant microploughing for very low carbon hypoeutectoid steel, and substantial cracking and spalling in higher carbon steels and in quenched and low temperature tempered medium carbon steels.

Introduction

Numerous empirical observations between abrasive wear of carbon steels and both hardness and carbon content have been established [1–5]. Kruschov and Babichev [1–3] proposed a linear relationship between wear resistance and hardness, and also an additive rule of wear resistance for structurally inhomogeneous materials. For tempered structures, Larsen-Badse and Mathew [5] and Larsen-Badse [6] suggested that wear resistance should be a linear function of the logarithm of the absolute tempering temperature above 2500C and the square root of distance between the dispersed carbides. The volume fraction of pearlite is evidently important in controlling the wear of annealed carbon steels, and it has been agreed [7, 8] that wear resistance is, in fact, proportional to this volume fraction in hypoeutectoid steels.

[5:16] (Contd)

Experimental details

The microstructures of the specimen materials were examined using optical microscopy. Wear mechanisms were elucidated by scanning electron microscopy of the wear debris, wear surface topography and subsurface. The subsurface was exposed by partially removing and polishing the slightly curved surface formed by the geometry of the drum. Precipitated carbides were studied using transmission electron microscopy, and retained austenite was measured using computer aided image analysis and by linear intercept analysis.

Results and Discussion

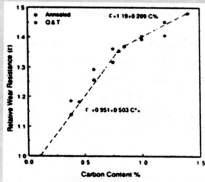

Fig. 2. Diagram showing relative wear resistance as a function of carbon content of annealed steels and quenched and tempered steels.

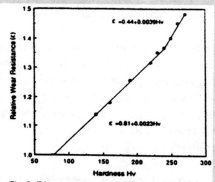

Fig. 3. Diagram showing relative wear resistance as a function of hardness of annealed steels.

Figure 5.15 Results charts (Figs 2–3)

The results presented in Figs 1–3 indicate that the grain boundary allotriomorphs of cementite and the cementite in pearlite have different effects with increasing hardness and wear resistance. Also it is clear that a linear relationship between wear resistance and hardness can exist only for steels having similar microstructural characteristics and, for this condition, hardness can be used as a predictor of wear resistance.

Therefore, for the steels with the same type of annealed structures, the linear relationship between relative wear resistance, e, and hardness, HV, can be expressed as

   $e = a + b\,HV$

where a and b are constants. This relationship is a modified form of the equation

   $e = b\,HV$

proposed by Kruschov and Babichev,

...

Conclusions

(1) For annealed steels, both the wear resistance and hardness were linearly related to carbon content with different slopes for hypoeutectoid and hypereutectoid steels. Similarly the the slope of the linear relationships between relative wear resistance and hardness was different for hypoeutectoid and hypereutectoid steels. Thus hardness can be used as a predictor of wear resistance only for annealed steels with the same type of microstructure.

...

Xu and Kennon 1991

First we'll look at the Introduction. In the Abstract of [5:16], the relationships between wearing and different kinds of steel were summarised. In the Introduction the nature of these relationships is expanded. Introductions to research articles typically have three functions:

- to locate the text in the development of the field, by reference to previous research

- to identify a problem that previous research has not successfully dealt with
- to outline the goals of the current research.

Establishing a position within the discourse of the field is part of the interpersonal dimension of the research article. The writers need to identify their own observations and interpretations in relation to other workers in the field, which include their own readers. Simultaneously they need to identify themselves with accepted ideas, and to question some of these ideas in order to create a position for their own research. References to other research are highlighted as follows (footnote numbers refer to References).

Numerous empirical observations between abrasive wear of carbon steels and both hardness and carbon content **have been established [1–5].**

Kruschov and Babichev [1–3] proposed a linear relationship between wear resistance and hardness, and also an additive rule of wear resistance for structurally inhomogeneous materials.

For tempered structures, **Larsen-Badse and Mathew [5] and Larsen-Badse [6] suggested** that wear resistance should be a linear function of the logarithm of the absolute tempering temperature above 250oC and the square root of distance between the dispersed carbides.

The volume fraction of pearlite **is evidently important** in controlling the wear of annealed carbon steels, and **it has been agreed [7, 8]** that wear resistance is, in fact, proportional to this volume fraction in hypoeutectoid steels.

It is worth noting that, while individual authors *propose* and *suggest* certain relationships, others have been *established* and *agreed* by members of the metallurgy field. The findings of these previous researchers consist of varying relationships between wearing and characteristics of different kinds of steel, which are packaged into long nominal groups. These relationships are first drawn in terms of location, *between x and y*:

> empirical observations **between** abrasive wear of carbon steels **and both** hardness **and** carbon content
>
> a linear relationship **between** wear resistance **and** hardness

But then these relationships 'between' are reconstrued as mathematical functions and proportions:

> a linear **function** of the logarithm of the absolute tempering temperature above 2500C **and** the square root of distance between the dispersed carbides
>
> wear resistance is, in fact, **proportional** to this volume fraction in hypoeutectoid steels

Or in other words, relationships 'between' *the logarithm... **and** the square root...,* and 'between' *wear resistance [**and**] this volume fraction.*

Next the Experimental Details (i.e. Method) stage. As in technical notes, the experimental methods are not spelt out step-by-step, but are simply named. Most of the methods are given in the Experimental Details stage, in which each sentence begins with the object studied, and ends with the technology used to study it, as follows:

> The microstructures of the specimen materials were examined using **optical microscopy**.
>
> Wear mechanisms were elucidated by **scanning electron microscopy** ...
>
> The subsurface was exposed by **partially removing and polishing** ...
>
> Precipitated carbides were studied using **transmission electron microscopy**,
>
> and retained austenite was measured using **computer aided image analysis** and by **linear intercept analysis**.

This pattern was actually established in the first sentence of the Abstract, which begins with the research problem, followed by characteristics of the material studied, as follows.

The abrasive wear behaviour	of 0.01%-1.4% carbon steels	heat-treated to	various micro-structures	and hard-nesses	was studied	using a pin-on-drum machine.
Research problem	Steel: composition	temper	structure	hardness		Research technology

It is by these various means that the extreme lexical density of the research article is organised in patterns that are recognisable and readable to the authors' peers in the scientific field.

Next Results and Discussion. Whereas the Investigation stage of the technical notes consisted of sequential explanations, compressed into a few sentences, the corresponding Results stage of the research article is more closely related to conditional explanations. That is, the characteristics of different steels constitute variable conditions with varying wear effects. However there are not just a few conditions, such as we saw in conditional explanations in Chapter 4, or in the conditional procedure [5:9] above. The research reported in this article has found numerous variations in both conditions and outcomes, so these are modelled mathematically and presented as graphs, shown here as Figure 5.15.

These mathematical results are then generalised verbally, as two kinds on conditional relations:

> The results presented in Figs 1–3 indicate that the grain boundary allotriomorphs of cementite and the cementite in pearlite have different effects with increasing hardness and wear resistance. Also it is clear that a linear relationship between wear resistance and hardness can exist only for steels having similar microstructural characteristics and, for this condition, hardness can be used as a predictor of wear resistance.

These two generalisations construe conditions and effects as follows:

Condition	Effect
with increasing hardness and wear resistance	grain boundary allotriomorphs of cementite and the cementite in pearlite have different effects
only for steels having similar microstructural characteristics	hardness can be used as a predictor of wear resistance

This last verbal generalisation is then expressed more exactly as a mathematical equation, that builds on previous research:

> Therefore, for the steels with the same type of annealed structures, the linear relationship between relative wear resistance, e, and hardness, HV, can be expressed as
>
> $e = a + b\,HV$
>
> where a and b are constants. This relationship is a modified form of the equation
>
> $e = b\,HV$
>
> proposed by Kruschov and Babichev.

Finally the Conclusion stage summarises the conditional relations between wear resistance, hardness, carbon content and different steel types, and the significance of this result for steel manufacturing is restated:

> Thus hardness can be used as a predictor of wear resistance only for annealed steels with the same type of microstructure.

5.3 Protocol

As we noted in Chapter 1 with reference to Conal's bus rules [1.8], procedures are complemented by a genre called protocol, which restricts rather than enables behaviour. Restrictions on behaviour are occasionally incorporated into procedural genres, at the point where they are relevant. Text [5:17] from the BHP steel mill, includes warnings at the beginning of the procedure (*no smoking...*) and between steps D and E of phase 2 (*do not proceed if...*).

[5:17] SAFETY

WARNING: NO SMOKING whilst working on preheater.

1   Isolate Tundish Car Long Travel Drives
Isolate and tag Tundish car long travel drives 1 & 2 at local centres in No. 2 switchroom.

2   Isolate Gas Systems
A) Light pilot flame by depressing 'Preheat Pilot On' push button at Tundish Preheat Control Station.
B) Observe pilot flame in end of burner. Small flame approx. 20mm in diameter and mostly blue in color.
C) Isolate and tag Main Gas Shut-off Valve.
D) Observe burners for presence of any additional flame other than Pilot flame.

WARNING: DO DOT PROCEED if additional flame present after 5 minutes.
            Contact Process Engineers to carry out further isolation.

E) Depress 'Preheat Pilot Off' push button to extinguish pilot flame.

F) Isolate and tag Pilot Natural Gas Shut-off valve.

3   Isolate 110 Volts Ignition Transformer Supply
Remove fuse from Burner Management Panel. Terminal Strip X1, Terminal No. 1.

Turning to domestic appliances, Jim's new kettle foregrounds warnings of this kind after what is labelled step 3 in its operation procedure – using special formatting to highlight the warnings. For some reason the steps before the warnings are numbered but those following are not.

[5:18] Operation of your kettle

1 To fill the kettle, remove it from the power base and open the lid by pressing the lid release button. Fill with the desired amount of water. Always fill the kettle between the minimum and maximum marks on the water window. Too little water will result in the kettle switching off before the water has boiled.

2 Ensure that the lid is locked firmly into place. Place the kettle firmly onto the power base. Plug the power cord into 230/240 power point and switch 'On'.

3 Press the On/Off switch to the 'On' position. The power 'On' light and water guage will illuminate.

> Always fill the kettle between the minimum (Min) and maximum (Max) marks on the exterior of the kettle. Too little water will result in the kettle switching "Off" before the water has boiled. Filling above the maximum mark on the exterior of the kettle may result in boiling water splashing from the kettle.
>
> **Note**

> The kettle must only be used with the power base supplied. Use caution when pouring water from your kettle, as boiling water will scald. Do not pour the water too quickly.
>
> **Note**

The kettle will automatically switch 'Off' once the water has boiled. Lift the kettle from the power base and pour the water. Take care to hold the kettle level, especially when filled to the maximum level. To re-boil it may be necessary to wait for a few seconds to allow the control to reset.

The kettle may be stored on its power base when not in use. The power point should be switched off and the appliance plug unplugged from the power base when not in use.

Texts like [5:17] and [5:18] are best interpreted as procedures, with a prosody of prohibition emerging now and again where required.

In other contexts, where understandings about how to undertake an activity sequence can be taken for granted or are spelled out elsewhere, the protocol genre itself may emerge as a list of restrictions. Alongside the kettle operating procedure in [5:18] Jim's instructions for use include a page of protocol genre including no less than 16 warnings – drawing on a range of congruent and grammatically metaphorical commands to do so (Martin 1991).

[5:19]

This appliance has been designed specifically for the purpose of boiling drinking quality water only. Under no circumstances should this product be used to boil any other liquids or foodstuffs.

- Always use the appliance on a dry, level surface.

- Do not touch hot surfaces. Use handle for lifting and carrying the appliance.

- Never immerse the kettle base, switch area, power base or cord in water, or allow moisture to come in contact with these parts. Keep clear of walls, curtains and other heat or steam sensitive materials. Minimum 200mm distance.

- The appliance is not intended for use by young children or infirm persons without supervision.

- Young children should be supervised to ensure that they do not play with the appliance.

- Do not let the cord hang over the edge of a table or counter, touch hot surfaces or become knotted.

- Do not place on or near a hot gas burner, electric element, or in a heated oven.

- This appliance is intended for household use only. Do not use this appliance for other than its intended use.

- Do not use outdoors.

- Do not operate the kettle on an inclined surface.

- Do not move while the kettle is switched on.

- Always turn the power off at the power outlet and then remove the plug fro the power outlet before attempting to move the appliance, when the appliance is not in use and before cleaning or storing.

- The installation of a residual current device (safety switch) is recommended to provide additional safety protection when using electrical appliances. It is advisable that a safety switch with a rated residual operating current not exceeding 20mA be installed in the electrical circuit supplying the appliance. See your electrician for professional advice.

- Regularly inspect the power supply cord, plug and actual appliance for any damage. If found damaged in any way, immediately cease use of the appliance and return unit to the nearest authorised Breville centre for examination, replacement or repair.

An appliance of this kind is arguably too dangerous to use, but at least Jim has been warned!

Protocol is a very important feature of bureaucratic discourse, deployed for rules, regulations, laws and legislation (see Martin & Rose 2003/2007 for discussion). Conal's bus rules were a proto-administrative discourse of this kind. In these contexts it functions alongside procedures to manage populations, and may incorporate features of legal discourse where these are required.

From a client perspective protocol can also be deployed as tips for running the gauntlet of unfamiliar activity sequences and regulations. Here are a few words of advice from the Sydney Morning Herald's 2005 *Student Survival Guide* for incoming University students – their *Golden Rules* for studying.

[5:20] Golden Rules

Put assignment/exam dates – and *start* dates – in your diary/wall planner

Ensure study time is proportionate to the value of assignments/exams

Study hard early on to develop good habits

Do the *essential* reading before *additional* texts

Don't read course material cover to cover – ask how

Re-read and summarise lecture notes

Talk to fellow students and tutors about the subject

If struggling, ask – before assignments are due

Keep up a social life

[*SMH* 1/2/3005: 18]

In Jim's experience Canadians are the world's experts in the protocol genre, something flowing on he expects from the deep grammar of prophylaxis which lies at the heart of their culture. During recent trips to Canada he has encountered lists of more than 30 rules governing behaviour at public swimming pools (prompting his Australian partner to suggest that it is impossible to go swimming in Canada without breaking at least 5 rules).[2] On his last trip he noted that even the small signs designating lap lanes as slow, medium and fast included a list of rules for using lap lanes on the back facing swimmers in the pool. Just in case readers think we're being too irreverent here (the deep grammar of Australia is surely responsible), we'll leave you with our favorite piece of anal retentive protocol – from a towel dispenser in the male toilet in a small diner north of Vancouver.

[5:21]

The Passive Restraint Guide is designed to prevent intentional abuse by children.

Excessive towel loop length could make intentional abuse more likely. Failure to follow loading instructions could result in serious injury or death.

This was for the maintenance operator, but dared we dry our hands?

In administrative discourse, changes to procedure and protocol are managed through a genre of text referred to as directive. Directives specify the change required with a Command nucleus, and in addition may motivate and enable this proposal in various ways. Directives are explored in Iedema et al. 1995, Iedema 1997. Procedures and protocol are also related to Jorden's policy genre, introduced in 6.2.1 below.

5.4   Procedural systems

In the diverse realm of 'doing' science, procedures and procedural recounts give complementary perspectives on activities, one prospective and the other retrospective – one directing what to do and the other telling what happened. For these reasons we will model them here in single system network, in Figure 5.16.

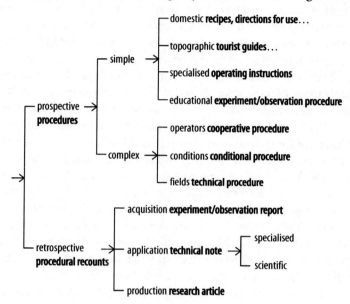

Figure 5.16 Procedural genres

We have included in domestic procedures all those texts associated with household activities such as recipes, directions for use on foods, medicines, cleaning products, and simple instructions for games. Topographic procedures include tourist guides but may also include certain games, particularly computer games, as well as directions for finding locations (both oral and written). Specialised simple procedures include operating instructions for industrial and domestic technologies (although operating manuals can also include complex procedures). And procedures for experiments or observations in school science have their own unique structure. The structures of complex procedures vary with multiple operators (cooperative procedures), multiple conditions (conditional procedures) and multiple fields, as the complexity of technical procedures involves both specialised and technical fields. With respect to procedural recounts, research articles recount the production of science, technical notes recount its application in industry, and reports of school science experiments and observations recount its acquisition in school. Finally all the members of this network contrast with protocols, as time structured vs non-time structured, but for reasons of space we have left this contrast out of the diagram.

5.5 Macrogenres

Most of the texts we have used to exemplify genres in the preceding chapters have been short; in larger font most would occupy half a page to a page. This was not merely for convenience of analysis – we haven't gone trawling through piles of texts selecting only those around this size. Rather it seems to have something to do with a text as a unit of discourse; genres tend to come in around these sizes (with plenty of room for variation up and down). This applies as much to technical written texts such as the reports, explanations and procedures we examined in Chapters 4 and 5 (although technical notes and research articles tend to be a bit longer), as it does to the historical explanations and arguments in Chapter 3, and the stories in Chapter 2. Intriguingly many of these were spoken stories, including traditional stories from cultures as diverse as Indigenous Australia, ancient Europe and southern India.

On the other hand, many of these short genres were extracts from longer texts. This was illustrated for spoken stories with Evie's observation and exemplum [2:7], both part of a much longer recounting of her experiences as a stolen child. For written stories we took extracts from novels such as *Follow the Rabbit-Proof Fence*, which we described as a series of smaller stories, following the girls' journey from their home to Moore River Native Settlement and back again; and from short stories such as Jennings' *Good Tip for Ghosts*, which we described as a serial narrative (following Rothery 1994), with five Complications, each with their own Orientation, Evaluation and (temporary) Resolution. In Chapter 3 we extracted genres from several books on Australian history and contemporary politics, and exemplified how short texts may be nested within larger ones, in Frank Brennan's recount of events surrounding the abuse of a child refugee [3:15]. In Chapters 4 and 5 many of the texts we used were from science textbooks or technical manuals.

In this section we will explore relations between short genres that go to make up larger texts, which we will refer to as **macrogenres**. Work on macrogenres includes Martin 1994, 2001a on science and geography textbooks as macrogenres. Christie 2002 deals insightfully with these issues in the context of classroom discourse as she develops her work on curriculum genres. Muntigl 2004 involves an intensive study of therapeutic discourse as it unfolds over several counselling sessions for couples. Jordens 2002 looks at story, policy and arguing genres as they unfold in his interviews with cancer patients, their family, and the health professionals involved in their treatment. And Iedema (2003a, b) follows a series of meetings culminating in the building of a new hospital wing, a process reconstituting language as material reality which he refers to as resemiotisation. For excellent work on the role of images in macro-generic texts, see O'Halloran 2004, especially the article by Guo Libo on biology textbooks. To explore macrogenres here, we will again use Halliday's logicosemantic relations, to model macrogenres as serial structures, as we did for relations between story phases in Chapter 2, and for multimodal texts in Chapter 4.

The notion of genre complexes has already been introduced in Chapter 4 in the context of the multimodal text in Figure 4.26. This double page spread described and explained the *Mulga plains* of Australia's arid lands with three verbal texts and three visual texts. The verbal texts include a descriptive report about *Mulga plains*, a factorial explanation *The mulga tree* (analysed as text [4:10]), and a conditional explanation *Flowering and setting seed*. These three texts are related by enhancement and extension, as follows.

[5:22] Mulga plains

The biggest shock for many arid land travellers is the dense scrub that covers much of the arid plains. This scrub can be so dense that it is difficult to walk through. Travellers begin to wonder if they really are in arid country.

It is the mulga tree that grows so densely across the desert plains. It is so well adapted to the arid climate that it covers one third of our arid desert ranges and rocky outcrops are surrounded by gently sloping hills and plains. This is red earth country and is the country of the mulga tree.

x (explaining adaptation)

The mulga tree
How can plant life grow so well in such dry, hot and infertile places?

Surviving the long drought

The mulga likes long droughts – if it is too wet mulga trees will not grow.

The shape of the mulga tree is a key to it surviving dry times. The branches of the mulga fan out from the bottom-like a huge half moon. The branching leaves and stems catch the rain and it trickles down to the soil. This traps more rainfall than if the tree grew straight up. The mulga catches more water than a gum tree. This water is stored in the soil to be used by the tree during

Even the leaves help it survive the drought. They are a silvery grey colour. The sun's rays bounce off the leaves helping the plant to stay cool. Also the mulga tree makes its own food by dropping thousands of leaves.

+ (adding further factor)

Flowering and setting seed
For many years geographers thought that our arid land shrubs and trees only flowered after rain. We now know this is not true. The long living plants flower each year. Even in a dry time mulga will flower in spring and summer. The tree simply makes less flowers. If it rains in spring the tree makes more flowers.

Even if a tree flowers it may not set seed. Setting a lot of energy, energy that may be needed to find water during a drought. If it has rained the tree does not have to use as much energy to find water. For the mulga to set seeds there must be rain in late summer and again in winter. When the seeds drop to the ground, rain is then needed if the seeds are to start growing.

These three texts, with their visual accompaniments, constitute one section in a chapter of a secondary school geography textbook *Australian Journey: environments and communities* (Scott & Robinson 1993). The organisation of this excellent textbook construes the field of geography in Australia in two parts, *Australian environments*, including four types of environment (arid lands, wetlands, woodlands, forests), and *Australian communities*, with three kinds of communities (urban, rural, remote). Each chapter includes reports and explanations that describe and explain these social and natural phenomena, but the book is also concerned to construe geography as a scientific activity, conducted by experts in their fields, and these activities are presented

[5:23] Australian Journey: environments and communities

Part one Australian Environments

1   Introduction
= What is Australia?
= Australia today
...

=   2   Exploring arid lands
= What are the features of Australia's arid lands?
x A useful tool to help geographers observe+The steps to being a good observer
= Types of arid lands
    = Desert ranges and rocky outcrops
    + Mulga plains
    + Spinifex plains
    + Saltbush and bluebush plains
    + Desert rivers and salt lakes
= Exploring Uluru National Park

x   3   Managing arid lands
x The issues involved in managing the arid lands
x Investigating an arid lands mystery
+ The world's arid lands

+   4   Exploring wetlands
...

x   5   Managing wetlands
...

+   6   Exploring woodlands
...

x   7   Managing woodlands
...

+   8   Exploring forests
...

x   9   Managing forests
...

+   Part two Australian Communities
10 Introduction
x Where are Australian communities found?
x Why are Australian communities where they are?
x How are Australian communities changing?

=   11 Living in urban communities
...

+   12 Living in rural communities
...

+   13 Living in remote communities
...

as primarily focused on environmental conservation. To this end, each chapter on environments is followed by a chapter on 'managing' this environment (cf Martin 2001a and Veel 1998 on the 'greening' of school geography). The key genres in these chapters on geography as an activity are procedures and procedural recounts. Hence apprenticeship into the field of geography is construed as learning both a hierarchically organised body of knowledge, realised in reports and explanations, and a set of technical practices, realised in procedures and procedural recounts. We will examine how the activity of geography is construed by relations among these procedural texts, but first let's look at how the field as a whole is organised in the book.

The organisation of the field is given by the headings throughout the book. This is analysed as a hierarchy of periodicity in [5:23] (left), and logical relations between each section and chapter are indicated by symbols for elaboration, extension and enhancement. The particular sections we analyse here are highlighted in bold.

The Introduction to *Part one* first elaborates the heading by describing Australia in relation to the world, and other lands. It then elaborates this description by classifying environmental regions in *Australia today* (northern, southern, coastal, arid). Chapter 2 *Exploring arid lands* exemplifies this classification with a specific environment type. The criteria for classifying environments as arid lands are then given in a report describing five of their *features* (soils, plants, animals, rainfall, temperature). The next section *A useful tool to help geographers observe,* enhances the whole text, describing how geography is done with specialised types of observation, which is then added to by a procedure for doing geographic observations *The steps to being a good observer.* This procedure is required for students to do the exercises associated with many sections of the textbook. It is immediately followed, for example, with exercise [5:24].

[5:24] Exercise

Being a good observer
Look carefully at Figs 2.1 to 2.5 and reread the information on pages 14–15.
[the section *What are the features of Australia's arid lands?* and photographs associated with each feature]

Figure 2.1 [an aerial photograph of a sand plain with sparse trees]
List the key features that you can observe. You must list the features of:
- vegetation
- landforms

Figures 2.3 and 2.4 [birds in a tree, and a wallaby among rocks]

- List the key features that you can observe.
- What animal can you observe or would you expect to see?

Figures 2.2 and 2.5 [people measuring rainfall, and in jumpers around a fire at night]
- List the key features that you can observe.
- What comments can you make about the:
  rainfall
  temperature
  evaporation

Such procedures function to engage the student in the field, mimicking the geo-graphic activities of observation, literature research and recording (cf procedure [5:5] above). Rather than being logically related to preceding texts, we can interpret them in terms of NEGOTIATION as moves in an exchange (Martin & Rose 2003/2007), where the writer first gives information, then demands a service from the readers (cf Chapter 1, section 1.5.6). This service requires them to reread the information given, and give it back in written form. The multimodal activities of observing, reading and writing are demanded here as both commands and questions.

Following this detour into geography as activity, the next section *Types of arid lands* then returns to geography as classification, and these types are detailed with a series of subsections, added one after another, that describe each type, and explain its features. The section analysed above as [5:22] *Mulga plains* is typical of these subsec-tions, describing the environment type in general and then explaining features such as strategies for surviving drought. The last section in this chapter then exemplifies these landscape types in a specific area of arid lands around Uluru (Ayers Rock).

Chapter 2 provides the factual basis on which chapter 3 argues that arid lands must be conserved through scientific management, and recounts how to do so. In these respects chapter 3 enhances chapter 2 with consequence and manner. This argument is developed, first with some explanations of former poor management *The issues involved in managing the arid lands*, then enhanced with a procedure and procedural recount of how to manage scientifically, *Investigating an arid lands mystery*. The last section *The world's arid lands* adds further arguments for manage-ment with respect to global environmental issues.

These patterns are repeated for the following chapters in Part one. There is thus an overall taxonomic movement in Part one, from Australia in comparison to other lands, to general kinds of Australian environments, to four types of environments recognised by geographers, to specific subtypes within each of these. The physi-cal geography of Australia is construed in a classifying taxonomy, as a system of environmental types and subtypes. Along the way, doing geography in Australia is construed as activities involving specialised observation of the environment, and these activities are motivated by concerns for environmental conservation.

Likewise, Part two classifies Australian communities on the criteria of their location, explains why they are so located, and accounts for how they are changing over time. Each chapter then describes and exemplifies these community types, explains how they are changing, and argues for scientifically informed planning on this basis. While the terms change from 'management' to 'planning' as we move from natural to social environments, the message continues that geographical observation must inform environmental policy. Martin 2001a and Veel 1998 describe how this complex construal of geography as scientific activity and environmental conserva-tion is woven into school curriculum texts, and must be reproduced by school students in their writing tasks.

In keeping with the focus of this chapter of *Genre Relations*, we will conclude with the procedure and procedural recount in chapter 3 *Managing arid lands*, introduced as texts [5:12] and [5:13] above, and their logical relations to its other sections. The chapter begins with an exposition arguing for scientifically informed management. This is enhanced by a factorial explanation of former poor management, each factor of which is added as a consequential explanation of changes since white settlement, with its own heading. This rationale is then enhanced by a generalised recount of geographers' role in management through case studies (for generalised recounts see Chapter 6 below, 6.2.1), and this is enhanced by a procedure for such case studies, which is in turn exemplified by the procedural recount of a case study at Uluru. Each step in this long procedural recount is a genre in itself, and within *Step 3 The field trip*, there are three subsections of varying genres. Only brief extracts of each section are presented here, and headings in the textbook are shown here in bold.

[5:25] 3 Managing arid lands

Exposition (rationale for geography informing management)
Imagine spending months at a time in Uluru National Park trying to find out about Australia's arid land animals. This is what Lynn Baker does. She spends long days in search of a small marsupial called the mulgara.
...
Much of Australia's unique desert fauna is vanishing before our eyes and most Australians have not heard of, let alone seen these animals.
...The second reason that all Australians should be concerned is that arid lands are a major grazing are for sheep and cattle.
...
If landowners can make sure that desert habitats are better managed, two things will happen:
- the desert will be able to continue to support grazing activity, and,
- Australia's unique flora and fauna will survive.

x   **The issues involved in managing the arid lands**
Factorial explanation (former poor management)
For thousands of years people have used the arid lands. With the arrival of European settlers the arid lands began to be used to graze cattle and sheep. The way the land was used or managed has changed.
...

= Consequential explanations x 4
   Issue number 1 Changes to burning
   ...
+ **Issue number 2 Changing land ownership and responsibilities**
   ...
+ **Issue number 3 Disappearing vegetation and soil**
   ...
+ **Issue number 4 Changing animal life**
   ...

[5:25] (contd)

x **Investigating an arid lands mystery**
Generalised recount (geographer's field trips)

Geographers are interested in the management issues that affect arid lands. To investigate these issues, it is important to go to the area to be studied. Geographers call these trips field trips.

The aim of field trips is to:
- observe what is happening
- collect and record information

When a field trip is finished the geographers study the information collected. They then:
- decide what is happening in the case study area
- develop ideas on how to improve or change what is happening

...

x Procedure

It is important that a geographer makes the best use of the time while on a field trip. To do this the geographer follows a number of steps:

Step 1 Identify the issue to be studied.
Step 2 Research the background to the issue.
Step 3 Go on the field trip. While on the field trip it is important to:
- observe and
- collect information.
Step 4 Use the observations to identify what is happening.
Step 5 Develop a plan to manage an environment.

= **The mulgara at Uluru National Park**
Procedural recount

Before leaving on the field trip to Uluru National Park, Lynn identified the issue she wished to study and spent time researching it.

= **Step 1 Identify the issue to be studied** (policy)

'I want to find out why mulgara appear to be in some areas and not in others. If I find that the mulgara are rare I want to be able to suggest ways to conserve their habitat.'

x **Step 2 Research background to the issue** (recount)

Lynn didn't just pack her bags and leave for Uluru. She spent time in the library reading what others have found out about arid zone animals.

...

x **Step 3 The field trip** (recount)

...

The work involved in step 3 can be divided into two parts:
1 Making observations
2 Collecting and recording information

= **Observing the mulgara and its environment** (recount)

During her first field trips to Uluru, Lynn spent time observing mulgara and the environments where it lives.

...

x **Collecting and recording information** (recount)

Now Lynn needed to collect information that would help her find out why the mulgara seemed to be found in different habitats during times of high rainfall and during times of drought. Her first task was to collect data that showed where mulgara were living and where they were not living.

...

[5:25] (contd)

+ **Using computer mapping to locate relict drainage environments** (generalised recount)
Earlier you learnt that old river systems can't be seen when walking over the ground. However, photographs taken by satellites, circling thousands of kilometres above the earth, do reveal these old rivers.
...

x **Step 4 Use the observations to identify what is happening** (sequential explanation)
Lynn's next step was to carefully study her observations to see what they told her... She started to develop a theory:
'The theory is that in the relict drainage area the vegetation remains in better condition than in areas outside its influence. This area is better able to support animals during drought. It becomes an important refuge area for animals like the mulgara during times of drought. The mulgara in this area are better able to survive than those living elsewhere. This is because the plants are able to collect the water from the underground drainage system. When it rains the habitat in the rest of the country improves. The mulgara are able to spread out over the country and I will find mulgara living away from this area again.'
...

x **Step 5 Developing plan to manage the environment** (exposition)
Geographers conduct field work to help them decide on ways to manage the environment. When Lynn Baker's work is complete she wants to be able to suggest things that can be done to protect and save the mulgara. This means protecting the environments where it lives.
At this stage Lynn believes the refuge areas that are found in our arid lands must be protected, as the research so far suggests that small animals like the mulgara do rely on them in droughts.
...

In summary, the rhetorical structure of the chapter is expository: it begins with why geographers are needed, then what it is they do, followed by an example of what they do; in genre terms, thesis, evidence and example. In terms of apprenticing potential geographers, the activity of geography is thus contextualised and made appealing from two perspectives. First it is logically related to the need for environmental conservation. The previous chapter motivates this need by describing the complexity and beauty of Australia's arid lands, so that the explanations of environmental degradation here are counterexpectant problems, and geographic study is construed as (part of) a solution. Secondly it is logically related to the activities of a specific geographer, with whom the readers are invited to personally identify. An appraisal analysis (Martin & White 2005) would provide more insights into the interpersonal relations enacted here between the reader, the land, geography and the geographer, but unfortunately we have run out of space.

What is usefully displayed here is the way that this pedagogic text frames relations between technical activities, social issues and personal actions. This is achieved by linking reports, explanations, procedures, procedural recounts and expositions in an intricate logical series. This series of genres apprentices students into a hierarchy of knowledge and specialised activities that could eventually give them the power to participate in controlling the natural and social worlds.

5.6 Education and production

In this chapter we have sketched parallel semiotic developments in the industrial hierarchy and in science education. Relationships between levels of education and economic production are schematised in Figure 5.17. The education field in this model is presented as a spiralling curriculum, in which learners acquire the discourse of science in steps, from junior secondary to post-graduate research. Bernstein 1990, 1996 makes the point that what they are learning is not science as it is produced and practised in the field of economic production, but science that has been recontextualised in the education field as pedagogic discourse. Nevertheless our research has shown relatively weak boundaries between production and education in the sciences, so that educational outcomes tend to match the requirements of science based industries, for workers with various levels of training. Correlating with each of the curriculum steps in education is a jumping off point into economic production. At the first level, if you have not learnt to read the genres of junior secondary science (and can demonstrate that you have in written assessments), you may be destined to supply industry with the de-skilled manual labour required by process line production. Those learners who do learn to read the reports and explanations described in Chapter 4, will also be able to read the operating procedures described above, and thus become skilled operators of industrial technology. Those who can successfully demonstrate their acquisition of junior secondary science are permitted to get further education at diploma level, to become technicians capable of carrying out technical procedures, such as text [5:11]. Those few who acquire the abstract technical discourse of senior secondary science are permitted to enter undergraduate programs that train professional applied scientists and engineers. And finally the handful who can demonstrate a special aptitude for reading and writing science may be permitted to go on to post-graduate study, and so contribute to the production of scientific knowledge.

The numbers of learners jumping off at each level of the education curriculum are far from equal, as shown in Figure 5:18. In Australia almost twice as many never enter further education (~55%) as those who acquire vocational qualifications at technical college (~30%), which are twice as many again as those who receive professional degrees at university (~15%), and these proportions have changed only slightly over the past twenty years at least (ABS 1994, 2004, Rose 2006a). In terms of occupations, the large lower group includes manual labour and skilled operators (and the unemployed), the middle group tradespeople and technicians, and the small upper group scientists, engineers, educators and managers at various levels. Unequal acquisition of the science genres described here thus has extensive consequences for both socio-economic structure and occupational options. The lower group have relatively few of these options, have little autonomy in the workplace, and earn the least, the middle group may have more options for autonomy and earning, but it is the upper group who primarily participate in the control of the natural and social world that these genres afford here.

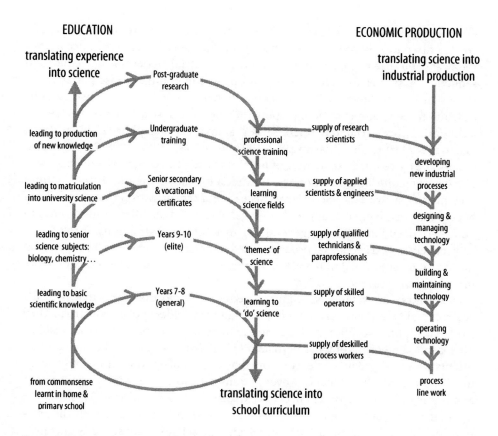

Figure 5.17 Stages in science education and levels in industry

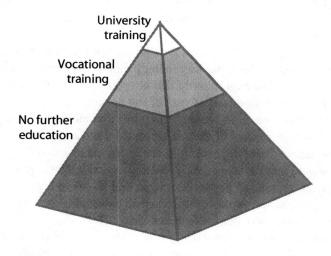

Figure 5.18 Proportions of educational qualifications

One of the reasons so few learners acquire the privileged genres of science is that written discourses become more remote from the construal of experience in everyday spoken discourse, as we move up the industrial ladder and the education sequence. Activities involving things and people in commonsense parlance are reconstrued in technical fields, as abstract things that act on other abstract entities, and these relations of 'acting upon' then become abstract things themselves, a semiotic process Halliday refers to as grammatical metaphor (Halliday 1998, Halliday & Martin 1993, Martin 1989, 1993, Rose 1993, 1997, 1998, 2004a, 2005c, to appear a). Eventually sequences of unfolding activities come to be re-expressed as parts of composition taxonomies, as criteria for classifying the abstract entities they modify, as we described above. Instead of a sensually experienced world of happenings involving actual people, things, places and qualities, reality comes to be experienced virtually as a generalised structure of abstractions. Instead of a subjectively negotiated social order, enacted in personal exchanges, interpersonal meanings are subsumed in the causal relations between abstract things, graded as more or less necessary or evident.

Of course the scientists, engineers, educators and managers that live this abstract reality in their working roles, also know the older spoken construal. They (we) learn it first as children and continue to deploy it in personal relationships. This is one dimension of what Bernstein (1971–96) has called elaborated coding orientations, that provide access to more than one set of options for making meaning. The scientific construal however is dominant in modern industrial society, and is integral to the maintenance and expansion of its stratified social structure; the theories of natural reality it realises have evolved in tandem with the relations of production in industrial capitalism. The scientific construal is currently the exclusive property of those socioeconomic classes which benefit most from this system, and its version of reality reflects the structures of institutional roles which members of these classes occupy in the course of making their living and negotiating power.

Today access to technical discourses is required not only by professionally and vocationally trained workers, but increasingly for employment at all levels of industry. As we stated at the beginning of this chapter, many of the texts in this chapter are from manuals produced as part of the national and global industry restructuring movement which increasingly requires that all workers are trained and accredited. Without control of written technical discourses, this training is not possible, and employment opportunities are restricted to a shrinking market for unskilled low-paid manual labour. As globalised capital is able to rapidly move manufacturing from regions of higher education and wages to regions of lower education and wages, it is only possible for workers in developing nations to achieve wage parity through control of literate technical discourses.

There is a view however, popularised by the 'new literacies' group among others, that teaching technical literacy 'is simply imposing western conceptions of literacy onto other cultures' (Street 1996:2). The ideological goal of literacy research in this view is to privilege literacy practices documented amongst disempowered peoples, over teaching literacy practices regarded as cultural imperialism. To this end, policies focused on vocational literacy training may be specifically rejected; Prinsloo & Breier (1996:15) for example, dismiss such literacy policies in post-apartheid South African as 'a quick fix by way of fast delivery by large-scale programmes'. Street (1996:1–2) characterises these literacy programs as 'the autonomous model of literacy', i.e. disconnected from the cultural contexts of learners, and suggests that developing nations naively and mistakenly assume that literacy training will bring social benefits such as ''modernisation', 'progress' and economic rationality, to name a few'. In the South African context, he associates literacy 'attached to formal education' with 'vested interests which depend upon the old views for their legitimacy', clearly implying a connection between advocates of state literacy programs and the racist ideology of apartheid. As research in this paradigm is concerned not with what workers need to know, but what they already do know, its results cannot be used to inform the literacy programs it opposes. Rather proposals emerging from such research focus on altering the attitudes of educators, administrators and workplace managers, rather than educating workers. For example, following their study of literacy practices in a Cape Town factory, Breier & Salt's (1996:83) recommendation is that management 'stop insisting that communication take place on its terms alone, with the onus on workers to acquire the necessary skills to participate'.

It is claimed that this new literacies position 'offers a more culturally sensitive view of literacy practices' (Street ibid), and there is no doubt that the documenting of diverse language practices serves valuable functions. It is of course a key goal of *Genre Relations*, in which we set out to explore the cultural contexts of language use. Unfortunately however, the associated disparaging of technical/vocational literacy teaching has the potential to undermine such programs where they are most needed, such as post-apartheid South Africa, where the gulf between rich and poor is reportedly second only to Brazil (cf Muller 2000 on this debate), or in Indigenous Australia which has among the worst education, employment, income and health statistics in the world (Rose 1999, 2004a, Rose et al 2004). In our opinion this ethnographic valorising of others' cultural practices over their educational needs is an example of what Bernstein 1990 considers the boundary maintaining function of agencies of symbolic control. At the socio-economic level, such apparently liberal views function to protect the economic interests of the new middle class, ensuring that the world's have-nots continue to be denied access to its semiotic resources. As an alternative we would like to suggest that access to the discursive resources of power is the democratic right of all citizens, and that as linguists and language educators it is our responsibility to make these resources available to all.

6 Keeping going with genre

Our main aim in writing this book has been to extend an invitation to readers to consider genres as configurations of meaning and to think paradigmatically about relations among genres – focussing our attention on stories, histories, reports, explanations and procedures. In this final chapter we want to explore a little further various issues arising from a project of this kind, which as we noted earlier tries to map culture as systems of genres. We begin with an obvious query – Is genre everything? And we then turn to the question of genre relations – one genre to another in the culture, and one genre to another as a text unfolds.

6.1 Is genre everything?

Is there life beyond communication? Is there meaning beyond genre? Just how much work can we make genre theory do?

6.1.1 Genre in a functional model of language and social context

The first thing we need to do in response to a query about the limits of genre is to place our work on genre within the functional model of language and social context in which it evolved. As we noted in Chapter 1, in this model (see Fig. 1.9) genre is positioned as an abstract level of analysis co-ordinating field, mode and tenor (known collectively as register), and register is realised in turn through language (discourse semantics, lexicogrammar and phonology/graphology). This picture means that of course there is more to genre than the descriptions in Chapter 2–6 entailed. Our treatment of linguistic realisations there was necessarily sketchy and exemplary; and as we apologised in Chapter 1, serious consideration of field, mode and tenor was beyond the scope of this volume.

In a model of this kind then, genre may have less work to do than in other frameworks (e.g. Berkenkotter & Huckin 1995, Bhatia 1993, Biber 1995, Miller 1984, Swales 1990), because the descriptive workload is distributed across strata and metafunctions (ideational, interpersonal and textual meaning). For example, the kind of 'knowledge' involved in genre is a matter for **field**, where professional, disciplinary, recreational and domestic activity would be described. Similarly, the effects of speaking and writing, and of mono-modal and multi-modal discourse is a matter for **mode**, where the amount of work language is doing has to be explored. Likewise for the negotiation of social relations, which is the concern of **tenor** and its implications for interpersonal meaning. When comparing our model of genre with that of others, it may be useful to treat analyses of field, mode and tenor as more delicate extensions of the genre descriptions offered in Chapters 2–5. It is often the case that genre plus aspects of field, mode or tenor in our model does the work of genre alone in alternative frameworks.[1] As noted in Chapter 1, we don't actually model register and genre in these terms because to do so would mean restating comparable field, mode and tenor descriptions from one genre to another and we in fact see field, mode and tenor as tools for generalising knowledge, multi/modality and social relations across genres.

Another important respect in which there is more to genre than canvassed here has to do with what Matthiessen 2003 has called 'individuation'. In Bernstein's terms, this has to do with the relationship between the reservoir of meanings in a culture and the repertoire a given individual can mobilise. For Bernstein this is a matter of coding orientation, which has been fruitfully explored in SFL by Hasan and her colleagues (see especially Cloran 1989, 1999, Hasan 1990, 1991, 1992, 1996, Hasan & Cloran 1990, Williams 1999, 2001). Access to genres is an important part of this picture, and a major political motivation behind literacy interventions based on our work. Studies of the factors influencing the relations of reservoir to repertoire in a given culture can be usefully related to work on ideology and subjectivity in other frameworks (for discussion of the relation of CDA to SFL see Chouliaraki & Fairclough 1999, Martin 2000a, Martin & Wodak 2003).

In short then, in a functional model of language and social context, there is more to say about genre as we move across strata and metafunctions. At the same time, the model assumed here does privilege genre as its ultimate level of abstraction, thereby giving genre responsibility for coordinating the recurrent configurations of meaning in a culture. In such terms, genre mediates the limits of our world – at the same time as offering systemic linguists a wholistic perspective on their metafunctionally and stratally diversified analyses.

6.1.2 Genre and chat

The idea that social life is delimited by genre is a controversial one in another respect, since it so readily conflicts with various modernist ideals (or one might say modernist conceits) – for example personal choice, individualism, spontaneity, creativity, freedom and liberation. Even those prepared to grant the recurrent closure of institutional genres, such as science reports or historical explanations, are less prepared to acknowledge the delimitation of informal spheres of social activity, in particular casual conversation. Eggins & Slade 2005 in fact demonstrate the utility of genre description in workplace conversation, recognising what they call 'chunk and chat' – recognisable generic chunks (eg. gossip and various story genres), with less clearly defined chatty transitions in between.

More problematic perhaps is Eggins & Slade's dinner table conversation data for which the major social imperative is 'keep talking', and where there is perhaps more chatty banter to be found than clearly bounded chunks of gossip or narration. One way to think about 'chat vs chunk' is to return to the notion of types of structure introduced in Chapter 1. In such terms the basic ideational organisation of chat is serial rather than orbital; chat involves an open-ended series of dialogic moves designed to keep the conversation going, and thus contrasts with orbital genres in which stages enable a nuclear move that consummates the telos of the genre. (cf. the narrative [2:10] or factorial explanation [4:10]). Compared with chat, the chunky genres also map culminative waves of information onto the orbital structure, further strengthening our sense of a beginning, middle and end. Chat on the other hand coasts along through a kind of prosodic extension of the attitudes under negotiation, weakening our sense of bounded wholes (Martin 2000). These contrasting modes of unfolding are illustrated in Figure 6.1.

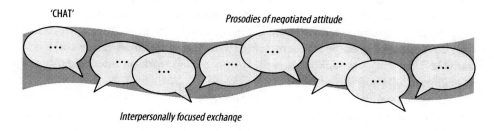

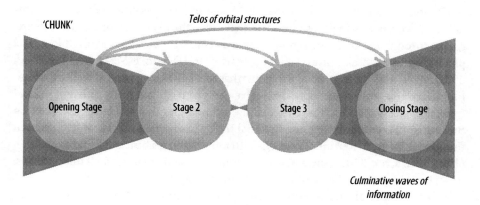

Figure 6.1 Contrasting modes of unfolding in chunk and chat genres

In a sense then, chat does give us the illusion of being 'outside of genre'. But this is because its more fluid structuring principles resonate with the modernist conceits noted above. We feel free, even though we're not. As Eggins & Slade show, chat does involve recurrent configurations of meaning that are the basis for the recognition of any spoken genre, whether informal (as in their data) or institutional (as in for example the work of Christie 2002 on classroom discourse or Ventola 1987 on service encounters) – including some very conservative ideological motifs, at times disguised and thus enabled by humour.

6.1.3 Genre and non-verbal communication

How else to get away from genre? Another popular refuge is extra-linguistic reality, including other forms of communication and physical and biological materiality. This may be accompanied by accusations of logocentricity as far as genre theory is concerned. By defining genres as configurations of meaning, we have tried to open the door to multimodal realisations of genres, including various modalities of communication (e.g. image, music and spatial design as introduced in Chapter 1). Work on multimodal genres is an important focus of innovative discourse analysis for the noughts, and presents a number of challenges for the register variable mode which have yet to be resolved (Baldry 1999, Kress & van Leeuwen 2001). The challenge posed by this research for genre lies in the development of models which not only co-ordinate discourse across metafunctions (i.e. across field, mode and tenor variables) but across modalities as well. For promising work on intermodality see O'Halloran 2004 and Royce 2006.

Alongside non-verbal modalities of communication, physical and biological systems are certainly significant dimensions of analysis around genres. But to bring them into the picture we have to analyse talk about them, by laypersons or by physicists, geologists, chemists, biologists and so on – in more and less common sense terms (including mathematical and technical language and various kinds of imaging). This talk is as close as we can get as discourse analysts to the material world outside genre, gazing through the lay or uncommon sense discourses which have evolved to model physical and biological reality (Halliday & Martin 1993, Martin & Veel 1998, O'Halloran 2003). We would like to stress at this point that specialists are gazing at reality through their discourse too; so our meta-discursive perspective is not really different in kind from the necessarily discursive modelling technologies that scientists use. And on the border of communicative and material reality lies human action, which has been the special focus of Martinec's research into movement, gesture and facial expression (1998, 2000 a, b, c, 2001). Since Martinec models this activity in social semiotic terms, it can be brought into the picture as an attendant 'paralinguistic' modality.

So yes, there are non-verbal modalities of communication to worry about. And yes, there is a material world outside, but one which we inevitably semioticise as we explore. We remain satisfied that genre is well positioned in our model as a resource for co-ordinating communication across modalities in multimodal texts as our understandings of inter-modality unfold.[2]

6.2   Relations among genres – paradigmatic relations

How do we tell one genre from another? Are there texts that are more one genre than another, and others in between? Is it possible to have mixed genres, which we treat as realising more than one genre at a time?

6.2.1 Family membership

As a general rule, the better our genre analysis, the easier it will be to recognise genres as we come across them. If we return to story genres, then we can draw on the body of work outlined in Chapter 2, and expect to find recounts, anecdotes, exemplums, narratives and observations. Looking at the stories in Elaine Russell's beautiful children's picture book, *The Shack that Dad Built* (2004), clear examples of these are easy to find. Elaine recounts moving from La Perouse to Murrin Bridge ('From the beach to the bush'):

[6:1]

We used to sit around the campfire at night, and Dad would tell us about how he travelled all over the place before he and Mum started a family. Sometimes he'd tell us scary ghost stories. But one night when I was about ten, he told us that we were going on a long trip. He had got a job as a handyman on a mission called Murrin Bridge, way out in the country. We would live in a house with floorboards and proper windows. Not long after that, we packed up our clothes (there weren't many!) and said goodbye to our friends, and to Violet, who was staying behind. We were all excited, but also sad at the thought of leaving La Perouse and the beach where we loved to swim and fish.

She tells a moving anecdote about a Christmas present she missed out on ('My saddest Christmas'):

[6:2]

One Christmas eve, my parents took me and my brothers and sisters to nearby Matraville, where a charity was giving away toys to Aboriginal children. It was a very hot day, and the queue was so long. I watched lots of kids going home, happy with their dolls and bikes and scooters and toy cars. My heart was set on a doll that said 'Mama, Mama'. When we finally reached the head of the queue, the people told my parents that they'd run out of toys. I cried and cried.

And she offers an equally moving exemplum about friendship and respect among outsiders ('The Hand of Friendship'):

[6:3]

One day, while we were playing outside our shack, we were surprised to see a family of gypsies coming down the road in a caravan pulled by a horse. They really seemed like strangers in a strange land. But my father extended the hand of friendship. The gypsy family said we were the first people to make them feel welcome. That night we all sat around a big campfire telling our stories to each other.

She includes a narrative about getting over her anxiety on her first day at school ('My school'):

[6:4]

My sister Violet walked me to school on my first day, saying 'Hurry up! We'll be late!' When we got to the school gate, she just left me there – she went to a different building because she was older. I was scared! I felt a lot better when we lined up to go to our classes. I soon made some new friends and we played games in the schoolyard. The next day I wasn't scared at all!

And in an observation she shares an insight into her Dad's character that led to him building a shack for the family at La Perouse:

[6:5]

When I was about five we moved to Sydney because my father, Clem, had found a job. We went to live in La Perouse. Some of Dad's cousins already lived there, and so did lots of other Aborigines – some in the mission, some in shacks. Dad didn't want to live in the mission, though. He preferred to be independent.

Like these stories, the biographical recount that introduces Elaine Russell [6:6] is about specific people, but instead of referring to a specific incident it hops through time (in bold).

[6:6]

Elaine Russell was born in Tinghua, northern New South Wales, **in 1941**. She spent her childhood in La Perouse, and **later**, on the Aboriginal mission at Murrin Bridge, where her father was a handyman. **In 1993**, Elaine enrolled in a visual arts course and was finally able to realise her lifelong ambition to become a painter. Her work has been exhibited in museums and galleries around the world. **In the 2001** Children's Book Council of Australia Awards her first book, *A is for Aunty*, was shortlisted for the Picture Book Award and was an Eve Pownall Information Book Honour Book.

Elaine has six children and ten grandchildren, and lives in Glebe, New South Wales.

And the historical recount that introduces her book [6:7] also hops through time, but here the participants are mostly generalised (in bold).

[6:7]

Aboriginal people have lived on the east coast of Australia for more than 40 000 years, and La Perouse, on the shores of Botany bay, has been used as a camping ground or meeting place for at least 7500 years. **People** followed the seasonal fishing between La Perouse and the south coast of New South Wales.

Records of **permanent Aboriginal habitation** at La Perouse date back to around 1880, when twenty-six Aborigines from the south coast took up permanent settlement. In the mid 1880s, the camp was officially established as an Aboriginal reserve. The camp was first run by **missionaries and a policeman**, and in later years by **resident managers**. Tin houses were built and in 1894, a mission church. But the sand dunes they stood on were too unstable, and the mission buildings were moved to higher ground in 1929–1930.

These were the Depression years, and **hundreds of unemployed people – black and white** – moved into the area around the mission and set up camp, building shacks out of whatever materials they could find. As the Depression ended, **many of the white people** moved on, and by the time Elaine Russell and her family moved to La Perouse, the area was **predominantly Aboriginal** once more.

So far these texts fit the story and history genres we identified in Chapters 2–3. But what about a text like the following [6:8]? This looks like a story, but instead of past tense, activities are modalised for usuality with *usually* and *would* (in bold).

[6:8]

On the weekends, when the tourists came out to La Perouse, they**'d usually make their way down** to the wharf. There they**'d throw** coins into the sea and watch the kids dive for them. I was too small to dive, so I **would sit** on the wharf and hold the coins that my brothers collected. Afterwards we**'d go** and buy the biggest bag of hot chips we could get, then **sit** on the beach and **have** a good feed. Yum! The golf course provided the local kids with another way to make money. Golfers **often lost** their balls in the long grass and bush around the course. Kids **would watch** where the balls went then **come back later** to find them. They**'d take** them home, **give** them a wash, and **sell** them back to the golfers – who **were usually** happy to get their favourite balls back!

This time round, instead of a specific incident and what it meant, Russell generalises across experience, telling us about two ways in which the kids at La Perouse would often make money. And instead of specific participants, we get mainly generic ones (tourists, coins, kids, golfers, balls):

> the tourists – they – their (way) – they
> coins – them – the coins – money
> the kids – the local kids – kids – they
> Golfers – their (balls) – the golfers – their (favourite balls)
> (their) balls – the balls – them – them – them – them – (their) favourite balls

The events related are sequenced in time, like stories rather than history or biography. But this time round we are looking at generalised activity sequences, not specific ones. What kind of genre is this?

Conservatively, we might argue that this is simply a generalised recount (or two generalised recounts, one after the other, to be precise – diving for coins, then selling golf balls). But would this be saying enough about the different focus of this genre? Is it too narrative a gaze?

Alternatively we might read Russell as shifting from narrative towards history here. Her generalised recount relies on generic participants engaged in recurrent behaviour. Unlike historical recounts and biographical recounts however, [6:8] does deal with specific activity sequences; it doesn't hop through time, like [6:6] and [6:7], but records habitual behaviour step by step.

Moreover each sequence in [6:8] culminates with an attitudinal burst, involving affect and appreciation (*Yum!* and *happy to get their favourite balls back!*), something we expect from narrative but not history. On balance then, while the generalised recount shares certain features with history discourse, on balance it seems more narrative than history.

What about the discourse of administration? Jordens (2002), in the course of his study of interviews with cancer patients, family and hospital staff involved in their care proposes a non-narrative genre he calls 'policy'. For Jordens, the policy genre proposes a behavioural routine, implemented in specific circumstances on the basis of a particular rationale. Its general structure is Scenario ^ Policy ^ Rationale, as in [6:9 below]. In the following example, one of his doctors discusses an aspect of his current institutional practice as far as warning patients about their prospects of recovery is concerned.

[6:9]

Scenario

Um in more recent years when I first came back into clinical practice after a time out of practice I again found myself being unduly *over*-supportive and talking about the negatives but emphasising the positives a little bit too much. And I found that in the first couple of years I was back in practice I think I was tending to carry the patients' burdens a little bit. And then when it did go bad then I felt like I'd failed {{CJ: Right}}, or they felt like this was really unexpected.

Policy

And nowadays I'm finding it more important for my own survival in this for the next twenty years of my practicing life *not* to carry their burdens. {{CJ: Right, so that involves being careful about how you talk to them in the beginning about prospects – {{Jon: Exactly}} and the possibilities of cure and –}} That's right. It really – I really find it vital now to make absolutely clear at the start that there's no guarantees that this is going to be fixed. 'We'll do our best' and, you know, 'We're hopeful' and 'There is a good chance. But there is no guarantees'. And I wouldn't have said –. I – you know, I would have made sure that they understood that message before. But now, at the end of my standard consultation at the end of treatment, I now deliberately say to people: 'Yes it has all gone well. I am quite happy with it. I think you're gonna be okay. But there are no guarantees.'

Rationale

And I guess that reflects scars of a few times when it went wrong. And even though they ought to have known, and they would have been told by me that it might go wrong, I still ended up feeling guilty that it did, or they felt that something had gone wrong when it hadn't. {{CJ: Right.}} [Jordens 2002: 163–164]

Unlike historical and biographical recounts, this text does focus on the details of activity – what the doctor now says at the beginning of treatment and at the end:

> I really find it vital now to make absolutely clear **at the start** that there's no guarantees that this is going to be fixed. 'We'll do our best' and, you know, 'We're hopeful' and 'There is a good chance. But there is no guarantees'…

> But now, **at the end of my standard consultation at the end of treatment**, I now deliberately say to people: 'Yes it has all gone well. I am quite happy with it. I think you're gonna be okay. But there are no guarantees.'

And like the generalised recount it does construe habitual behaviour. In policies however, the behaviour in question is current practice, not what happened in the past (although the doctor does contrast his current practice with his past):

> **nowadays** I'm **finding** it more important… *not* to carry their burdens

> **now** I really **find** it vital to make …clear that there's no guarantees

> **now** I deliberately **say** to people, '… But there are no guarantees.'

> **before** I **would have made** sure that they understood that message

And current practice is explicitly motivated through a rationale stage giving reasons for what is done.

Attitude in this policy focuses on appreciation of the significance of what to say and the quality of service provided:

> **more important**…*not* to carry their burdens.

> **vital**…to make **absolutely clear**…that there's no guarantees…

> We'll do our **best**

> There is a **good** chance

> it has all gone **well**

> I am quite **happy** with it.

> you're gonna be **okay**.

Once again then, though the generalised recount leans towards some relevant administrative discourse, its overall configuration of meanings is closer to those of the narrative genres. Critically, when we look at the phasing of these meanings, the generalised recount unfolds through sequence in time (in the case of [6:8], one activity sequence after another); historical and biographical recounts on the other hand hop from one setting in time to another. The policy's phasing is different from both of these in that it culminates with a rationale, motivating the behaviour specified in its nucleus. These differences show the importance of taking staging into account when considering relations among genres.

Topologically speaking we might place generalised recounts like [6:8] towards the periphery of the narrative family, drawn 'outwards' by the semiotic 'gravity' of both historical and administrative genres, illustrated in Figure 6.2, and summarised in more detail in Table 6.1 below. Whatever its position in a universe of meaning as genre analysis unfolds, the critical point is that where it belongs depends on the configurations of meaning it shares and does not share with other genres and how these are phased as the genre unfolds. Since sharing meaning is ultimately a matter of degree, topology provides a better modelling strategy than typology for such 'intermediate' genres.

Table 6.1 Configurations of meaning across generalised recount, historical recount and policy genres

	GENERALISED RECOUNT	HISTORICAL RECOUNT	POLICY
PARTICIPANTS	mainly generic	mainly generic	specific & generic
TENSE/MODALITY	modalised usuality	past	habitual present
ACTIVITY SEQUENCE	step by step	setting to setting	specific steps
ATTITUDE	affect, appreciation	some judgement	appreciation
CAUSE	implicit motivation	implicit motivation	explicit motivation
PHASING	activity sequencing	resetting in time	routine ^ rationale

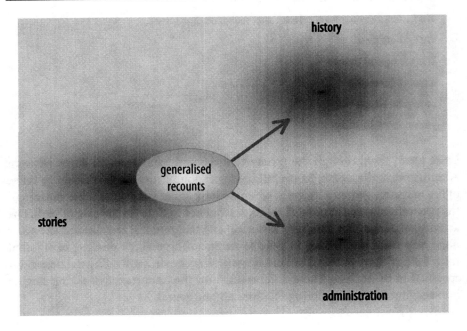

Figure 6.2 Generalised recounts drawn 'outwards'

6.2.2 Shifting gears

Not all individual texts of course fit neatly into one genre or another. Some texts shift gears, from one configuration of meaning to another. Elaine Russell's text 'Our New Home' begins with a paragraph of description and moves on to a paragraph of generalised recount. Whereas night-time behaviour is managed as a single event in the first paragraph (*us kids would all sleep...*), day-time behaviour is unpacked as an activity sequence in paragraph two.

[6:10]

We only had one big room in our shack. The walls were lined with newspaper to help keep out the cold and heat. At night, us kids would all sleep on a big mattress on the floor, the girls up one end and the boys down the other.

During the day we would put the mattress away, and Violet and I would sweep the floor. I sprinkled water on the first so it didn't fly everywhere. Then Mum would put down an old piece of lino. I thought it looked lovely!

We might be tempted to treat paragraph one as the Orientation stage of a generalised recount; but this would gloss over the contrast Russell makes between night and day routines.

Another shift in gears is found in [6:11] which starts out as a report in paragraph one and moves to hortatory exposition in paragraph two: the text begins by generalising about threats to animals, and continues by arguing why they need to be conserved (Martin 2001a).

[6:11]

At one time overhunting was the greatest threat to animals. Since 1600 78 mammals and 94 birds have become extinct. At least one third were wiped out by hunting. Although overhunting is still a serious threat, the destruction of the habitat has become more important. Extinct animals can never be brought back to life. For every species of animal which has been wiped out by man, there are many more which are endangered.

Animals need to be conserved not just because they are beautiful or unusual. The survival of all species, including people, depends upon the maintenance of a wide range of native species in their natural habitat. Survival of species is not a competition between people and animals – it is a matter of living together, with people conserving and managing natural environments to ensure that native species continue to play their roles in the world we all share. These following animals are but a mere few of the species currently battling extinction.

Texts like [6:10] and [6:11] are often referred to as examples of 'mixed genres', by way of capturing the transitions from one genre determined configuration of meaning to another. Strictly speaking of course we should refer to examples such as these as mixed **texts**, which happen to instantiate more than one genre. The concept of a 'mixed genre' is in itself contradictory, since recognising such phenomena entails acknowledging the typologically distinct systemic categories we find in our mix. For example, calling something a mixture of report and exposition means that we already know what reports and expositions are, and regularly recognise them as discrete relatively bounded categories. It's not the genres that are mixed, but the individual texts that instantiate them.

6.2.3 Genesis

At this point we need to bring time into the picture, since 'mixed texts' are one obvious source of new genres. If the mix gets instantiated often enough, because the social purpose of such texts recurs often enough, then we soon stop seeing it as a mix of genres and accept it as a new genre in which the shift in gears is treated as a predictable move from one stage to the next – each partaking in the accomplishment of the telos of the new genre.

In our work on secondary school geography for example we began to wonder if we were witnessing the emergence of a new green genre, such was the impact of ecology and environmentalism on the Australian curriculum (Martin 2001a, Veel 1998). In [6:12–14] below for example (taken from a Year 10 Geography assignment), we begin with traditional reports on three rainforest animals, of the kind we'd find in modernist geography textbooks and encyclopaedias. In each case this is followed by discussion of status of the animal in question as a threatened species (highlighted in **_bold italic_** font).

[6:12] THE JAGUAR

In South America, the jaguar is the greatest of the hunters and its vantage point is a tree, the jaguar leaps onto its unsuspecting prey. Ranging to eight feet in length and 125 to 120 pounds in weight, the jaguar is the largest of all the cats. It is stocky, muscled body, short legs and massive chest make the jaguar a powerful and efficient hunter. Although the jungles of Brazil form the centre of the jaguar's homeland they have been spotted as far away as Mexico.

Through its range, the jaguar adapts to many habitats from the swampy marshes to the stifling rainforests. The jaguar is also a good climber but does most of its hunting on the ground. Deer, tapir, peccary and toucans are frequent victims but the big cat is also fond of fish.

**Jaguars have always been prized for their beautiful spotted coats. For many years the jaguar skins were exported annually to the fur markets of the world. In recent years some 23,000 were exported. Many South American countries now protect the jaguar, but unfortunately the big cat can still be legally hunted even where they have already become endangered. In the Amazon Basin, its last stronghold, it is threatened today not only by hunting, but by the loss of suitable habitat as the rainforest is being opened up to timbering, farming, livestock raising and other human activities.**

[6:13] Gorilla

The gorilla is commonly known as the gentle giant of the rainforest. The biggest of the apes, sometimes reaching a weight of 300 kilograms and a height of 1.75 metres. The gorilla is quite a friendly creature unless threatened or provoked.

The rainforests which these gorillas inhabit supply all the fruits and plants they need, *but the troubling thing is that these forests are shrinking because the land is continually being cleared for farming. Many of these are sold to zoos or hunted for their fur and paws. As a result, their numbers have dropped alarmingly. Today the gorillas number only a few thousand, while there are fewer than 400 mountain gorillas.*

In zoos and wildlife parks it has taken more than a hundred years for the first of these animals in captivity and with the raising of animals being so difficult it will not be easy to try and restock the wild.

[6:14] Orangutan

Orangutan means man of the woods. They are called this because like other great apes, gorillas and chimpanzees they are like humans in many ways.

At 80 kilograms the male orangutan is by far the largest truly tree-dwelling. Treetop life for such a heavy animal would be impossible if it did not possess remarkable hooked hands, hand-like feet, long arms and tremendous strength. These adaptions allow the orangutan to hang tirelessly, for hours at a stretch, suspended by only three limbs while picking fruit with the spare hand. It can only hang upside down, clinging with only one foot. *Orangutans once lived in all of the forests in South East Asia but today they are only found on the islands of Sumatra and Borneo. They now number fewer than 5000. There are many reasons, for the declining populations during the last 200 years: – their rainforests are being cleared, they are shot for sport and some were killed as they were thought of as extremely dangerous. Many were collected for zoos, while a lot of the young ones were taken for pets.*

Today about a third of those in zoos were bred in captivity, and many pet animals are being taken back to their natural habitats. All of the governments concerned give them full protection. Forest reserves have been set aside to save the orangutan. Since most of the world's tropical forests are being cut for timber, these parks are vital.

In the 'extensions' our student writer's attitude to their plight is made explicit (*unfortunately, troubling, alarmingly*) and concessive adjuncts are deployed to engage a sense of urgency in the reader (*still, even, already, not only... but, only, only*). There are no explicit exhortations, but the play of inscribed and evoked attitude paints a dire picture of what is going wrong and the challenging nature of protection measures (zoos, wildlife parks and forest reserves). This evaluation clearly functions as an implicit call for action, and in this respect we can interpret the green reports as subsuming an expository stance. So where report and arguments once stood as complementary geography genres, as we showed for the textbook *Australian*

Journey: environments and communities in section 5.5 above, these genres are now fusing to occupy a niche of environmental sensitivity in Australian secondary school curricula and practice.

One relatively well documented example of the emergence of a new genre is provided by Iedema 1997b and White 1997 who describe the development of the 20th century news story of out of 19th century recounts, focusing on the disruption of the time line as newspapers foreground highly charged evaluative meaning by way of attracting a more diversified readership. So instead of recounts beginning with initial events and culminating with final ones we have news stories beginning with a Headline/Lead and unfolding through a series of dependent satellites each elaborating that Headline/Lead nucleus and not the satellite before. The changing social conditions behind this, according to Iedema and White, have to do with the centralisation of print media ownership, and the need to appeal to a much wider range of readers than newspapers were concerned with in the 19th century.

News stories were considered in Chapter 2 above and so will not be exemplified again here. Note however that the change in organisation canvassed here pushes news stories to the periphery of the family of story genres, since they are no longer chronologically structured and unfolding through time is such a central dimension of the meaning of narrative genres. The only thing holding news stories in the family perhaps is the fact that we can still usually reconstruct the sequence of events from what is reported even though sequential conjunctive links are not deployed. If this residue of chronology were to be lost, as a result perhaps of 20th century marketing pressures or web based transmission, then news stories would certainly have to be reconsidered as card carrying members of the narrative family of genres (and perhaps change their name from news stories to news reports in the process).

We'll finish this section with one more example of generic change, this time considered from the perspective of inter-cultural communication. In Chapter 2 we noted the infantilising of Australian Indigenous culture through the just-so story genre, a genre fostered in Australian primary schools as we illustrated in Chapter 1 with text [1.10]. This raises important questions about how we read a text arising in one culture and recontextualised into another. One Australian publisher, Ashton Scholastic, has published a series of 'Aboriginal Stories' which attempt to speak across the cultural divide. One of these, The Echnida and the Shade Tree (Green 1984), is reproduced as [6:15] below (for representations of echidna see Figure 6.3); the publisher presents the story as 'Told by Mona Green (Compiled by Pamela Lofts)'. Inside the front cover it describes the book as 'based on a story told by Mona Green, of the Djaru Tribe, to Aboriginal children living in Halls Creek, Western Australia. The illustrations are adapted from their paintings of the story.' [For this monomodal presentation, '/' separates text on facing pages of a two page spread, and '//' separates one two page spread from the next.]

Figure 6.3   Echidna in the flesh and as ancient Aboriginal rock art

[6:15] The Echidna and the Shade Tree

Away out in the middle of the desert, there once grew a huge tree. //

It was so big, that it shaded the whole land from the scorching sun. //

All the animals lived in the shade of the this tree. Each day, they would hunt for food, while old Echidna stayed behind. He looked after the children. //

Each time, when the animals returned with the food, they would give the children the tastiest bits – / but poor old Echidna got only the scraps. //

This made Echidna very angry! He grabbed hold of that giant shade tree and shook it. He pulled it. And, with a mighty tug, tore it right out of the ground – roots and all.

//He put the tree on his back and stomped off. / Soon, the animals realised that their shade was moving and that they would die of thirst in the hot sun. //

They chased after Echidna and begged him to stop. They begged him to put the tree back. //

But he just marched on in anger. / The animals threw a boomerang. Surely that would stop him! //

But it didn't. it hit him on the feet and broke his toes – //

But he still shuffled on! / At last, the animals hurled their spears. //

Echidna howled in pain. Soon, he was completely covered with spears. //

The giant tree crashed to the ground. It rolled over and over across the plain – / and it's huge branches broke off and stuck into the ground. //

Poor Echidna lay dying. Soon the animals began to feel sorry for him. / Cockatoo flew up and asked, 'Where would you like to be buried? //

In an antbed? / In a clump of spinifex grass? In between some rocks?' Echidna chose the rocks. When he died the animals buried him there and covered him up. Only the spears were sticking out. //

To this day echidnas have spears on their backs. They still shuffle about on little bent and broken feet, as they hunt for ants among the rocks. //

The animals, too, still live in the desert. They hunt in the shade of the small trees that grew from the branches of that one giant tree. //

And they will never die of thirst, because water filled up the hole left by the shade tree – and made a huge lake, called Nongra. //

We believe that publishing the story in this way is a genuine attempt to open up an Indigenous perspective for non-indigenous children. But how will they read this genre? The last three paragraphs invite a reading of the story as an explanation of natural phenomena – why the echidnas have spines, how they walk, what they hunt, and how Nongra Lake was formed. And this invites a reading of the story through a just-so story template – rendering it a fanciful childish native tale about how the world was formed. On the book's back cover, Mona Green comments that 'when my husband was a stockman, we used to go out to Nongra Lake to see if the cattle had enough water. I had heard the story about this giant lake and I think that, from the air, it would look a tree with roots stretching out.'

This comment seems to reinforce the creation reading of the story foregrounded in the 'just-so' genre, but to the Djaru elders who told the story to Mona Green, it may have several quite different interpretations. For example, at the level of social obligation, echidna clearly represents the aged grandparents who often stayed in camp to care for young children while their parents foraged, so that his anger at being given only scraps is morally justified. As the senior members of the society are custodians of its sacred cultural capital, the shade tree that echidna uprooted and carried off probably stands for an aspect of this. Indeed, in the context of sacred ceremonies in Australia's Western Desert, society is divided into a 'shade' moiety and a 'sun' moiety, that play complementary ceremonial roles. So at the level of religious theory, the hijacking of the shade tree may represent a threatened withdrawal of half the society's sacred repertoire, which it could not survive, any more than the people could survive burning by the sun. The slaying of echidna would then represent the rescue of this repertoire through the ritual transformation of the offender from echidna the man to echidna the animal. This interpretation is reinforced by his burial in the rocks, leaving only his quills/spears sticking out. This is clearly a reference to the species of cane bush that grows in the rocky hillsides of arid Australia, from which are obtained the shafts for making spears; as men obtain their primary economic tools from the buried corpse of echidna, so too they obtain their most valued semiotic resources from the cultural heritage of their ancestors. If this interpretation is correct, then the key activities in the story would undoubtedly be reenacted in ceremonial performances, accompanied by a series of songs. Such sacred songs and rituals, like the echidna myth, are immeasurably old. They are not invented by any individuals past or present, but come down to us mysteriously through deep time, along with the rest of the social and natural worlds we are heir to (cf Rose 2001a, 2006b, to appear a).

Djaru children would be apprenticed into this system of esoteric knowledge and practices in stages. They would hear this story repeatedly from an early age. At some stage they would recognise the analogy between the spearing of echidna and the quills on the animal they know, and they would recognise the offended behaviour of the old man in that of their own grandparents, and its ethical implications. They would learn to respond to the narrative pattern of expectancy and counterexpect-ancy that makes repeated retelling always pleasurable, and to identify themselves with the protagonists' victory and the wonder of Nongra Lake's everlasting waters that resulted. But at some time as they become adults, the esoteric layers of meaning encoded in the story would be revealed to them. At that moment the familiar childish entertainment the story gave them would be transformed in a flash of adult insight into the deep principles and origins of their society. This is the experience of initiation, the pleasure of discovery that we experience as a metamorphosis from ignorance to wisdom. The knowledge is derived from the elders who reveal it to us, but the experience of discovery is ours. This experience is a powerful force for socialisation, as much in contemporary urban societies as in the hunting-gathering cultures of Australia. Indeed it underlies the whole academic enterprise in which we are engaged, as well as the school education that prepares us for it.

How many steps would it be from say Conal's understanding of this story to that of the Aboriginal children living in Halls Creek today, to that of Mona Green, to that of the elders who told her the story, and back further to the elders who had assumed custody of it over tens of thousands of years in Indigenous languages and cultures? It is doubtful Conal would recognise any of the significance of the social relations and obligations described in the story. He wouldn't see that as part of this meaning of this genre, because he can only read in terms of the social purpose of the genres he knows; and he knows just-so stories are make-believe – the stuff of legends (a term often used to refer to stories recontextualised from Indigenous traditions along these lines). Non-Indigenous adults reading the story may recognise some of the moral message implied in the story; certainly these messages are often emphasised in retellings of Aboriginal stories for a general audience. But it is highly unlikely that many would recognise the abstract principles of social and natural order that the story encodes, and certainly not its relation to the religious practices that reenact and so reproduce this social and natural order. Rather for the average reader these stories remain firmly in the just-so genre, entertaining tales that give child-like explanations of natural phenomena and social behaviours.

As a genre is recontextualised from one culture to another it cannot help but become something else, a new genre (a transformative process that Bernstein described for texts that are recontextualised from production to education). When this occurs for significant texts of Indigenous cultures, the Indigenous meaning of these genres is bound to be transformed in this process, especially where colonialist templates such as Kipling's just-so-stories are available for their appropriation. Of course reconciliation necessarily involves communication across incommensurable cultures. But semiotically speaking, handler beware!

6.2.4 Contextual metaphor

We'll conclude this discussion of relations among genres with reference to what Martin (e.g. 1997) calls contextual metaphor, defined as the process whereby one genre is deployed to stand for another. One well-known example of this is Eric Carle's

(1970) children's story *The Very Hungry Caterpillar* in which a caterpillar eats and eats, builds himself a cocoon and turns into a beautiful butterfly – a recount genre standing for a scientific explanation of metamorphosis. Genre symbolism of this kind was popularised in Australian schools in the late 1980s as progressive literacy pedagogy spread across the curriculum, promoting narrative as a primary act of mind (sic) and encouraging story writing to promote real learning (sic) in science and other content areas (Martin 1990). This gave rise to recounts with titles such as 'Emma's egg' (about conception) or 'Journey to the Brain' (about sound waves in the ear). Of course recounts and scientific explanations are every bit as incommensurable as Indigenous narratives and just-so stories, and the project degenerated into farce – although at times we couldn't help applauding the play of humour that contextual metaphor affords. One of our favourite examples, from a different context, is the following land rights recipe from *Pulp* (the student magazine of Southern Cross University [1998]), a procedure standing for a hortatory exposition.

[6:16] Terra Nullius Pie

INGREDIENTS...

1   * 'Empty' continent (a wide brown one will do nicely)

10   * Point Plan, OR

100 Litres 'Sorry Tears'

Some live Cultures

Plenty of re-written history to garnish

METHOD
Take the land and thoroughly clean of any people. Remove as much of the forest and minerals as you can. Next liberally pour wastes into waterways until nicely blue-green. At this point you'll be tempted to carve the pie up into 10 big slices, but this may cause heartburn or even armed insurrection later!

ALTERNATIVELY, sprinkle well with sorry tears and leave to reconcile for a while. When cool, share it out – if no one is too greedy there'll be plenty to go round...

Contextual metaphors, like grammatical metaphors, operate by offering readers a literal 'surface' reading implicating one genre, but providing in addition 'other genre' indicators signalling the presence of a 'deeper' genre lurking behind. There may in fact be more than one layer to this. Text [6:17] for example is literally a personal recount, about a trip to the library.

[6:17]

Yesterday I went to the library and found a book about dolphins. I had seen dolphins on TV and I was interested in them. I wanted to find the answer to the question, why are dolphins so interesting to humans?

The book said that dolphins were sea mammals. I bet you didn't know that dolphins have to breathe air! If they don't breathe air, they will die.

I have often wondered what dolphins like to eat, so I looked in the book for information about this. Do they eat other fish, I wondered? I found out that they do.

I suppose you know what dolphins look like, of course. I found out some interesting things, such as what that dorsal fin is for and how they keep warm. Why do we humans like dolphins so much, I often wonder. I searched in the book for the answer to this question, but could not get down to the real reason. The book talked about their tricks and stunts and their general friendliness. As I thought about it, I came to the conclusion that it had something to do with the fact that they, like us, are mammals.

But it uses projection to mount a second field, which is concerned with dolphins:

The book said	that dolphins were sea mammals.
I bet you didn't know	that dolphins have to breathe air!
I have often wondered	what dolphins like to eat,
I wondered	do they eat other fish
I often wonder	why do we humans like dolphins so much
I came to the conclusion	that it had something to do with the fact that they, like us, are mammals.

In this sense the text is a recount (about a trip to the library) standing for a report (about dolphins). Beyond this however, the text unfolds dialogically though a question and answer format:

I wanted to find the answer to the question, why ...?
- The book said that ...

I have often wondered what...
- so I looked in the book for information about this.

Do they...I wondered?
- I found out that ...

I suppose you know what...of course.
- I found out some interesting things, such as what ...and how...

Why do we ...so much, I often wonder.
- I searched in the book for the answer to this question, but could not get down to the real reason. The book talked about ... As I thought about it, I came to the conclusion that ....

As we can see, this mock Socratic dialogue culminates with a conclusion about why we like dolphins, and so might be additionally construed as an argumentative genre focussing on why this is indeed the case... so that we end up with a recount standing for a report standing for an argument perhaps, if we try and tie up all the loose ends and push our contextual metaphor reading to its limits. Confirming this reading is the title given to the text by its author: 'Is this a report or a recount or a discussion?'. The title reflects the fact that the text was contrived by a secondary school English consultant as a challenge to genre theory, mounting the argument (discredited above) that mixed genres show that there aren't genres and so genre-based literacy programs should be expunged as a base line for designing pedagogy and organising curriculum. Our response of course was that anyone writing contextual metaphors of this order had already learned what recounts, reports and arguments were like, and had the literacy facility to compose a text in which one symbolised another. The working class, migrant and Indigenous kids we were working with were operating far from middle class currency of this order.

In short then, our genre theory, like any other, has to take responsibility for mixed texts which instantiate more than one genre. The challenge lies in understanding the ways in which they do this. And this involves mapping out the system of genres a culture deploys, and carefully considering the ways in a text might draw on one or more of them and thus 'mix genres' (sic) or not. In this section we've looked at various issues as far as recognising genres is concerned, including texts that change gears from one genre to another, genre evolution, cross-cultural appropriation, and contextual metaphor. Below we shift from a paradigmatic to a syntagmatic perspective and ask how genres can be extended or combined to form much longer texts than those we've been considering in this chapter thus far.

6.3   Relations between genres – syntagmatic relations

How do we tell where a genre begins and ends? Are there always sharp boundaries? How do genres combine and grow to form long texts?

6.3.1 Combining genres – expansion

In section 5.5 we introduced the notion of macrogenres, drawing on Halliday's 2004 model of logicosemantic relations. We return to this conception here, beginning this time round with story genres, and focussing on story genres, and their recontextualisation as steps in longer texts. We begin with expansion, and its subtypes – elaboration, extension and enhancement, followed by projection.

First, expansion by elaboration. Once upon a time...

> **[6:17]**
>
> A small child asked her father, 'Why aren't you with us?' And her father said: 'There are other children like you, a great many of them...' and then his voice trailed off.

...which we might read as a bare anecdote. Add some appreciation...

> **[6:17']**
>
> A small child asked her father, 'Why can you not be with us?' And her father had to utter some **terrible** words: 'There are other children like you, a great many of them...' and then his voice trailed off.

... and the family's pain of separation is directly inscribed. Add some more appreciation...

> **[6:17″]**
>
> It was **as simple and yet as incomprehensible as** the moment a small child asks her father, 'Why can you not be with us?' And the father must utter the terrible words: 'There are other children like you, a great many of them...' and then his voice trails off.

and the pain is further inscribed as bewildering. Generalise the deixis, and we know it is the author talking about his own family, not someone else's...

> **[6:17‴]**
>
> It was as simple and yet as incomprehensible as the moment a small child asks her father, 'Why can you not be with us?' And the father must utter the terrible words: 'There are other children like you, a great many of them...' and then **one's** voice trails off.

...the agony is a personal one. Reframe the story as an example of the price paid by the family of a political leader...

> **[6:17⁗]**
>
> In that way, my commitment to my people, to the millions of South Africans I would never know or meet, was at the expense of the people I knew best and loved most. = It was as simple and yet as incomprehensible as the moment a small child asks her father, 'Why can you not be with us?' And the father must utter the terrible words: 'There are other children like you, a great many of them...' and then one's voice trails off.

...and we re-read the text as an exemplum – an instance of the effect of a moral dilemma. Contextualise the dilemma, as part of the politics of apartheid South Africa...

> **[6:18]**
>
> In life, every man has twin obligations – obligations to his family, to his parents, to his wife and children; and he has an obligation to his people, his community, his country. In a civil and humane society, each man is able to fulfil those obligations according to his own inclinations and abilities. But in a country like South Africa, it was almost impossible for a man of my birth and colour to fulfil both of those obligations. In South Africa, a man of colour who attempted to live as a human being was punished and isolated. In South Africa, a man who tried to fulfil his duty to his people was inevitably ripped from his family and his home and was forced to live a life apart, a twilight existence of secrecy and rebellion. I did not in the beginning choose to place my people above my family, but in attempting to serve my people, I found that I was prevented from fulfilling my obligations as a son, a brother, a father and a husband.
>
> =
>
> In that way, my commitment to my people, to the millions of South Africans I would never know or meet, was at the expense of the people I knew best and loved most. = It was as simple and yet as incomprehensible as the moment a small child asks her father, 'Why can you not be with us?' And the father must utter the terrible words: 'There are other children like you, a great many of them…' and then one's voice trails off.
>
> [Mandela 1995: 746–750]

…and we move into a discussion by Mandela of the personal cost of his decision to serve his people (Mandela's text is further discussed in Martin & Rose 2003/2007, Chapter 7). The text now illustrates one way in which discourse expands through elaboration, with a story serving as an illustration in expository discourse. It also illustrates the way in which our reading of a story will be shaped by its co-textualisation. What started off in [6:17] looking like a moving anecdote, inviting us to empathise with a family's pain, ends up in [6:18] as an exemplum provoking judgment about the cruel consequences for his family of a rebel's courage. The critical point here is that expansion of one genre by another always involves some degree of recontextualisation. We cannot help but read text in terms of what has gone before, and to some extent reinterpret what has gone before with respect to what in fact follows. Since reading is a process, genre analysis has to be a matter of contingent interpretation – attuned to unfolding discourse, not just chunks of de-co-textualised discourse taken out of time.

Expansion through extension can be illustrated through texts [6:12–14] above, which reported on three rainforest animals. In the secondary school geography report from which these text were taken these combined with a forth report on butterflies (parts of which were impossible to decipher) to form four step additive chain (Martin 2001a):

THE JAGUAR

...

+ GORILLA

...

+ ORANGUTAN

...

+

[6:19] BUTTERFLY

Tropical forests are the home of many beautiful butterflies. The ?xxx Rajah birdwing lives in Borner. Also the giant ?xxx, which has the same wingspan as a bird inhabits the ?xxx rain forest of the Amazon. These two butterflies have become extremely rare. Butterflies are netted and killed, then preserved ?xxx. Sometimes their wings are made into souvenirs. Most ?xxx have become extinct due to the destruction of the forests.

These four reports in fact function as an elaboration of text [6:11] – the report cum exposition interpreted as shifting gears in 6.2.1.2 above. The green culmination of each report supports the urgency of the implicit call for action in [6:11], a co-contextualisation reinforcing the environmentalist orientation of the report as a whole.

VICTIMS UNDER THREAT
... These following animals are but a mere few of the species currently battling extinction.
= THE JAGUAR

...

+ GORILLA

...

+ ORANGUTAN

...

+ BUTTERFLY

The following stories illustrate expansion through enhancement, as they present South East Asian responses to 9/11 (Martin 2004a). The Singapore detention is presented as overlapping in time with the arrests in Macau (*meanwhile*); and the reactions on public transport in Hong Kong, where the texts were written, are compared with these (*similarly*).

[6:20]

The Macau police found themselves in a *Keystone Cops* episode, arresting and detaining seven 'suspected Pakistani terrorists.' The scare was enough to close the U.S. Consulate in Hong Kong for a day, though the men turned out to be tourists, a word which is spelled somewhat like terrorists, and we suppose to some people, just as frightening. One of the arrested people in fact was a Hindu, a chef from Hong Kong, who had been cleverly tracked down by undercover cops sitting peacefully at the Hotel Lisboa bar.

x

> **[6:21]**
>
> **Meanwhile** (and we're not making this up), two Indian nationals on a flight from Singapore to Hong Kong were detained at Changi Airport after an American passenger said he heard one of the men calling himself a 'Bosnian terrorist.' (The man in fact said he was a 'bass guitarist.')

x

> **[6:22]**
>
> **Similarly**, there have already been reports of taxis putting up 'out of service' signs and people changing seats on buses when confronted by dark-skinned people – as if changing your seat would save you if a bomb went off, anyway. But such is the logic of xenophobia.

Taken one at a time, we would probably read [6:20] as an exemplum (mocking the stupidity of the Macau police), [6:21] as an anecdote (poking fun at the American passenger in Singapore) and [6:22] as an observation (explicitly judging the racist responses in Hong Kong and implicitly appreciating the break-down of social order). The editorial from which these stories were taken in fact positions them as three examples of what it refers to as *some unfortunate cases locally of backlash*, appreciating the incidents and their like as regrettable, but not judging the perpetrators too harshly, and not really inviting empathy with the victims. And this survey of the local scene contrasts sharply with the preceding discussion of reactions in America, which are strongly criticised using explicit judgment and considerable amplification (Martin 2004a, Martin & White 2005):

> [strong negative judgment of America's response]
>
> +   On a smaller and closer scale, we have already begun to see some unfortunate cases locally of backlash against members of the Muslim community (or even just people who look like they *might* be Muslim).
>
> =   The Macau police
>
> ...
>
> x   Meanwhile... at Changi Airport
>
> ...
>
> x   Similarly.. reports of taxis
>
> ...

As the editorial concludes, *If, as all the pundits are saying, there is no hope of normalcy returning soon, let's at least hope that sanity does.* (*HK Magazine* Friday Sept 21 2001: 5), the breakdown in social order, and by implication its threat to business, is what concerns the editor and his readership in Hong Kong. So ultimately, the point of the stories is to exemplify the need for a speedy return to business as usual; we're not invited to respond by prosecuting perpetrators of racist discrimination or making reparations to their victims.

As we can see, both the geography report and *HK Magazine* editorial make use of different types of expansion as the texts are elaborated, extended and enhanced. At a glance, the report scaffolds this more overtly than the editorial by using headings to punctuate the moves. But a range of discourse semantic devices are also at play managing the transitions, including cataphoric deixis (*these following*), general lexis (*animals, Muslim community*), comparative text reference (*on a smaller and closer scale*), metadiscourse (*cases*), nominalisation (*extinction, backlash*) and conjunction (*meanwhile, similarly*). As with clause complexing, expansion enables genres to unfold indefinitely, one to another, until the large scale goals of the macro-genre are achieved.

Since we have already drawn on several of the genres from Russell's picture book, it may be useful to outline their relation to one another and the rest of *The Shack that Dad Built* here, as [6:23]. Basically the stories take us through Russell's childhood, from birth to the bush, via temporal succession (enhancement); this progression is extended by two series of extending vignettes, arranged before and after starting school.

[6:23] The Shack that Dad Built

    When I was little
    ... (observation)
x Moving to Sydney
    ...(observation)
x The Shack the Dad Built
    ... (observation)
    + Our New Home
       ... (description/generalised recount)
    + The Biggest Backyard on the World
       ... (observation)
    + Bush Tucker
       ...(generalised recount)
    + Fish for Supper
       ...(generalised recount)
x My School
    ... (narrative)
    + Money for Hot Chips
       ...(generalised recount
    + My Secret Garden
       ... (observation)
    + The Hand of Friendship
       ...(exemplum)
    + My Saddest Christmas
       ... (anecdote)
x From the Beach to the Bush
    ...(recount)
x Leaving
    ... (recount)

Compared with many other picture books, Russell's stories are strongly punctuated with headings that demarcate one story from another. This segmentation reinforces the relative lack of discourse semantic continuity as we hop from one memory to the next and encourages us to hear Russell not just telling stories but looking back at what happened, at a much later stage of life. And this indeed is how the inside front jacket cover constructs the picture book – as a collection of memories:

[6:24]

When Elaine Russell was five, her dad built the family a shack just outside the Aboriginal mission at La Perouse. In The Shack the Dad Built, Elaine's vivid paintings illustrate her happy memories of hide-and-seek in the sand dunes and hunting for bush tucker along with more poignant memories, such as 'My Saddest Christmas Ever.'

Warm, funny, and sometimes sad, this true story of an indigenous childhood on the sores of Botany Bay is for everyone to share.

6.3.2 Combining genres – projection

One obvious way in which genres combine through projection is for a character in one genre, a story let's say, to project another genre by verbalising it (telling another story for example, or writing a letter). We are all familiar with this strategy from classic macro-genres such as Chaucer's *Canterbury Tales* and *Tales of the Arabian Nights*. Russell's exemplum, 'The Hand of Friendship', which we presented above, recalls sitting round the campfire exchanging stories with the gypsy family; and we can easily imagine this text unfolding through some of the stories told that night. Later on in her recount 'From the Beach to the Bush' she recalls her father telling scary ghost stories, another opportunity for projecting one or more tales. Some of the stories used as examples in Chapter 3 were projected along these lines in the stolen generations report, *Bringing Them Home* (for discussion of the projection of Indigenous voices in Australia see Martin 2003a, 2004a).

One version of this gambit addressed by Rothery and Stenglin in their work on the development of narrative writing in schools involves 'reality' projecting 'fantasy', by imagining it as it were (Rothery & Stenglin 1997, 2000). In such texts a recount of everyday life is taken as a jumping off point for an excursion into a fantastic world where different rules apply. Conal, writing at age 9 (a year or so after he wrote the texts reviewed in Chapter 1), plays with this motif in his story 'The Golden Rings'. The activity sequence of coming home from school unfolds as usual until he enters the garage a second time. There he discovers a treasure box with jewels, one of which transports him into a whole new world in which he is kidnapped by pirates, who take him to a shop, where he is knocked out, waking up to realise he is dead.

[6:25] The Golden Rings

On a sunny and bright day I was walking home. My house is just around the corner. My house is white with a white door. It has a white window and the walls are white.

Everything is white except for the garage. The garage is yellow with a blue door. I got to my house, went inside and put my bag in my bedroom. Then I went out side again and into the garage. The garage has completely changed. On the inside there are splintery old walls, not painted white but just plain. There was a dusty old table with a treasure box on the old dusty table. In that treasure box there were golden rings with diamonds in them. The diamonds were red, orange, yellow, blue, purple and green. I didn't know if it was a mirage. So I picked one up and put it on my finger. It was real. It was the blue one I put on. I looked down at the ring and then looked up again and I was in a whole new world. I was standing in a pool. I don't know why and my feet where soaking wet. I got out of the pool and a pirate ship came. A man grabbed me and pulled me onto the pirate ship with two other men. We stopped at a shop. There was a plank that we walked up onto the entrance to the strange shop. The shop had a picture of a crab on the top of the shop. The door opened and I walked in with the two other men.

There was an old man with a knife; he said 'Hello. So you have brought him.' They put me on a chain. One of the men came up to me with a stick and banged me on the head with it and everything went black. I was in a place and I saw Zeus and Jesus. I realized that I was dead.

Then I saw my body in the garage, dead on the ground.

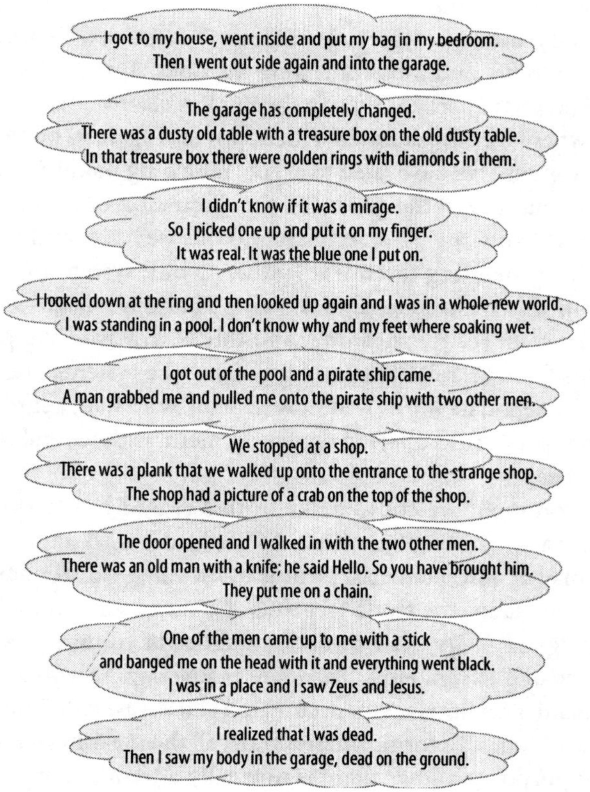

Figure 6.4 Conal projects 'fantasy' from 'reality'

Rothery and Stenglin see this strategy for developing discourse as an important step towards writing modernist narratives in which the story symbolises an underlying moral message (sometimes called 'theme'; Martin 1996a). Along this path Conal still has to learn to get the projected field to comment more judgmentally on the projecting one, and later on to subsume one field into the other so that 'reality' stands for a deeper transcendent truth. His successes to date are schematised in Figure 6.4.

6.3   Rules and resources

Genres makes some people nervous. They offend modernity, which prefers to hide its genericity beneath its creed of individualism. They upset post-modernity, which is entranced by the surface play of intertextuality in instances of discourse, and is suspicious of systems that might constrain the carnivale. But modernity and post-modernity are fashions of meaning, posing against what went before. If we develop theories that are overly imbued by these cultural dispositions we end up with rules for scholarly etiquette perhaps, but not a theory of discourse – not at least a theory of discourse that seriously interrogates the how and why of texts in social contexts, our mission in *Genre Relations*.

For modernity, the main worry about genre is creativity. Genre is read as rules prescribing what to do, and thus contesting freedom. This is a powerful rhetoric, nowhere more powerful perhaps than in the English classrooms of western secondary education where we have collided with it now and again in our work on literacy in schools. In response we have tried to argue, following Bakhtin, that creativity in fact depends on mastery of the genre (cf. the discussion of contextual metaphors above in text [6:16] and [6:17]). And further to this we have tried to position genre as a resource for generating discourse (rather than a system of rules delimiting what we do). In this we are simply following Halliday's (e.g. 1978) conception of language as a resource for meaning, and this is why we have placed so much emphasis in this book on relations among genres– the systems of genres on which speakers draw to negotiate life as we know it. Seen as system, genre is not so much about imposing structure as offering choice – a menu with several courses of social purpose to choose.

A further comment we could make in this regard has to do with modular perspective on making meaning which SFL affords, with genre coordinating a complex interplay of complementary kinds of meaning (ideational, interpersonal and textual) across language strata (register, discourse semantics, lexicogrammar and phonology/graphology) and across modalities of communication (language, image, music, spatial design etc.). There are many ways in which metafunctions, strata and modalities can interact to instantiate a genre. Overwhelmingly, developing a text is not like filling out a form, where almost all the meaning has been frozen for administrative purposes; rather there is normally a tremendous playoff of meanings going on. But without genre we would be puzzled as to what was going on, confounded perhaps. Because we cannot not mean genre.

For post-modernity, the main worry about genre is hegemony. Genre is read as rules inscribing power – effacing the powerless and contesting possible futures. This has been a fashionable rhetoric, voiced on behalf of the 'other' in populist queer, feminist and post-colonial literature. This is an engaging arena of debate, to which we offer three main observations here.

Our first point is that the status of a genre derives from its power, not the other way round. In post-Fordist global capitalist world order, power has to do with controlling the environment (for production, via discourses of science and technology) and managing people (for consumption, via discourses of government and bureaucracy). The more power a genre has in these respects, the higher its status will be, and the more powerful the people deploying the genre will be (and so the higher their status). There is nothing in the genre theory developed here that privileges more powerful genres over less powerful ones, although it is certainly the case in practice that we have concentrated in our literacy initiatives on providing universal access to what we consider to be powerful genres. We concentrate on redistributing access to powerful genres because we think this is a significant step in subverting a social order in which middle aged, middle class, anglo-saxon, able-bodied men preside over the accelerating destruction of our planets' material resources and pitiless exploitation of its disempowered people. As humanists, we put our faith, however naively, in the imaginary futures to which subversion of this kind might lead.

This raises the issue of change, and our second point about genre and power. This is that genres are always changing. They are like all semiotic resources in this respect. As life would have it, texts unfold, individual repertoires develop, and a culture's reservoir expands; and by the same token, as mortality would have it, texts abort, repertoires decline, and cultures disappear. In this flux, the key to understanding genre and change is metastability. As system, genre functions as a kind of inertia; it stabilises social life to the point where we have time to learn how things are done and negotiate our repertoire for a few decades with significant others. As process, genre allows for gradual change, as texts unfold in relation to both recurrent and divergent material and social conditions; as divergence recurs, innovative configurations of meaning stabilise, and new texts become familiar genres (cf. the recount to news story evolution outlined above). The key to modelling change is setting genre up in such a way that it dictates familiarity (so we know where we are coming from) at the same time as enabling innovation (so we can see where we are going). This makes instantiation a major focus of genesis oriented research in SFL (for further discussion see Halliday & Matthiessen 2004).

The third and final observation we would make as far as genre and power is concerned has to do with the discourse of critique itself and who has access to it. We have always found it an instructive exercise to take the language of critical theory and compare it with the language of the disempowered voices it purports to speak for.

Our general impression is that the discourse of critique represents the most abstract academic written discourse to have evolved in human history (Martin 2003b) – a discourse which we suspect takes a least an undergraduate education to read and a post-graduate education to write. Who, we wonder, will teach this discourse to the other, if we listen to the critical theorists and stop teaching powerful genres and the language that realises them? Or are we being called upon to imagine a utopian plenum in which abstract discourse is not required and alternative discourses, enjoying equal status one to another, abound?

To our mind, in a world under threat from the rapidly technologising pursuit of profit, that relentlessly seeks out whatever resources it can to exploit, this is a silly fantasy; ecologically, economically, socially, culturally, too much damage has been done, and there is just no time left to waste. We now need our powerful genres and those which will evolve from them more than ever; and for life as we know it to have any chance of survival we have to pass those genres around – and have them reworked by people who will use them a lot more sensibly than the remorseless short-sighted patriarchs who manage them now.

6.4 Dialogue

As we noted at the beginning of this final chapter, we have written this book as an invitation to consider genres as configurations of meaning and, following on from this, an invitation to map cultures as systems of genres. This is an extroverted enterprise as far as linguistics is concerned, since it involves going beyond language in several directions at the same time. For one thing it means treating social context as more abstract levels of meaning, stratified as register and genre. And for another, it means modelling alternative and attendant modalities of communication as linguistically as possible, in order to bring them into the picture for multimodal genres. Beyond this it means finding some way of taking into account the physical and biological materiality from which social semiotic systems have evolved, and in which there are ongoingly embedded; the strategy we proposed for managing this here was to take both lay and professional discourse about these material systems as data, and bring material reality into the picture via this semiotic veil.

In an enterprise of this kind no single discipline can presume to have a monopoly on meaning, let alone insight. We have learned a lot, and have much more to learn, from our affine disciplines in the humanities and social sciences, and from science and mathematics as we bring materiality into the picture. And beyond this there are lay discourses from all walks of life, and from all kinds of subjectivities, each of which is infused with talk about social life, drawing on the everyday terms they use to talk over what is going on. With respect to all of this complementary insight, our basic strategy is trespass. We try our best to go in and model what is going on as functional linguists, and thus produce a social semiotic account which reads practices as genres. This means treating everything as information, an imperial recontextualisation if ever there was one – privileging linguistics as its informing discipline, and involving massive reconstitutions of perspective, most radically perhaps in the context of physical and biological materiality.

But we intend our incursion as a friendly one. We visit the territories of others because in our experience productive dialogue across disciplines is only possible when they focus on a comparable object of inquiry, map out overlapping claims, and then begin to talk – a process which is considerably enhanced by shared political commitment. We have to intrude we have found, to listen; trespass to hear. That at least is our experience in language education, where our interest in schooling, together with Bernstein's conception of pedagogic discourse, engendered negotiations that we are proud to look upon as genuine transdisciplinary work (Bernstein 1990, 1996, Christie 1999). Yes we are intruding, but with our ears and eyes open, trying our best to learn.

Notes

Chapter 1

1   Texts [1:1–1.10] were in fact written in 2003 by Conal (age 8) in Year 3 in a primary school in Sydney; we're using them as examples of the kinds of writing we found in Australian schools from the beginning of our research in 1979.

2   The American guru of the process writing movement was Donald Graves, and his ideas were promoted in Australia by Jan Turbill, Brian Cambourne and others; later on in the eighties the Goodmans' whole language philosophy was to further propagate the recount genre.

3   This version of Conal's description has been edited by his teacher; aspects of this editing process are discussed in relation to grammatical metaphor in section 4 below.

4   Ventola, who had done an MA with Hasan at Macquarie, did her PhD with Jim in the early 80s at Sydney University (see Ventola 1987) and so provided a direct link with Hasan's work.

5   In 1997, the thirtieth anniversary of Labov & Waletzky's publication, Michael Bamberg guest edited a special commemorative issue of the *Journal of Narrative and Life History* in its honour; Martin & Plum's contribution to this volume reflects our ongoing engagement with Labov & Waletzky's initiative.

6   An alternative perspective on the relationship between register and generic structure in SFL has been developed by Hasan and her colleagues, who model it on the 'axial' relationship between system and structure (cf. Hasan 1995, 1996, 1999, Matthiessen 1993).

7   Ironically, by 1994 the name was already well out of date, since the model we're presenting here was being developed at all the metropolitan Sydney universities, at Wollongong University, at the Northern Territory University, at Melbourne University and beyond. By 2000 the work had become an export industry, with centres in Singapore and Hong Kong, and around Britain ('the empire strikes back' as it were).

8   Compare however Halliday & Matthiessen's 2004 invitation to treat concepts as meanings in a language based approach to cognition.

9   For discussion and exemplification of the relation of SFL to Critical Discourse Analysis see Martin & Wodak 2003.

10   Note that Biber reserves the term genre (later register) for 'folk' categorisations of discourse glossed in terms of social purpose, and packages his corpora for both analysis

and interpretation in relation to such criteria, which he sees as language external; his text type is closer to what we mean by genre.

11 To simplify the discussion we'll set aside graphology and signing as alternative forms of expression here.

12 Since constituency is an important dimension of analysis in all theories we won't review it here, although SFL's approach to constituency is distinctive in that it is organised by rank (a specific type of composition hierarchy); see Butler 2003 for discussion.

13 Grammatically speaking *they got so annoyed that they got a gun out* is an attributive clause with *that they got a gun out* embedded in the attribute *so annoyed*; but semantically we can treat the two clauses as conjunctively linked.

14 As noted, we are only concerned here with minimal New; everything except the crocodiles is arguably New in this report.

15 We haven't analysed a Theme in this non-finite clause.

16 Dependent clauses such as *when we got off the plain* which precede the clause they depend on can be themselves treated as marked Themes, an analysis which would reinforce the realisation of transition here.

17 The fifth heading, **equipment**, is a general term for the things Conal needed for the experiment rather than a grammatical metaphor.

18 Although obviously derived historically from the process *inform*, *information* is no longer a live metaphor, but merely a general term for the facts Conal finds (comparable to *food* and *habitat*); in order to re-activate the metaphor we'd have to use a wording such as *information process*.

19 Upon learning Jim was using some of his writing in this book Conal immediately began negotiating a share of the royalties (how he found out about such his dad Jim is not sure); so we hope he'll forgive us one day for enjoying him here.

Chapter 2

1 Labov's deficit model of narrative variation resonates ironically with his construal of Basil Bernstein's theory of coding orientation in deficit terms.

2 Philip Noyce's film *Rabbit Proof Fence* (based on Doris Pilkington's novel *Follow the Rabbit-Proof Fence*) introduces an international audience to the genocide.

3 Indigenous humour is also a counterpoint to jokes exploiting racist stereotypes that were a distinctive feature of Anglo-Australian culture for generations, but are thankfully becoming less and less acceptable.

4 Of course Uncle Mick's joke is ultimately on the absurdity of certain religious beliefs abouty divine intervention.

5 The grave of King Togee is to be found 29 km west of Coolah on the left-hand side of the Neilrex Rd, just past the 'Langdon' homestead. There is little to see other than a weather-worn sandstone headstone surrounded by four white posts with a sign overhead reading: 'TOGEE KING OF THE BUTHEROE TRIBE'. King Togee was friendly with the early settlers.

6   Nganyintja and husband Charlie Ilyatjari adopted David as a son when he first came to work for their community in the early 1980s.

7   The English translation of the *Piltati* myth here is not a 'free translation', rather there are consistent careful steps in translating it from the Pitjantjatjara. Firstly, most word groups realising an experiential or interpersonal function are directly translatable from Pitjantjatjara to English. These are then arranged in each clause rank translation to reflect the textual structure of the original, and finally re-interpreted in relation to discourse patterns beyond the clause. For example:

a *wati kutjara pula a-nu malu-ku*
   man two they go-did kangaroo-for
   'Those two men went hunting for kangaroos.'

b *kuka kanyila-ku   tati-nu puli-ngka*
   game wallaby-for   climb-did   hill-on
   'For wallabies, that is, they climbed up in the hills.'

8   In general languages seem to differ most at lower levels of phonology and morphology, less at higher ranks in grammar, and less still in discourse semantics patterns, depending on genre and register. See Rose 2001a&b, 2005a for further discussion of these principles.

9   Serpent killing origin heroes are a common trope in Indo-European mythology, from *Indra* the Aryan killer of the Indus serpent *Vithrahan*, to *Apollo* killing the *Python* of Delphi, *St George* slaying the 'dragon' of Silene in Libya, and Norse *Beowulf's* destruction of the 'great worm' *Grendel*. They are often associated with the conquest of serpent worshipping farmers by Indo-European pastoralist invaders, such as the Aryans in India or the Hellenes in Greece (Dumezil 1968, Graves 1955). Zeus' defeat of Typhon in Thrace and Sicily may encode the Hellenic conquests of these peoples. Semitic origin myths also demonise serpents and their worshippers. Egypt's cattle-herding founder hero *Osiris* was temporarily defeated by the Nile serpent *Set*, Babylonian *Marduk* slew the sea-serpent *Tiamat*, and in current missionary bible translations in central Australia, *Jehovah's* enemy *Lucifer* is explicitly described as a *wanampi* serpent (Rose 2001a).

10   Kipling was himself of course bastardising Middle Eastern, South Asian and African cultures, as an agent of British colonialism and its race driven prejudice.

11   A message is defined as a unit of discourse realised by an independent clause, or by a dominant clause together with its non-finite dependent clauses, or by a projecting clause together with its projected clauses.

12   The river is in fact the Ganges, and the woman is the goddess Ganga. This is the first half of the *Shantenu Raaje* myth. In the second half of the story Shantenu falls in love with the daughter of a fishmonger, who refuses to let her marry him as he already has a son who will inherit his kingdom. Accordingly his son selflessly leaves home and becomes a great religious sage *Bishma*. This episode commences the *Mahabharata* epic.

13   This analysis differs from those of Hoey (1983) and Jordan (1984), who interpret the problem-solution relation on the model of grammatical relations of cause and effect. However problems are rarely the cause of solutions, which are more often fortuitous, i.e. counterexpectant. On the other hand, reactions <u>are</u> expectant consequences of preceding phases, for example a problem may engender fear or flight, or a setting, description or solution may engender a positive attitude.

Chapter 3

1   Lavina Gray's recount was recorded by the NSW AMES as part of their Wanyarri project, which was developed to encourage migrants in Australia to learn about Indigenous cultures as part of their ESL program (Wanyarri 1997). It appears here as it was transcribed by Jim from the Wanyarri video (an alternative version is found in the Wanyarri teacher's resource book, p 102). In these materials a number of Indigenous Australians tell their life stories. For a comparable set of autobiographical recounts from the Western Desert see *Stories from Lajamanu* 1985.

2   The episodes in her biography were told to David by Nganyintja and her family, or were shared by David in the years he lived and worked with her.

3   Including one adverbial clause which has a closely related function (*when the third Vietnamese boat of the first wave arrived*).

4   Following Halliday 1994 we are treating adjectival groups as a kind of nominal group, functioning as Head of the Attribute here.

5   The distinction was formulated in unpublished material; cf Gleason 1968.

6   Introducing our third variable, person, would result in a 3 dimensional model, which we can certainly visualise (and imagine constructing, materially or electronically); conceptually speaking however, we know that genre topology is much more complicated – involving multi-dimensionality we can conceive (but not literally perceive).

7   It is important not to confuse texts such as those imagined here, which blend one genre with another, with texts that combine genres one after another and/or one including another (e.g. 3.15 above).

8   History programs foregrounding oral history and post-colonial critique may well require literacy leaps of this magnitude, at the same time as their irreverent approach to grand narratives expunges historical recounts, accounts and explanations from the curriculum; for discussion of post-colonial history discourse see Martin 2003.

9   Following Halliday 1994 we are treating adjectival groups as a kind of nominal group, functioning as Head of the Attribute here.

Chapter 4

1   In the history of sciences, theories explaining causes commonly have one or more false starts, that are nevertheless widely accepted, such as the pre-Darwinian theory of of the 'great chain of being' in biology, or 'phlogiston' in physics. A comparable false start in linguistic theory would be Chomsky's attempt to explain linguistic variation as deep-surface structure transformations, 'hard-wired' in the human brain.

2   Kress & van Leeuwen 2006 and Unsworth 2001a classify images by analogy with grammatical process types rather than discourse semantics, using terms partly derived from functional grammar and partly invented anew. In keeping with the discourse oriented approach here, and to keep labels more manageable, we have used the same terms as for verbal texts wherever possible. For example, where Kress & van Leeuwen use the cryptogrammatical terms 'overt/covert', we use 'explicit/implicit'; and where Kress & van Leeuwen use polysemous terms 'concrete/abstract', we prefer the semiotic terms 'iconic/indexical/symbolic'.

3   Kress & van Leeuwen 2006 use the term 'framing' to refer to boundaries between visual and verbal texts, presumably adapted from commonsense 'picture framing', but this usage conflicts with Bernstein's technical use of 'framing' to refer to relative control of interactants in an exchange. We prefer CLASSIFICATION to refer to boundary strength, consistent with Bernstein's usage. Kress & van Leeuwen do not offer general terms for the ideal-real and centre-margin contrasts, where we have used SUBSTANCE and RELEVANCE, and the interpretation of the central-marginal contrast as relevance is our own. 'Salience' is used by Kress & van Leeuwen, but the values of high/neutral/low are our own.

Chapter 5

1   Due to its religious importance, the correct procedure for cooking a kangaroo was one of the first skills taught to David when he first lived with the Pitjantjatjara communities. First a small incision is made in the kangaroo's belly, the intestines are removed for separate cooking, and the incision sewn up with a stick. A long pit is then dug and a large fire of sticks is prepared, onto which the carcase is thrown and turned until all the fur is burnt. The feet are removed by twisting, to extract sinews for binding spearheads and other wooden tools, and the tail is cut off. When the fire has burnt down, the coals are scraped out of the pit, the carcase and tail are laid in it, and coals scraped back over them. When cooked, the carcase is removed and butchered in a precisely prescribed sequence. The legs are first cut away, then the pelvis and lower back are disjointed at a particular vertebra, the upper torso is split in two and the head removed. The various parts are shared out according to work done – hunting and cooking – and obligations to and needs of various kin.

2   This contrasts with the typical three rules in Australian pools: No running. No spitting. No bombing.

Chapter 6

1   Kress 2003 for example employs a 'tenor' flavoured concept of genre, complemented by mode (multimodally oriented) and discourse (ideologised field) in his unstratified model of social context variables.

2   We have not included a cognition dimension of analysis in this survey because in our model we do not operate with a concept of mind; readers perplexed by this omission may find Halliday & Matthiessen's 2004 invitation to reconsider concepts as meanings an engaging argument. Basically our position is that contemporary models of perception and semiosis make the mind redundant with respect to evolutionary accounts of brain function (Edelman 1992, Edelman & Tononi 2000).

References

A., J. (1998) Emma fries to death in own pan. *Pulp*. (Student Magazine of Southern Cross University)

Abeyasingha, K. (1991) *No 4 Blast Furnace Gas Cleaning Manual*. Port Kembla, NSW: BHP Steel, Slab & Plate Products Division 1990–91.

ABS (1994, 2004) *Australian Social Trends 1994 & 2004: Education – National summary tables*. Canberra: Australian Bureau of Statistics, www.abs.gov.au/ausstats

Anderson, L. & Nyholm, M. (1996) *The Action Pack: technology*. (Activites for teaching factual writing. Language and Social Power Project.) Sydney: Metropolitan East Disadvantaged Schools Program.

Baldry, A. (ed.) (1999) *Multimodality and Multimediality in the Distance Learning Age*. Campo Basso: Lampo.

Bamberg, G.W. (1997) *Oral Versions of Personal Experience: three decades of narrative analysis*. London: Lawrence Erlbaum Associates.

Barthes, R. (1966) Introduction to the structural analysis of narratives. *Communications* 8. [reprinted 1977 in *Image-Music-Text*. London: Collins. 79–124.]

Barnard, C. (2000) The rape of Nanking in Japanese high school textbooks: history tests as closed texts. *Revista Canaria de Estudios Ingleses* 40: 155-70.

Bazerman, C. (1988) *Shaping Written Knowledge: the genre and activity of the experimental article in science*. Madison, Wisconsin: University of Wisconsin Press (Rhetoric of the Human Sciences).

Berkenkotter, C. & Huckin, T. (1995) *Genre Knowledge in Disciplinary Communication: cognition/culture/power*. Hillsdale, NJ: Erlbaum.

Bernstein, B. (1975) *Class and Pedagogies: visible and invisible*. London: Routledge.

Bernstein, B. (1990) *The Structuring of Pedagogic Discourse*. London: Routledge.

Bernstein, B. (1996) *Pedagogy, Symbolic Control and Identity: theory, research, critique*. London: Taylor & Francis.

Bernstein, B. (1999) Vertical and horizontal discourse: an essay. *British Journal of Sociology of Education* 20(2): 157–73.

Bhatia, V. J. (1993) *Analysing Genre: language use in professional settings*. London: Longman.

Biber, D. (1995) *Dimensions of register variation: a cross-linguistic perspective*. New York: Cambridge University Press.

Biber, D. & Finnegan, E. (1994) *Sociolinguistic Perspectives on Register*. Oxford: Oxford University Press.

Boyce, J. (2003) Fantasy island. In R. Manne (ed.) *Whitewash: on Keith Windschuttle's fabrication of Aboriginal history*. Melbourne: Black Inc. 17-78.

Boyce, R. (2003) Fantasy Island. In R. Manne (ed.) *Whitewash: on Keith Windschuttle's fabrication of Aboriginal history*. Melbourne: Black Inc.

Breier, M. & Sait, L. (1996) Literacy and communication in a Cape factory. In M. Prinsloo & M. Breier (eds) *The Social Uses of Literacy: theory and practice in contemporary South Africa*. Bertsham, South Africa: Sached Books. Philadelphia: Benjamins. 64-84.

Brennan, F. (2003) *Tampering with Asylum: a universal humanitarian problem*. Brisbane: University of Queensland Press.

Brown, F. (1984) The weapon. In P. Forrestal & J. Reid (eds) *The Brighter Side of School*. Melbourne: Thomas Nelson.

Bruner, J.S. (1986) *Actual Minds, Possible Worlds*. Cambridge, Mass: Harvard University Press.

Bruner, J.S. (1997) *The Culture of Education*. Cambridge, Mass: Harvard University Press.

Butler, C.S. (2003) *Structure and Function: a guide to three major structural-functional theories. Part I: Approaches to the simplex clause. Part II: From clause to discourse and beyond*. Amsterdam: Bejamins.

Caffarel, A., Martin, J.R. and Matthiessen, C.M.I.M. (eds) (2004) *Language Typology: a functional perspective*. Amsterdam: Bejamins.

Caldas-Coulthard, C. & Coulthard, M. (eds) (1996) *Text and Practices: readings in critical discourse analysis*. London: Routledge.

Callow, J. (1996) *The Action Pack: environment*. (Activites for teaching factual writing. Language and Social Power Project.) Sydney: Metropolitan East Disadvantaged Schools Program.

Callow, J. (1999) *Image Matters: visual texts in the classroom*. Sydney: PETA.

Carle, E. (1970) *The Very Hungry Caterpillar*. Puffin: Hammondsworth.

Cazden, C. (1996) A report on reports: two dilemmas of genre teaching. In F. Christie & J. Foley (ed.) *Literacy in Mother Tongue Teaching*. (Mother Tongue Education Research Series 2). New York: Waxman. 248–65.

Cha, J. S. (1995) *Towards Communication Linguistics: essays by Michael Gregory and associates*. Seoul: Department of English Language and Literature, Sookmyung Women's University. 154-95.

Chafe, W.L. (1980) *The Pear Stories: cognitive, cultural, and linguistic aspects of narrative production*. Norwood, NJ: Ablex.

Chouliaraki, L. & Fairclough, N. (1999) *Discourse in Late Modernity: rethinking critical discourse analysis*. Edinburgh: University of Edinburgh Press.

Christie, F. (1994) *On Pedagogic Discourse*. Melbourne: University of Melbourne.

Christie, F. (1996) *An ARC Study in the Pedagogic Discourse of Secondary School Social Sciences – Report 1: Geography*. Melbourne: Faculty of Education, University of Melbourne.

Christie, F. (ed.) (1999) *Pedagogy and the Shaping of Consciousness: linguistic and social processes*. (Open Linguistics Series) London: Cassell.

Christie, F. (2002) *Classroom Discourse Analysis: a functional perspective*. London: Continuum.

Christie, F. & Martin, J.R. (eds) (1997) *Genre and Institutions: social processes in the workplace and school*. (Open Linguistics Series) London: Pinter.

Christie, F. & J. R. Martin (eds) (2007) *Language, Knowledge and Pedagogy: functional linguistic and sociological perspectives*. London: Continuum. 2007

Christie, F. & Misson, R. (1998) *Literacy & Schooling*. London: Routledge.

Cloran, C. (1989) Learning through language: the social construction of gender. In R. Hasan & J.R. Martin (eds) *Language Development: learning language, learning culture*. (Meaning and Choices in Language: studies for Michael Halliday) Norwood, NJ: Ablex. 361–403.

Cloran, C. (1999) Contexts for learning. In F. Christie (ed.) *Pedagogy and the Shaping of Consciousness: linguistic and social processes*. London: Cassell. 31-65.

Cloran, C. (2000) Socio-semantic variation: different wordings, different meanings. In L. Unsworth (ed.) *Researching Language in Schools and Communities: functional linguistic perspectives*. London: Cassell. 152–183.

Coe, R., Lingard, L. and Teslenko, T. (eds) (2002) *The Rhetoric and Ideology of Genre: strategies for stability and change*. Cresskill, NJ: Hampton Press.

Coffin, C. (1997) Constructing and giving value to the past: an investigation into secondary school history. In F. Christie and J.R. Martin (eds) *Genre and Institutions: social processes in the workplace and school*. (Open Linguistics Series.) London: Pinter. 196–230.

Coffin, C. (2000) Defending and challenging interpretations of the past. *Revista Canaria de Estudios Ingleses* 40: 135–54.

Coffin, C. (2003) *Reconstruals of the past – settlement or invasion?* The role of judgement analysis. In J.R. Martin & R.Wodak (eds) *Re/reading the past: critical and functional perspectives on time and value*. Amsterdam: Benjamins. 219–46.

Coffin, C. (2006) *Historical Discourse: the language of time, cause and evaluation*. London: Continuum.

Coke Ovens Byproducts Department (1991) *Standard Procedure: Isoltae No 12 Precipitator*. Port Kembla, NSW: BHP Steel, Slab & Plate Products Division 1990–91.

Colombi, C. and Schleppergrell, M. (eds) (2002) *Developing Advanced Literacy in First and Second Languages*. Mahwah, NJ: Erlbaum.

Cope, W. & Kalantzis, M. (eds) (1993) *The Powers of Literacy: a genre approach to teaching literacy*. London: Falmer (Critical Perspectives on Literacy and Education) & Pittsburg: University of Pittsburg Press (Pittsburg Series in Composition, Literacy, and Culture).

Corrigan, C. (1991) *Changes and Contrasts: VCE geography units 1 & 2*. Milton, Qld: Jacaranda Press.

Derewianka, B. (2003) 'Grammatical metaphor in the transition to adolescence'. *Grammatical Metaphor: views from systemic functional linguistics*. In A.-M. Simon-Vandenbergen, M. Taverniers & L. Ravelli (eds). Amsterdam/ Philadelphia: J. Benjamins Pub. Co. 185–219.

Drmota, R. & Draper, P. (1991) *GTA Welds On Hi-Silicon Coil Platses Without Filler Rod Addition*. Port Kembla, NSW: BHP Steel, Slab & Plate Products Division 1990–91.

Dudley-Evans, T. (1994) Genre analysis: an approach to text analysis in ESP. In M. Coulthard (ed.) *Advances in Written Text Analysis*. London: Routledge. 219–28.

Ebert, K. (1996) *Kodava, Languages of the World*. Munchen: Lincom Europa.

Edelman, G. (1992) *Bright Air, Brilliant Fire: on the matter of the mind*. London: Harper Collins Basic Books.

Edelman, G.M. & Tononi, G. (2000) *A Universe of Consciousness: how matter becomes imagination*. New York: Basic Books.

Eggins, S. & Slade, D. (2005) *Analysing Casual Conversation*. London: Equinox.

Evans, R. (1997) *Deng Xiaoping and the Making of Modern China*. London: Penguin.

Feez, S. & Joyce, H. (1998) *Writing Skills: narrative & non-fiction text types*. Sydney: Phoenix Education.

Firth, J.R. (1957b) A synopsis of linguistic theory, 1930–1955 *Studies in Linguistic Analysis* (Special volume of the Philological Society). London: Blackwell. 1–31. [reprinted in F. R. Palmer 1968 (ed.) *Selected Papers of J.R. Firth, 1952–1959*. London: Longman. 168–205.]

Francis, G. (1985) Anaphoric nouns. *Discourse Analysis Monographs* 11. English Language Research, University of Birmingham.

Freedman, A. and Medway, P. (eds) (1994a) *Learning and Teaching Genre*. Portsmouth, NH: Boynton/Cook.

Gee, J. P., Hull, G. & Lankshear, C. (1996) *The New Work Order: behind the language of the new capitalism*. Sydney: Allen & Unwin.

Ghadessy, M. (ed.) (1993) *Register Analysis: theory and practice*. London: Pinter.

Gleason, H. A. Jr. (1968) Contrastive analysis in discourse structure. *Monograph Series on Languages and Linguistics 21*. (Georgetown University Institute of Languages and Linguistics) [reprinted in A. Makkai and D. Lockwood (eds) (1973) *Readings in Stratificational Linguistics*. University, Al: Alabama University Press. 258–76.]

Golding, B., Marginson, S. & Pascoe, R. (1996) *Changing Context, Moving Skills: generic skills in the context of credit transfer and the recognition of prior learning*. Canberra: National Board of Employment, Education and Training.

Goodman, S. (1996) Visual English. In S. Goodman & D. Graddol (eds) *Redesigning English: new texts, new identities*. London: Routledge. 38–105.

Gordon, M. & Harvey, C. (1997) A divided nation: PM's advice on payouts in question. *The Weekend Australian* 31 May, p. 11.

Graves (1955/1992) *The Greek Myths*. London: Penguin Books.

Green, B. and Lee, A. (1994) *Writing geography lessons: literacy, identity and schooling* 207–24. Freedman and Medway.

Green, M. (Compiled by P. Lofts) (1984) *The Echidna and the Shade Tree.* (An Aboriginal story.) Sydney: Scholastic.

Grossbard, A.M. & Grossbard, J.R. (1978) *The Sense of Science.* Sydney: McGraw-Hill.

Halliday, M.A.K. (1967) *Intonation and Grammar in British English.* The Hague: Mouton.

Halliday, M.A.K. (1970) *A Course in Spoken English: intonation.* London: Oxford University Press.

Halliday, M.A.K. (1978) *Language as a Social Semiotic: the social interpretation of language and meaning.* London: Edward Arnold.

Halliday, M.A.K. (1979) Modes of meaning and modes of expression: types of grammatical structure, and their determination by different semantic functions. In D. J. Allerton, E. Carney and D. Holdcroft (eds) *Function and Context in Linguistic Analysis: essays offers to William Haas.* (Republished in Halliday, 2002: 196–218.) Cambridge: Cambridge University Press. 57–79.

Halliday, M.A.K. (1985) *Spoken and Written Language.* (Republished by Oxford University Press, 1989.) Geelong, Vic.: Deakin University Press.

Halliday, M.A.K. (1990) *New Ways of Meaning: a challenge to applied linguistics.* Journal of Applied Linguistics 6.

Halliday, M.A.K. (1992) Language as system and language as instance: the corpus as a theoretical construct. In J. Svartvik (ed.) *Directions in Corpus Linguistics: proceedings of Nobel Symposium 82, Stockholm, 4–8 August (1991)* Berlin: De Gruyter. (Trends in Linguistics Studies and Monographs 65). 61–77.

Halliday, M.A.K. (1993a) *Language in a Changing World.* (Occasional paper 13.) Canberra, Australian Capital Territory: Applied Linguistics Association of Australia.

Halliday, M.A.K. (1993b) *On the Language of Physical Science.* In M.A.K. Halliday & J.R. Martin (eds) *Writing Science: literacy and discursive power.* London: Falmer. Pittsburgh: University of Pittsburgh Press.54–68 (Reprinted in M.A.K. Halliday 2005 *The Language of Science.* London: Continuum, 140–158)

Halliday, M.A.K. (1994) *An Introduction to Functional Grammar.* London: Edward Arnold. Revised edition, by C.M.I.M. Matthiessen, 2004)

Halliday, M.A.K. (1998) Things and relations: regrammaticising experience as scientific knowledge. In J.R. Martin & R. Veel. 185–235.

Halliday, M.A.K. (2002) *On Grammar.* London: Continuum.

Halliday, M.A.K. (2004) The language of science. London: Continuum (Volume 5 in the *Collected Works of M.A.K. Halliday,* Edited by J. J. Webster).

Halliday M.A.K. & Hasan, R. (1976) *Cohesion in English.* London: Longman (English Language Series 9).

Halliday, M.A.K. & Martin, J.R. (1993) *Writing Science: literacy and discursive power.* London: Falmer (Critical Perspectives on Literacy and Education) & Pittsburg: University of Pittsburg Press (Pittsburg Series in Composition, Literacy, and Culture).

Halliday, M.A.K. & Matthiessen, C.M.I.M. (2004) *Construing Experience through Language: a language-based approach to cognition.* London: Continuum.

Hasan, R. (1977) Text in the systemic-functional model. In W. Dressler (ed.) *Current Trends in Textlinguistics.* Berlin: Walter de Gruyter. 228–46.

Hasan, R. (1984) The nursery tale as a genre. (Special issue on systemic linguistics.) *Nottingham Linguistic Circular* 13: 71–102.

Hasan, R. (1985) The structure of a text. In M.A.K. Halliday and R. Hasan. *Language, Context and Text.* (Republished by Oxford University Press 1989.) Geelong, Vic.: Deakin University Press. 52–69.

Hasan, R. (1990) Semantic variation and sociolinguistics. *Australian Journal of Linguistics* 9(2): 221–76.

Hasan, R. (1991) Questions as a mode of learning in everyday talk. In M. McCausland (ed.) *Language Education: interaction and development.* Launceston: University of Tasmania. 70–119.

Hasan, R. (1992) Meaning in sociolinguistic theory. In K. Bolton & H. Kwok (eds) *Sociolinguistics Today: international perspectives.* London: Routledge. 80–119.

Hasan, R. (1995) The conception of context in text. In P. Fries and M. Gregory (eds) *Discourse in Society: systemic functional perspectives.* (Advances in Discourse Processes L: meaning and choices in language - studies for Michael Halliday.) Norwood, NJ: Ablex. 183–283.

Hasan, R. (1996) *Ways of Saying: ways of meaning: selected papers of Ruqaiya Hasan* (Open Linguistics Series. Edited by C. Cloran, D. Butt & G. Williams.) London: Cassell.

Hasan, R. (1999) Speaking with reference to context. In M. Ghadessy (ed.) *Text and Context in Functional Linguistics.* (CILT Series IV) Amsterdam: Benjamins. 219–328.

Hasan, R. & Cloran, C. (1990) A sociolinguistic interpretation of everyday talk between mothers and children. In M.A.K. Halliday, J. Gibbons & H. Nicholas (eds) *Learning, Keeping and Using Language. Vol. 1: selected papers from the 8th World Congress of Applied Linguistics.* Amsterdam: Benjamins.

Hasan, R. & Williams, G. (eds) (1996) *Literacy in Society.* (Language and Social Life) London: Longman.

Heading, K.E.G., Provis, D.F., Scott, T.D., Smith, J.E. & Smith, R.T. (1967) *Science for Secondary Schools*, 2. Adelaide: Rigby.

Hjelmslev, L. (1961) *Prolegomena to a Theory of Language.* Madison: University of Wisconsin Press.

Hoey, M. (1983) *On the Surface of Discourse.* Boston: Allen & Unwin.

Hood, S. (2004) Managing attitude in undergraduate academic writing: a focus on the introductions to research reports. In L. Ravelli & R. Ellis (eds) *Analysing Academic Writing: contextualised frameworks*. London: Continuum. 24–44.

Hopkins, A. & Dudley-Evans, T. (1988) A genre-based investigation of the discussion sections in articles and dissertations. In *English for Specific Purposes* 5: 107–20.

Horton, D. (ed.) (1994) *The Encyclopaedia of Aboriginal Australia: Aboriginal and Torres Strait Islander history, society and culture*. Canberra: Aboriginal Studies Press for the Australian Institute of Aboriginal and Torres Strait Islander Studies.

HREOC (1997) *Bringing Them Home: the 'Stolen Children' report*. Canberra: Human Rights and Equal Opportunity Commission. http://www.hreoc.gov.au/social_justice/stolen_children/

Humphrey, S. (1996) *Exploring Literacy in School Geography*. Sydney: Metropolitan East Disadvantaged Schools Program.

Humphrey, S. & Takans, P. (1996) *Explaining the Weather: a unit of work for Junior Secondary Geography*. Sydney: Metropolitan East Disadvantaged Schools Program.

Hyland, K. (2000) *Disciplinary Discourses: social interactions in academic writing*. Harlow, UK: Pearson Education.

Hyland, K. (2002) Genre: language, context and literacy. *ARAL* 113–35.

Hyland, K. (2004) *Genre and Second Language Writing*. Ann Arbor: University of Michigan.

Hymes, D. (1981) *In Vain I Tried To Tell You. Essays in Native American Ethnopoetics*. Philadelphia: University of Pennsylvania Press.

Hyon, S. (1996) Genre in three traditions: implications for ESL. *TESOL Quarterly* 30(4): 693–722.

Iedema, R. (1997a) The language of ddministration: organizing human activity in formal institutions. In F. Christie and J.R. Martin (eds) *Genre and Institutions: social processes in the workplace and school*. (Open Linguistics Series.) London: Pinter. 73–100.

Iedema, R. (1997b) The history of the accident news story. *Australian Review of Applied Linguistics* 20(2): 95–119.

Iedema, R. (2001) Analysing film and television. In T. van Leeuwen and C. Jewitt (eds) *Handbook of Visual Analysis*. London: Sage. 183–204.

Iedema, R. (2003a) *Discourse of Post-Bureaucratic Organization*. (Document Design Companion Series.) Amsterdam: Benjamins.

Iedema, R. (2003b) Multimodality, resemiotization: extending the analysis of discourse as multi-semiotic practice. *Visual Communication* 2(1): 2003. 29–57.

Iedema, R., Feez, S. & White, P. (1994) *Media Literacy (Write it Right Literacy in Industry Project: Stage Two)*. Sydney: Metropolitan East Region's Disadvantaged Schools Program.

Jennings, P. (1997) *Uncanny*. Ringwood, Vic: Puffin/Penguin.

Jewitt, C. (2002) The move from page to screen: the multimodal reshaping of school English. *Visual Communication* 1(2): 171–96.

Jewitt, C. & Oyama, R. (2001) Visual Meaning: a social semiotic approach. In T. van Leeuwen & C. Jewitt (eds) *Handbook of Visual Analysis*. London: Sage. 134–56.

Johns, A. M. (ed.) (2002) *Genre in the Classroom: multiple perspectives*. Mahwah, NJ: Lawrence Erlbaum.

Johnson, D. (2002) *Lighting the Way: reconciliation stories*. Sydney: The Federation press.

Jordens, C. (2002) Reading spoken stories for values: a discursive study of cancer survivors and their professional carers. PhD thesis (Medicine). University of Sydney.

Jordens, C. & Little, M. (2004) 'In this scenario, I do this, for these reasons': narrative, genre and ethical reasoning in the clinic. *Social Science and Medicine* 58: 1635–45.

Jordens C.F.C., Little, M., Paul, K. & Sayers, E.-J. (2001) Life disruption and generic complexity: a social linguistic analysis of narratives of cancer illness. *Social Science and Medicine* 53: 1227–36.

JVC (2000) *Video Cassette Recorder HR-J777MS: Instructions*. Tokyo: Victor Company of Japan, Ltd.

Kinnear, J. & Martin, M. (2004) *Biology 1: preliminary course*. Milton, Qld: Jacaranda.

Koop, C. & Rose, D. (2008) Reading to Learn in Murdi Paaki: Changing Outcomes for Indigenous Students. *Literacy Learning: the Middle Years* 16(1): 41-46 http://alea.edu.au/html/publications/121/llfeb08

Korff, J. (2004) *Web review of Follow the Rabbit-Proof Fence*. www.creativespirits.de

Kress, G. (1997) *Before Writing: rethinking the paths to literacy*. London: Routledge.

Kress, G. (2003) *Literacy in the New Media Age*. London: Routledge (Literacies).

Kress, G., Jewitt, C., Ogborn, J. & Tsatsarelis, C. (2001) *Multimodal Teaching and Learning: the rhetorics of the classroom*. (Advances in Applied Linguistics) London: Continuum.

Kress, G. & van Leeuwen, T. (2006) *Reading Images: the grammar of visual design*. London: Routledge.

Kress, G. & van Leeuwen, T. (2001) *Multimodal Discourse – The Modes and Media of Contemporary Communication*. London: Arnold.

Kress, G. & van Leeuwen, T. (2002) Colour as a semiotic mode: notes for a grammar of colour. *Visual Communication* 1(3): 343–68.

Labov, W. (1972) *The Transformation of Experience in Narrative Syntax. Language in the Inner City*. Philadephia: Pennsylvania University Press. 354–96.

Labov, W. (1982) Speech actions and reactions in personal narrative. In D. Tannen (ed.) *Analysing Discourse: text and talk*. (Georgetown University Round Table on Language and Linguistics 1981) Washington, DC: Georgetown University Press. 217–47.

Labov, W. (1984) Intensity. In D. Schiffrin (ed.) *Meaning, Form and Use in Context: linguistic applications*. (Georgetown University Roundtable on Language and Linguistics) Washington, DC: Georgetown University Press. 43–70.

Labov, W. (1997) Some further steps in narrative analysis. *Journal of Narrative and Life History* 7(1–4): 395–415.

Labov, W. and Waletzky, J. (1967) Narrative analysis: oral versions of personal experience. In J. Helm (ed.) *Essays on the Verbal and Visual Arts.* (Proceedings of the 1966 Spring Meeting of the American Ethnological Society) Seattle: University of Washington Press. 12–44. (reprinted in G.W. Bamberg 1997 *Oral Versions of Personal Experience: three decades of narrative analysis.* London: Lawrence Erlbaum Associates)

Lamkshear, C., Gee, J. P., Knobel, M. & Searle, C. (1997) *Changing Literacies.* Buckingham: Open University Press (Changing Education).

Lemke, J.L. (1990a) Technical Discourse and Technocratic Ideology. In M.A.K. Halliday, J. Gibbons & H. Nicholas (eds) *Learning, Keeping and Using Language.* Vol II. Amsterdam/Philadelphia: Benjamins. 435–60.

Lemke, J.L. (1990b) *Talking Science: Language, Learning, and Values.* Norwood, NJ: Ablex Publishing.

Lemke, J.L. (1998) Multiplying meaning: visual and verbal semiotics in scientific text. In J.R. Martin & R. Veel (eds) *Reading Science: critical and functional perspectives on discourses of science.* London: Routledge. 87–113.

Lemke, J.L. (2002) Travels in hypermodality. *Visual Communication* 1(3): 299–325.

Lepetit, P. (2002) New Releases: Rabbit-Proof Fence. In *The Sunday Telegraph* 24 February, p. 107.

Levine, P. & Scollon, R. (2004) *Discourse and Technology: multimodal discourse analysis.* (Georgetown University Round Table on Languages and Linguistics) Washington, DC: Georgetown University Press.

Levi-Strauss, C. (1970–78) *Introduction to a Science of Mythology,* Volumes 1, 2 & 3. London: Jonathan Cape.

Lyotard, J. (1984) *The Postmodern Condition.* Minneapolis: University of Minnesota Press.

Macken-Horarik, M. (1996a) Literacy and learning across the curriculum: towards a model of register for secondary school teachers. In R. Hasan & G. Williams (eds) *Literacy in Society.* (Language and Social Life) London: Longman. 232–306.

Macken-Horarik, M. (1996b) *Construing the Invisible: Specialized Literacy Practices in Junior Secondary English.* PhD thesis. University of Sydney.

Macken-Horarik, M. (1998) Exploring the requirements of critical school literacy: a view from two classrooms. In F. Christie & R. Misson (eds) *Literacy & Schooling.* London: Routledge. 74–103.

Macken-Horarik, M. (2002) 'Something to shoot for': a systemic functional approach to teaching genre in secondary school science. In A. M. Johns (ed.) *Genres in the Classroom: applying theory and research to practice.* 17–42.

Macken-Horarik, M. (2003) A telling symbiosis in the discourse of hatred: multimodal news texts about he 'children overboard' affair. *ARAL* 26(2): 1–16.

Macken-Horarik, M. (2004) Interacting with the multimodal text: reflections on image and verbiage in *ArtExpress. Visual Communication* 3(1): 5–26.

Macken-Horarik, M. & Martin, J.R. (eds) (2003) Negotiating heteroglossia: social perspectives on evaluation. (Special issue) *Text* 23(2).

Malinowski, B. (1935) *Coral Gardens and their Magic*. London: Allen & Unwin

Mandela, N. (1995) *Long Walk to Freedom: the autobiography of Nelson Mandela*. London: Abacus.

Manne, R. (2001) *In Denial: the stolen generations and the new right*. (First published in *Quarterly Essay*) Melbourne: Black Inc.

Manne, R. (ed.) (2003) *Whitewash: on Keith Windschuttle's fabrication of Aboriginal History*. Melbourne: Black Inc.

Mares, P. (2001) *Borderline: Australia's treatment of refugees and asylum seekers*. Sydney: UNSW Press (Reportage Series).

Marr, D. and Wilkinson, M. (2003) *Dark Victory*. Sydney: Allen and Unwin.

Manne, R. (1998) The stolen generations. *Quadrant* XLII(343). Number 6. 1–2. 53–63.

Martin, J.R. (1986) Grammaticalising ecology: the politics of baby seals and kangaroos. In T. Threadgold, E.A. Grosz, G. Kress & M.A.K. Halliday (eds) *Semiotics, Ideology, Language*. (Sydney Studies in Society and Culture 3) Sydney: Sydney Association for Studies in Society and Culture. 225–68.

Martin, J.R. (1989) Technicality and abstraction: language for the creation of specialised texts. In F. Christie (ed.) *Writing in Schools: reader*. Geelong, Vic.: Deakin University Press. 36–44. [republished in M.A.K. Halliday & J.R. Martin, 1993.]

Martin, J.R. (1990) Literacy in science: learning to handle text as technology. In F. Christie (ed.) *Literacy for a Changing World*. Melbourne: Australian Council for Educational Research (Fresh Look at the Basics). 79–117. [Republished in M.A.K. Halliday & J.R. Martin 1993 166–202] [Norwegian translation in *Å Skape Mening Med Språk: en samling artikler av M.A.K. Halliday, R. Hasan og J.R. Martin* (presentery og redigert av K. L. Berge, P. Coppock & E. Maagero) Oslo: Landslaget for norskundervisning (LNU) og Cappelen Akademisk Forlag. 1998.]

Martin, J.R. (1991) Intrinsic functionality: implications for contextual theory. *Social Semiotics* 1(1): 99–162.

Martin, J.R. (1992) *English Text: system and structure*. Amsterdam: Benjamins.

Martin, J.R. (1993) Life as a noun. In M.A.K. Halliday & J.R. Martin. *Writing Science: literacy and discursive power*. London: Falmer.

Martin, J.R. (1994) Macro-genres: the ecology of the page. *Network* 21: 29–52.

Martin, J.R. (1996a) Evaluating disruption: symbolising theme in junior secondary narrative. In R. Hasan & G. Williams (eds) *Literacy in Society*. (Language in Social Life) London: Longman. 124–71.

Martin, J.R. (1996b) Types of structure: deconstructing notions of constituency in clause and text. In E.H. Hovy and D.R. Scott (eds) *Computational and Conversational Discourse: burning issues – an interdisciplinary account*. Heidelberg: Springer. 39–66.

Martin, J.R. (1997) Analysing genre: functional parameters. In F. Christie & J.R. Martin (eds) *Genre and Institutions: social processes in the workplace and school.* London: Pinter. 3–39.

Martin, J.R. (1998a) Discourses of science: genesis, intertextuality and hegemony. In J.R. Martin and R. Veel (eds) *Reading Science: critical and functional perspectives on discourses of science.* London: Routledge. 3–14.

Martin, J.R. (1998b) Practice into theory: catalysing change. In S. Hunston (ed.) *Language at Work.* (British Studies in Applied Linguistics 13.) Clevedon: Multilingual Matters. 151–67.

Martin, J.R. (1999a) Mentoring semogenesis: 'genre-based' literacy pedagogy. In F. Christie (ed.) *Pedagogy and the Shaping of Consciousness: linguistic and social processes.* London: Cassell. 123–55.

Martin, J.R. (1999b) Modelling context: a crooked path of progress in contextual linguistics (Sydney SFL). In M. Ghadessy (ed.) *Text and Context in Functional Linguistics* 25–61. (CILT Series IV) Amsterdam: Benjamins.

Martin, J.R. (2000a) Factoring out exchange: types of structure. In M. Coulthard, J. Cotterill & F. Rock (eds) *Working with Dialogue.* Tubingen: Niemeyer. 19–40.

Martin, J.R. (2000b) Beyond exchange: appraisal systems in English. In S. Hunston & G. Thompson (eds) *Evaluation in text: authorial stance and the construction of discourse.* Oxford: Oxford University Press. 142–75.

Martin, J.R. (2000c) Close reading: functional linguistics as a tool for critical analysis. In L. Unsworth (ed.) 275–303.

Martin, J.R. (2000d) Design and practice: enacting functional linguistics in Australia. *Annual Review of Applied Linguistics* 20 (20th Anniversary Volume 'Applied Linguistics as an Emerging Discipline'). 116–26.

Martin, J.R. (2001a) From little things big things grow: ecogenesis in school geography. In R. Coe, L. Lingard & T. Teslenko (eds) *The Rhetoric and Ideology of Genre: strategies for stability and change.* Cresskill, NJ: Hampton Press. 243–71.

Martin, J.R. (2001b) Giving the game away: explicitness, diversity and genre-based literacy in Australia. In R. de Cilla, H. Krumm & R. Wodak (eds) *Functional Il/literacy.* Vienna: Verlag der Osterreichischen Akadamie der Wissenschaften. 155–74.

Martin, J.R. (2001c) Fair trade: negotiating meaning in multimodal texts. In P. Coppock (ed.) *The Semiotics of Writing: transdisciplinary perspectives on the technology of writing.* Brepols (Semiotic & Cognitive Studies X). 311–38.

Martin, J.R. (2001d) A context for genre: modelling social processes in functional linguistics. In R. Stainton & J. Devilliers (eds) *Communication in Linguistics.* Toronto: GREF (Collection Theoria). 1–41.

Martin, J.R. (2002a) A universe of meaning – how many practices? In A. M. Johns (ed.) *Genre in the Classroom: multiple perspectives.* Mahwah, NJ: Lawrence Erlbaum. 269–78.

Martin, J.R. (2003a) Voicing the 'other': reading and writing Indigenous Australians. In G. Weiss & R. Wodak (eds) *Critical Discourse Analysis: theory and interdisciplinarity*. London: Palgrave. 199–219.

Martin, J.R. (2003b) Making history: grammar for explanation. In J.R. Martin & R. Wodak (eds) *Re/reading the past: critical and functional perspectives on time and value* 19–57. Amsterdam: Benjamins.

Martin, J.R. (2004a) Mourning – how we get aligned. *Discourse & Society* (Special Issue on 'Discourse around 9/11') 15(2/3): 321–44.

Martin, J.R. (2004b) Negotiating difference: ideology and reconciliation. In M. Pütz, J.N. van Aertselaer & T.A. van Dijk (eds) *Communicating Ideologies: language, discourse and social practice*. (Duisburg Papers on Research in Language and Culture) Frankfurt: Peter Lang. 85–177.

Martin, J.R. (2004c) Sense and sensibility: texturing evaluation. In J. Foley (ed.) *Language, Education and Discourse: functional approaches*. London: Continuum. 270–304.

Martin, J. R. (2004d) Positive discourse analysis: solidarity and change. *Revista Canaria de Estudios Ingleses*. 49 (Special Issue on Discourse Analysis at Work: Recent Perspectives in the Study of Language and Social Practice). 179-200. [reprinted in The Journal of English Studies (Special Issue on Discourse Analysis). Guest Editor: HUANG Guowen). Vol.4.14. 21-35. Sichuan International Studies University, Chongqing, China. 2006]

Martin, J. R. (2006) Genre, ideology and intertextuality: a systemic functional perspective. *Linguistics and the Human Sciences*. 2.2. 275-298.

Martin, J.R. 2007 Genre and field: social processes and knowledge structures in systemic functional semiotics. In L. Barbara & T. Berber Sardinha (eds) *Proceedings of the 33rd International Systemic Functional Congress*. São Paulo: PUCSP. (Online publication available at http://www.pucsp.br/isfc/proceedings/index.htm)

Martin, J R (2008) Negotiating values: narrative and exposition. *Journal of Bioethical Inquiry* 5.1. 41-55.

Martin, J.R. & Painter, C. (1986) *Writing to Mean: teaching genres across the curriculum*. (ed. with C. Painter) Applied Linguistics Association of Australia (Occasional Papers 9).

Martin, J.R. & Plum, G. (1997) Construing experience: some story genres. (Special issue. Edited by M. Bamberg. Oral versions of personal experience: three decades of narrative analysis.) *Journal of Narrative and Life History* 7(1–4): 299–308.

Martin, J.R. & Rose, D. (2003, 2nd edition 2007) *Working with Discourse: meaning beyond the clause*. London: Continuum.

Martin, J.R. & Stenglin, M. (2006) Materialising reconciliation: negotiating difference in a post-colonial exhibition. In T. Royce & W. Bowcher (eds) *New Directions in the Analysis of Multimodal Discourse*. Mahwah, NJ: Lawrence Erlbaum Associates. 215–238.

Martin, J.R. & Veel, R. (eds) (1998) *Reading Science: critical and functional perspectives on discourses of science.* London: Routledge.

Martin, J.R. & White, P.R.R. (2005) *The Language of Evaluation: appraisal in English.* London: Palgrave.

Martin, J.R. & Wodak, R. (eds) (2004) *Re/reading the past: critical and functional perspectives on discourses of history* Amsterdam: Benjamins.

Martinec, R. (1998) Cohesion in action. *Semiotica* 120(1/2): 161–80.

Martinec, R. (2000a) Rhythm in multimodal texts. *Leonardo* 33(4): 289–97.

Martinec, R. (2000b) Types of process in action. *Semiotica* 130–3/4: 243–68.

Martinec, R. (2000c) Construction of identity in M. Jackson's 'Jam'. *Social Semiotics* 10(3): 313–29.

Martinec, R. (2001) Interpersonal resources in action. *Semiotica*, 135(1/4): 117–45.

Matthiessen, C.M.I.M. (1993) Register in the round: diversity in a unified theory of register analysis. In M. Ghadessy (ed.) *Register Analysis: theory and practice.* London: Pinter. 221–92.

Matthiessen, C.M.I.M. (2003) Language, social life and discursive maps. Plenary for *Australian Systemic Functional Linguistics Conference*, July, Adelaide.

Metallurgical Technology (1991) *CTS Testing Procedure.* Port Kembla, NSW: BHP Steel, Slab & Plate Products Division 1990–91.

Milan, L. (1999) *Plates. Real Food for Fast People.* Sydney: New Holland Publishers.

Miller, C. (1984) Genre as social action. *Quarterly Journal of Speech* 70: 151–67.

Mitchell, T.F. (1957) The language of buying and selling in Cyrenaica: a situational statement. *Hesperis* 26: 31–71. (Reprinted in T.F. Mitchell, 1975, *Principles of Neo-Firthian Linguistics* 167–200. London: Longman.)

Mourning (2001) Editorial. *HK Magazine.* 21 September, Vol. 5.

Muller, J. (2000) *Reclaiming Knowledge: social theory, curriculum and education policy.* (Knowledge, Identity and School Life Series 8) London: Routledge.

Muller, J., Davies, B. & Morais, A. (eds) (2004) *Reading Bernstein, Researching Bernstein.* London: Routledge Falmer.

Muntigl, P. (2004) *Narrative Counselling: social and linguistic processes of change.* (Discourse Approaches to Politics, Society and Culture). Amsterdam: Benjamins.

Murray, N. & Zammit, K. (1992) *The Action Pack: animals.* Sydney: Met East DSP (Language and Social Power Project).

Myers, G. (1990) *Writing Biology.* Madison: University of Wisconsin Press.

Nareanddera Koori Community Gathering (2002) www.dulwichcentre.com.au

National Library of Australia (2002) *NLA News* XIII: 2.

National Training Board (1991) *National Competency Standards: policy and guidelines.* Canberra: National Training Board.

Ogborn, J., Kress, G., Martins, I. & McGillicuddy, K. (1996) *Explaining Science in the Classroom.* Buckingham, UK: Open University Press.

O'Halloran, K.L. (1999a) Interdependence, interaction and metaphor in multisemiotic texts. *Social Semiotics* 9(3): 317–54.

O'Halloran, K.L. (1999b) Towards a systemic functional analysis of multisemiotic mathematics texts. *Semiotica* 124(1/2): 1–29.

O'Halloran, K.L. (2000) Classroom discourse in mathematics: a multisemiotic analysis. (Special edition: Language and other semiotic systems in education.) *Linguistics and Education* 10(3): 359–88.

O'Halloran, K.L. (ed.) (2004) *Multimodal Discourse Analysis: systemic functional perspectives*. (Open Linguistics Series) London: Continuum.

O'Halloran, K.L. (2008) *Mathematical Discourse: language, visual images and mathematical symbolism*. London: Continuum.

O'Toole, M. (1994) *The Language of Displayed Art*. London: Leicester University Press (a division of Pinter).

Painter, C. (1984) *Into the Mother Tongue: a case study of early language development*. London: Pinter.

Painter, C. (1998) *Learning through Language in Early Childhood*. London: Cassell.

Painter, C. (2003) The use of a metaphorical mode of meaning in early language development. In A.M. Simon-Vandenbergen, M. Taverniers & L. Ravelli (eds) *Metaphor: systemic-functional perspectives*. Amsterdam: Benjamins. 151–67.

Paltridge, B. (1997) *Genre, Frames and Writing in Research Settings*. Amsterdam: Benjamins.

Paltridge, B. (2001) *Genre and the Language Learning Classroom*. Ann Arbor: University of Michigan Press.

Pearson, N. (2000) Aboriginal disadvantage. In M. Gratton (ed.) *Reconciliation: essays on Australian reconciliation*. Melbourne: Bookman. 165–75.

Pilkington, D. (1996) *Follow the Rabbit-Proof Fence*. St Lucia, Qld: University of Queensland Press.

Plum, G. (1988) Text and contextual conditioning in spoken English: A genre-based approach. Unpublished PhD thesis. University of Sydney.

Plum, G. (1998) *Text and contextual conditioning in spoken English: A genre-based approach*. Nottingham: University of Nottingham

Prinsloo, M. & Breier, M. (eds) (1996) *The Social Uses of Literacy: theory and practice in contemporary South Africa*. (Preface by B.V. Street) Bertsham, South Africa: Sached Books. Philadelphia: Benjamins.

Poynton, C. (1984) Names as vocatives: forms and functions. (Special Issue on Systemic Linguistics) *Nottingham Linguistic Circular* 13: 1–34.

Poynton, C. (1985) *Language and Gender: making the difference*. Geelong, Vic.: Deakin University Press [republished London: Oxford University Press. 1989].

Poynton, C. (1990a) *Address and the Semiotics of Social Relations: a systemic-functional account of address forms and practices in Australian English*. PhD thesis, Department of Linguistics. University of Sydney.

Poynton, C. (1990b) The privileging of representation and the marginalising of the interpersonal: a metaphor (and more) for contemporary gender relations. In T. Threadgold & A. Cranny-Francis (eds) *Feminine/Masculine and Representation*. Sydney: Allen and Unwin. 231–55.

Poynton, C. (1993) Grammar, language and the social: poststructuralism and systemic functional linguistics. *Social Semiotics* 3(1): 1–22.

Poynton, C. (1996) Amplification as a grammatical prosody: attitudinal modification in the nominal group. In M. Berry, C. Butler & R. Fawcett (eds) *Meaning and Form: systemic functional interpretations.* (Meaning and Choice in Language: studies for Michael Halliday) Norwood, NJ: Ablex. 211–27.

Propp, V. (1958) *Morphology of the Folktale.* International Journal of American Linguistics.

Ravelli, L. J. (2000) Beyond shopping: constructing the Sydney Olympics in three-dimensional text. *Text* 20(4): 1–27.

Roach, A. (1990) Took the children away, from the album *Charcoal Lane.* Melbourne: Mushroom Records.

Rose, D. (1993) On becoming: the grammar of causality in English and Pitjantjatjara. *Cultural Dynamics.* VI(1–2): 42–83.

Rose, D. (1996) Pitjantjatjara processes: an Australian grammar of experience. In R. Hasan, D. Butt & C. Cloran (eds) *Functional Descriptions: language form & linguistic theory.* Amsterdam: Benjamins. 287–322.

Rose, D. (1997) Science, technology and technical literacies. In F. Christie & J.R. Martin (eds) 40–72.

Rose, D. (1998) Science discourse & industrial hierarchy. In J.R. Martin & R. Veel (eds) *Reading Science: critical and functional perspectives on discourses of science.* London: Routledge. 236–65.

Rose, D. (1999) Culture, competence and schooling: approaches to literacy teaching in Indigenous school education. In F. Christie (ed.) 217–45.

Rose, D. (2001a) *The Western Desert Code: an Australian cryptogrammar.* Canberra: Pacific Linguistics.

Rose, D. (2001b) Some variations in theme across languages. In *Functions of Language* 8(1): 109–45.

Rose, D. (2004a) The structuring of experience in the grammar of Pitjantjatjara and English. In K. Davidse & L. Heyvaert (eds) *Functional Linguistics and Contrastive Description.* (Special issue of *Languages in Contrast*) 4(1): 45–74.

Rose, D. (2004b) Sequencing and pacing of the hidden curriculum: how Indigenous children are left out of the chain. In J. Muller, A. Morais & B. Davies (eds) *Reading Bernstein, Researching Bernstein.* London: Routledge Falmer. 91–107.

Rose, D. (2005a) Pitjantjatjara: a metafunctional profile. In A. Caffarel, J.R. Martin & C.M.I.M Matthiessen (eds) *Language Typology: a functional perspective.* Amsterdam: Benjamins. 479–537.

Rose, D. (2005c) Narrative and the origins of discourse: patterns of discourse semantics in stories around the world. *Australian Review of Applied Linguistics* Series S19, 151–173 http://readingtolearn.com.au/#articles

Rose, D. (2005d) Grammatical metaphor. In *Encyclopaedia of Language and Linguistics 2nd Edition.* Oxford: Elsevier.

Rose, D. (2006a) Democratising the classroom: a literacy pedagogy for the new generation. *Journal of Education* Vol 37 (Durban: University of KwaZulu Natal), 127–164. http://www.ukzn.ac.za/joe/joe_issues.htm

Rose, D. (2006b) A systemic functional model of language evolution. *Cambridge Archaeological Journal* 16:1 73–96.

Rose, D. (2006c) *Scaffolding the English curriculum for Indigenous secondary students: Final Report for NSW 7–10 English Syllabus,* Aboriginal Support Pilot Project. Sydney: Office of the Board of Studies http://abed.boardofstudies.nsw.edu.au/go/english-literacy-7-10.

Rose, D. (2007a) Towards a reading-based theory of teaching. L. Barbara & T. Berber Sardinha [eds] *Proceedings of the 33rd International Systemic Functional Congress.* São Paulo: PUCSP. ISBN 85-283-0342-X, 36-77. Online publication available at http://www.pucsp.br/isfc/proceedings/index.htm

Rose, D. (2007b) Reading Genre: a new wave of analysis. *Linguistics and the Human Sciences.* 2(1), 185-204

Rose, D. (2007c) A reading based model of schooling. *Pesquisas em Discurso Pedagógico,* 2007(1), 1-22 http://www.maxwell.lambda.ele.puc-rio.br

Rose, D. (2008a) Writing as linguistic mastery: the development of genre-based literacy pedagogy. In D. Myhill, D. Beard, M. Nystrand & J. Riley (eds) *Handbook of Writing Development.* London: Sage, 33-51

Rose, D. (2008b) Reading to Learn: Accelerating learning and closing the gap. Sydney: Reading to Learn http://www.readingtolearn.com.au

Rose, D. (to appear a) History, science and dreams: genres in Australian and European cultures. http://readingtolearn.com.au/#articles

Rose, D. (to appear b) Negotiating kinship: interpersonal prosodies in Pitjantjatjara. *Word* 20pp. http://readingtolearn.com.au/#articles

Rose, D. & Acevedo, C. (2006) Closing the gap and accelerating learning in the Middle Years of Schooling. *Literacy Learning: the Middle Years,* 14(2): 32-45 http://www.alea.edu.au/site-content/publications/documents/llmy/llmy0606.htm

Rose, D., Lui-Chivizhe, L., McKnight, A. & Smith, A. (2004) Scaffolding academic reading and writing at the Koori Centre. *Australian Journal of Indigenous Education,* 30th Anniversary Edition, www.atsis.uq.edu.au/ajie 41–9.

Rose, D., McInnes, D. & Korner, H. (1992) *Scientific Literacy (Literacy in Industry).* Sydney: Adult Migrant Education Service.

Rose, D., Rose, M., Farrington, S and Page, S. (2008) Scaffolding Literacy for Indigenous Health Sciences Students. *Journal of English for Academic Purposes* 7 (3), 34-50.

Rothery, J. (1990) *Story Writing in Primary School: assessing narrative type genres.* PhD thesis. University of Sydney.

Rothery, J. (1994) *Exploring Literacy in School English (Write it Right Resources for Literacy and Learning).* Sydney: Metropolitan East Disadvantaged Schools Program.

Rothery, J. and Macken, M. R. (1991) Developing critical literacy through Systemic Functional Linguistics: unpacking the 'hidden curriculum' for writing in junior secondary English in New South Wales. In *Monograph 1 in Issues in education for the socially and economically disadvantaged*. Metropolitan East Disadvantaged Schools Program.

Rothery, J. & Stenglin, M. (1997) Entertaining and instructing: exploring experience through story. In F. Christie & J.R. Martin (eds) 231–63.

Rothery, J. & Stenglin, M. (2000) Interpreting literature: the role of appraisal. In L Unsworth (ed.) 222–44.

Rowley, E. (2004) Different visions, different visuals: semiotic analysis of field-specific visual composition in scientific conference presentations. *Visual Communication* 3(2): 145–75.

Royce, T. (1998) Synergy on the page: exploring intersemiotic complementarity in page-based multimodal text. *Japan Association Systemic Functional Linguistics Occasional Papers* 1(1): 25–50.

Royce, T. & Bowcher, W. (eds) (2006) *New Directions in the Analysis of Multimodal Discourse*. Mahwah, New Jersey: Lawrence Erlbaum Associates.

Russell, E. (2004) *The Shack that Dad Built*. Sydney: Little Hare Books.

Salager-Meyer, F. (1990) A text type and move analysis study of verb tenses and modality distribution in medical English abstracts. *English for Specific Purposes* 11: 93–114.

Schiess, R. (2004) Reading and television sceen: text, texture and screen design. D. Banks (ed.) *Text and Textures: systemic functional viewpoints on the nature and structure of text*. Brest: L'Harmattan. 411–28.

Schleppegrell, M.J. (1998) Grammar as a resource: writing a description. *Research in the Teaching of English* 32(2): 182–211.

Schleppegrell, M.J. (2004) *The Language of Schooling: a functional linguistics perspective*. Mahwah, NJ: Erlbaum.

Scollon, R., & Scollon, S. (1981) *Narrative, Literacy and Face in Interethnic Communication: advances in discourse processes*. Norwood, NJ: Ablex.

Scott, L. & Robinson, S. (1993) *Australian Journey: environments and communities*. Melbourne: Longman Cheshire.

Sikes, D. & Humphrey, S. (1996) *Australia – Place and Space: a unit of work for Junior Secondary Geography*. Sydney: Metropolitan East Disadvantaged Schools Program. [Bridge & Swanson St., Erskineville, NSW, Australia]

Silkstone, B. (1994) *Australian Reptiles: lizards*. Sydney: Longman Cheshire.

Stenglin, M. & Iedema, R. (2001) How to analyse visual images: a guide for TESOL teachers. In A. Burns & C. Coffin (eds) *Analysing English in a Global Context: a reader*. (Teaching English Language Worldwide) London: Routledge. 194–208.

Street, B. (1996) Preface in Prinsloo & Breier (eds) 1–9.

Stories from Lajamanu (1985) Darwin: N.T. Department of Education Curriculum and Assessment Branch.

Sutherland, T. & Windsor, G. (1997) Government rejects genocide finding, compensation. In *The Australian* 22 May, p. 3.

Swales, J. (1990) *Genre Analysis: English in academic and research settings.* (Cambridge Applied Linguistics) Cambridge: Cambridge University Press.

Swales, J. (2004) *Research genres: exploration and applications.* (Cambridge Applied Linguistics) Cambridge: Cambridge University Press.

Swales, J.M. & Lindemann, S. (2000) Teaching the literature review to international graduate students. In A. Johns (ed.) *Genre in the Classroom: multiple perspectives.* London: Erlbaum. 105–19.

sweetprincess (2004) www.imdb.com/title/tt0252444/board/nest/5105043

traveloneline.com (2004) *Uluru Sunrise Climb and Base Tour.* www.northernterritory. visitorsbureau.com.au/itineraries/index.html

Tsavdaridis, N. (2001) TURNED AWAY 'We have a lot of sick people on board. These people are in really bad shape'. In *The Daily Telegraph* 28 August, p. 1.

Tutu, D. (1999) *No Future Without Forgiveness.* London: Rider.

Unsworth, L. (1997a) 'Sound' explanations in school science: a functional linguistic perspective on effective apprenticing texts. *Linguistics and Education* 9(2): 199–226.

Unsworth, L. (1997b) Scaffolding reading of science explanations: Accessing the grammatical and visual forms of specialised knowledge. *Reading* 313: 30–42.

Unsworth, L. (1997c) Explaining explanations: Enhancing science learning and literacy development. *Australian Science Teachers Journal* 43(1): 34–49.

Unsworth, L. (ed.) (2000) *Researching Language in Schools and Communities: functional linguistic perspectives.* London: Cassell.

Unsworth, L. (1999) Teaching about explanations: talking out the grammar of written language. In A. Watson & L. Giorcelli (eds) *Accepting the Literacy Challenge.* Sydney: Scholastic.

Unsworth, L (2001a) *Teaching Multiliteracies across the Curriculum: changing contexts of text and image in classroom practice.* Buckingham: Open University Press.

Unsworth, L. (2001b) Evaluating the language of different types of explanations in junior high school science texts. *International Journal of Science Education* 236: 585–609.

Unsworth, L. (2004) Comparing school science explanations in books and computer-based formats: the role of images, image/text relations and hyperlinks. *International Journal of Instructional Media* 31(3): 283–301.

van Dijk, T.A. (1977) *Text and Context. Explorations in the semantics and pragmatics of discourse.* London: Longman.

van Leeuwen, T. (1992) The schoolbook as a multimodal text. *Internationale Schulbuchforschung* 14(1): 35–58.

van Leeuwen, T. (1999) *Speech, Music, Sound.* London: Macmillan.

van Leeuwen, T. (2000) It was just like magic – a multimodal analysis of children's writing. *Linguistics and Education* 10: 273–305.

van Leeuwen, T. & Caldas-Coulthard, C. (2004) The semiotic of kinetic design. In D. Banks (ed.) *Text and Textures: systemic functional viewpoints on he nature and structure of text.* Brest: L'Harmattan. 355–82.

van Leeuwen, T. & Humphrey, S. (1996) On learning to look through a geographer's eyes. in Hasan & Williams. 29–49.

van Leeuwen, T. & Jewitt, C. (2001) *Handbook of Visual Analysis.* London: Sage.

Veel, R. (1992) Engaging with scientific language: a functional approach to the language of school science. *Australian Science Teachers Journal* 38(4): 31–5.

Veel, R. (1995) Making informed choices or jumping through hoops? The role of functional linguistics in an outcomes-based curriculum. *Interpretations* 28(3): 62–76.

Veel, R. (1997) Learning how to mean – scientifically speaking: apprenticeship into scientific discourse in the secondary school. In F. Christie & J.R. Martin (eds) 161–95.

Veel, R. (1998) The greening of school science: ecogenesis in secondary classrooms. In J.R. Martin & R. Veel (eds) 114–51.

Ventola, E (1987) *The Structure of Social Interaction: a systemic approach to the semiotics of service encounters.* London: Pinter.

Warner, N., Owen, R., Taylor, H., Barnett, A., Riley, M., Hindle, K., Watson, M. & Floey, J. (1995) *Studies in Senior Design and Technology.* Milton, Qld: Jacaranda.

Watson, G. (1999) *Science Works: Book 3.* Melbourne: Oxford University Press.

White, P. (1997) Death, disruption and the moral order: the narrative impulse in mass 'hard news' reporting. In F. Christie & J.R. Martin (eds) 101–33.

White, P.R.R. (1998) Extended reality, proto-nouns and the vernacular: distinguishing the technological from the scientific. In J.R. Martin & R. Veel (eds) 266–96.

Wignell, P. (1997) *Making The Abstract Technical: on the evolution of the discourse of social science.* PhD thesis. University of Sydney.

Williams, E. (2002) Journey into a nation's soul. In *The Weekend Australian* 23 February, Review, p. 12.

Williams, G. (1999) The pedagogic device and the production of pedagogic discourse: a case example in early literacy education. In F. Christie (ed.) 88–122.

Williams, G. (2001) Literacy pedagogy prior to schooling: relations between social positioning and semantic variation. In A. Morais, H. Baillie & B. Thomas (eds) *Towards a Sociology of Pedagogy: the contribution of Basil Bernstein to research.* (History of Schools & Schooling 23) New York: Peter Lang. 17–45.

Xu, L. & Kenyon, N.F. (1991) A study of the abrasive wear of carbon steels. In *Wear* 148: 101–12.

Yang Ruiying & Allison, D. (2003) Research articles in applied linguistics: moving from results to conclusions. *English for Specific Purposes* 22(4): 365–85.

Index

Lightning Source UK Ltd.
Milton Keynes UK
UKOW02f1820260514

232336UK00001B/2/P